THE FOOLISH JOURNEY

INTO FEAR ENDS HERE

The FOOLISH JOURNEY *into* FEAR ENDS HERE

The Lelystad Teachings

by Rananda

MAGNUM OPUS MINISTRIES NEDERLAND

More information:

www.rananda.com
www.mom-nederland.nl

ISBN 978-90-78582-05-2

TABLE OF CONTENTS

The moment will come, in what you call your life, when the holding on is more painful than the letting go... You do have a choice when this moment will be... If you are wise, you will choose wisely and choose it to be THIS moment! (Because there is no other, you dummy!)

Here It is, in these very pages! The help you have called out for in your lonely nights and you say no one answered! Here It is!!! Let The Light and Love of these words touch you... absorb you... let them have you!!!

God bless you and everyone of us!

Suzanne Moran

INTRODUCTION

The teaching of Pure Non-Duality has been available in the World for many years now, but has been rejected by the majority of people for centuries. This rejection, however, does not establish The Truth, for Truth is true and nothing else is true! Truth does not rely on the number of people believing. Truth is established outside of people's wishes and desires. We all should be very glad that the nature of Reality in no way can be affected by what happens in this world.

My teaching comes from direct revealing experiences that are beyond the ability to make myself. I share my message with those who care to listen, because they will change one's earthly experiences like no other teaching. Masters like Jesus have tried to reach people, but many still do not understand their message or misrepresent what they gave from their hearts. Many, like Jesus, have paid a price that for man is considered very dear, but to turn against The Truth is a more dear price to pay because Reality Itself is the cost! However, this cost will never be paid by the Masters because their devotion is like that shared by John the Baptist, who lost his head but found Life Eternal!

Whomever wants The Truth can now find It. It is no longer hidden by secret societies etcetera, and I am not afraid to reveal the secrets of all time and space. This world and its inhabitants may do or say whatever they will about what I share, but nothing will change what has been shared with me by The Light Itself. I am but a messenger, one who cries out the message of Love into the darkness, one who cares about you more than you do at this present moment.

I present a challenge to you... are you brave enough to find the answer to the question, Who am I really? Do you have the courage to find out that you have made a nonexistent self in a vain attempt to replace the Divine Self that is your true Self? This book is dedicated to the Masters who have gone on before me, carrying this message in their hearts and doing whatever they could to help a dying humanity to remember that there is no such thing as death, except in an illusion, and therefore it has no meaning except to a dream world.

We each were and are created to enjoy the gifts of Reality. This world is not Reality. It is a dream of our own making and does not exist! All suffering, pain and death are necessary for an illusion but can never exist in Reality! The acceptance of this message is required for us to awaken from this world of illusion. Our own self-identity, characterization, role, personality, is a part of the illusion and therefore will disappear along with the rest of the perceptual universe as we accept The Truth.

I warn you... that to read this book will ruin you for this world. If the world as you perceive it has great value to you, then please do not read this book. If you are willing to go past your fears and into The Love within, then this book can change your life here on earth immeasurably. You have choice and I encourage you to use it wisely.

Blessings,

rananda

FOREWORD

I have known Rananda for many years now and have been deeply touched by his devotion to God. I have watched it manifest in so many ways and have seen many peoples' lives be transformed and touched by God's Hand. We joined in our journey of remembering and serving God in 1998 and have been serving together ever since. However, if, after listening to his message a person does not follow the wisdom taught, then they will be just as if they have never heard him at all.

The talks that have made up this book were held over a few years' time in the little town of Lelystad, The Netherlands, at the house of Beate Kohnen and attended by about 35-50 people each night.

Many of the ideas that Rananda speaks about, from his experiences, can be very disturbing to one's mind or perhaps they will be ideas that you have held dear for many years and have been sure are true. No matter what tradition you have decided to practise, you will find that what Rananda teaches is the heart of all spiritual teachings, as he never preaches a specific tradition other than the timeless tradition of reliance upon our Creator for everything.

Although transcripts of talks are helpful as information, it is sharing the living frequency of The Truth that quickly changes lives. People came to these talks for different reasons but Rananda always directed them to attend to their transformation, to remember that their relationship with their Creator is to take priority over all other relationships. Rananda has a unique and at times very humorous way of leading people into the recognition of where the need for healing takes place in the mind.

I am sure that those who read this book with an open mind and grateful heart will benefit greatly from whatever effort that requires. You are not being asked to agree with what Rananda has to say but just the reading of his talks will have a profound effect upon your life's journey and the remembering of your True Self. We all seek happiness and some need help to find the path and even more to walk it without straying into the darkness of the tempting world of the senses. As Buddha would say, your desires are what bring you all your pain and suffering. Rananda helps us to see how our mind makes choices and the results that will follow from those choices. Because we make the choices we also are the answer to whatever problem arises from those thoughts. We can choose again and obtain the happiness that we say we are missing.

I am grateful to be able to take part in our journey together and thank God for this opportunity to help bring this book to a dying world that thirsts for Love while seeking It where It can never be found. Rananda has been and is dedicating his life to helping people to remember how and where to find The Peace of God within.

I hope that you enjoy this book and share it with those who long for peace of mind and heart but have yet to find it.

Suzanne Moran

FROM THE EDITOR

This book comes from Love, the only Love there is. The channels for the Love in this book are Suzanne and Rananda, our masters and teachers.

First of all I need to mention the Love that is being poured on us through Suzanne. Her being is sheer Love and Beauty and she showers It on us in so many ways; totally tender and totally powerful, totally compassionate and totally devoted. Her support makes it possible for all of us to carry this message into the world.

Being with a master is a gift of great magnitude. It has been given us in Rananda. His Love for Our Creator is deeply moving and his devotion to the vision he shares with Suzanne is not of this world! All are welcome to join in this vision of instantaneous healing, which will occur when we are truly willing to accept our Real Identity as Sons of God. Thank you, Rananda and Suzanne, for insisting on the Purity and the Power of our Being.

I bow deep to you both in total gratitude.

* * *

For this book to make it to print, it has required a joint effort of many people and we sincerely thank all of you who have been involved in it.

Beate Kohnen for welcoming us into her house; Janine Brüll, Rob Slijper, Rob Smit and Lily Faber for recording the sessions; Anneke Sennema, Annette Oostinga, Goedele Goossens, Josien Heesen and Lovie Pleisner for making the transcriptions; Frans Vermeulen and Karin Feekes for proof reading the manuscript; Lily Faber for the lay-out; Anje Rasker for the cover painting; Rob Slijper for the cover design.

The chapters in *The Foolish Journey into Fear Ends Here* are mostly presented in chronological order of dates in which the meetings took place.

You will find the use of capitals in this book to deviate from what is common usage. The reason is that Rananda likes to make an unambiguous distinction between what belongs to Reality and what belongs to the illusion. It will also help the reader – you – to immediately see whether he speaks of the True You or the you that you think you are in this illusion. All words pertaining to Reality are capitalized as well.

With great joy and gratitude I compiled these teachings into this book – it has been a privilege indeed, and I hope you will be inspired by Rananda and Suzanne like I am.

Chandra Moonen

1

ILLUSIONS ARE IMPOSSIBLE

Remembering Who You Are /
Illusion versus Reality / Language of Light

R: So, I'd like to start by telling you I don't give lectures, in case you didn't know that. I don' t like lectures at all! I don't do that! But, if you have questions, I will respond. If you don't, thanks a lot for coming. It was nice to sit with you in quiet for a moment.[1] Part of what I have discovered is that those who are serious about remembering Who They are, in that journey of remembering there are questions that arise in your mind that are very important about the path that you are choosing to walk. And although there are many teachers in your world, it's an opportunity to be able to talk with one that is not upstate somewhere or some way removed from you. Here you have an opportunity. So, I am not giving you a lecture.

Q: Remembering Who You are, how does it work? What do you remember? Do you already know that You know? How do you do it?

R: How do you not do it? What do you do to not remember? Have you sat with yourself long enough to prevent remembering when? So, if you don't do that, then you remember. So, if you want to know what to do to

---

[1] *Rananda always makes a clear distinction between a lecture and a Remembering Event. A lecture he sees as a meeting where you come to gather information. During a Remembering Event you are invited to join with his mind, so that his experience becomes available to you, which is the activity of forgiving.*

remember, don't do what you're doing to forget. I mean, that sounds really way too simple, doesn't it? Can it be that simple? Could it be that simple? That you're actively wanting to forget?

Q: I'm trying to remember all kinds of different possibilities.

R: Yes. Isn't that great? In your mind there are all kinds of possibilities! That should be exciting, I would think, no? Look at the nature of the world. Your possibilities are extremely small, like that big. [Rananda is holding his thumb and forefinger close.]

Q: To remember Who You are, different options arise in my mind about who I am. Mmmm. Maybe I'm nothing! That's an option.

R: What would happen if you were nothing? That's very interesting. Because it's true!

Q: The concept of nothingness is fullness, that comes up in my mind. Only if it's complete, if it's total, they are the same. If it's not total, then they're not the same. Could I ask you, is remembering also a process?

R: It's not a process.

Q: Does remembering in the right way also have effects in the world?

R: Yes, it would disappear! Isn't that good news? Then you're left with nothing. No, with Everything. Nothing disappears. Nothing you've been trying to make something will disappear, and Everything that always was, will be what You're with. Including the you that you think is something is nothing that disappears with everything else that's nothing.

And the You that has been Eternal is what You're aware of and what You're left with. Isn't that good news?[2]

Q: Eternal nothingness, I have my doubts.

R: Well, then it is not eternal nothingness, if you have doubts. It must be total. I don't teach nothingness. I don't teach void. I teach Everything. I teach the impossibility of anything but Everything. Isn't that good news? The fulfillment of our possibilities is how you begin to understand the nature of your mind and The Truth of the nature of You. Otherwise, you remain limited and serving a world trying to figure out what it means to you, based upon the value that you give what you perceive. Your mind is a part of Reality; it's a part of The Eternal. It's not something that comes and goes. So, the nature of You is Eternal.

Q: And the body is a way for the mind to manifest itself?

R: No, the body is an illusion! It's an attempt to prove that You're not Eternal. And it failed, by the way. Isn't that good news? You don't have to suffer eternally. Isn't that good news? Yes, it is, isn't it? But yes, when you know that the body is an illusion! In Reality the mind manifests itself as Creation.

Q: Doesn't the Bible speak of "Eternal Love"?

R: You know, the last time I carefully looked at the Bible, it said a lot of things. It says, "An eye for an eye", if you have teeth, "A tooth for a tooth" and "Turn the other cheek." There's all kinds of things in there. Not all of that I agree with.

Q: I wonder, why shouldn't it work? That's what you say.

---

[2] *Rananda calls the world, which is an illusion in its entirety, nothing and Heaven, Reality, Everything.*

R: Because it's impossible!

Q: What is impossible?

R: Illusions. Illusions are impossible! It's not possible for an illusion to replace Reality! That's why you call it an illusion. You can experience illusions if you want to. I think you are, right now. I'm not here to debate whether or not you are capable of experiencing you are an illusion. I'm not even here to debate with you whether or not your illusion is considered reality by you. If you want to give value to an illusion, you're only going to be doing one thing at a time, which means you're not going to be valuing Reality.

Q: Why do we do it?

R: You know, I've been asking that question for a long time. And nobody knows, and no one has an answer for me. Because, when they talk to me reasonably enough to actually hold a conversation, they come to the same conclusion. They have no idea why! That's why they usually create a God who made them do it.

Q: I've been in workshops a few months ago, working with what I experience, what I think you call a void, with nothing. And just someone transmitted a primal energy. I was nothing. I couldn't feel anything. I didn't have anything. I didn't have a name. I had nothing. I was nothing. I wasn't pleased by it.

R: I wouldn't be either. Doesn't sound Eternal to me!

Q: Later on in the workshop I came into the experience of a flow of things.

R: Flow is a part of the illusion, because it has to go from one point to another. The Eternal doesn't flow from one point to another. The Eternal is Everywhere. There's no flowing from one thing to something else. Now, saying, "I had an experience," I understand there's all kinds of experiences that are available to a mind that has all kinds of possibilities. And all I'm asking you to do is to consider possibilities that you have not allowed yourself to consider before. Let one of them be that You're actually Eternal! Not only actually Eternal, but You're Eternal right now! The reason you don't know The Eternal that You are right now, is because you are having fun using perception, thinking that you are going to learn something through having an illusionary body. As if, when You're Eternal, You don't know Everything needed to be known; as if You're not everything that there is. If that's true, then Oneness is just an illusion too, isn't It? And It's not! Is that helpful?

Q: No, I think...

R: OK. So, I gave you the answer you are looking for and you are rejecting it. Is that what you are saying?

Q: No.

R: You are accepting it then?

Q: No, it's...

R: Then you are rejecting it.

Q: But I had...

R: No, wait a minute. You're either accepting it or you're rejecting it.

Q: Oh, then I return.

R: OK, at least you're honest, a kind of...

* * *

Q: You have to break out of an illusion?

R: Well, the first thing you might want to look at is the way you phrased the question. OK? Because, the way you phrased the question indicates that you believe that you're bound. If it's an illusion how could you be bound, unless you accept that the illusion is something that can bind you? So, when you begin to want the illusion to not bind you, it won't. And you won't have to break out of anything, because there's nothing binding you except for your own thoughts. The question is, would you enjoy accessing a different Source of thought? Would you like to access a different Source of thought than the one that you are currently using? Because, that's where the different possibilities are going to come from. So, the first thing I would assume – and I know that you're not supposed to do that stuff – if you were to look at the idea that it's possible that there is A Source of thought other than the one that you've been entertaining, when you come to that, liking that idea, then it will begin to unfold in your mind for you. Because there *is* another Source of thought!

Q: How do you stop your mind?

R: What do you want to do that for?

Q: I thought it was the way to do it.

R: Oh, well, try it then! I don't do that! My mind is doing perfectly fine being focused on Oneness. I'm not trying to stop it from doing anything. It's doing fine! I recognized I was getting pain and suffering. I recognized there were thoughts in association with that. I also recognized there were thoughts that I valued. I believed that the thought and the resulting phenomena were connected. OK? When I recognized that they were connected, I also recognized where they're connected, which is in my mind. When I didn't want to suffer the results of those thoughts any longer, I began to explore my own mind to find out how it works.

Why do I do what I do? When I started to see what I put in the way of Love, I wanted Love more than what I put in the way. So, I let go of what I was putting in the way and Love was there immediately. Then I began to discover that It's Eternal, and that It's always there. It has nothing to do with circumstances of an illusion. What you call love comes and goes. That love has nothing to do with Eternal Love and I'm not interested in love that comes and goes. And, I'm not interested in being something that comes and goes from Love. You hear what I'm saying? I'm looking for The Eternal and I want to know that I am That! The only way I can know that is to let go of the ideas that I associate as self, that are less than Eternal. Is that helpful?

Q: Yes, well.

R: I've got one! Two! I got you too?

Q: You said there is nothing, so there is no... nothing.

R: No, I'm not saying there is nothing. I'm saying that this illusion is the attempt to make nothing something. I never said there is nothing. I've said and declared there is only Everything and nothing is not a part of Everything. Nothing is an illusion! Which, if you choose, you can experience. But, when you choose to experience that, you're choosing not to experience The Eternal, Oneness, The Truth of Who and What It is You are. Instead, you take on a personality. You take on a body. You take on all the phenomena that make up the illusion. Isn't that good news? It is, isn't it? It's good news to see it clearly, isn't it?

Q: If I listen to you it sounds quite easy.

R: That's because it is!!!

Q: The only thing you have to think, a new way of thinking, is, I'm Eternal?

R: Well, that would help. That's a start. Yes, that would help. The way I looked at it and the way it happened for me personally was, I looked at what I was experiencing, which was sometimes kind of happy, sometimes kind of sad, sometimes really joyful. You know, like really joyful and other times like really sad. So, there were degrees of what I was experiencing and I wanted something different. I didn't want to be tossed back and forth, based upon what was happening according to me at that time, outside of me. At that point I did not understand it was all happening in my own mind. So, it started with me wanting something different. And then, as I looked for possibilities, one of them was, I'm actually Eternal.

Because this is an illusion, you can come to know that it is an illusion, and when you come to know it's an illusion, the illusion will disappear! When it disappears, you will recognize or be aware of What has always been, which is what you call Eternal. At that point, it was like your question, "How is that going to happen?" And even like, "What do I have to do?" But, who thinks that they have to do something? That's the self you made to know about the illusion, because The Eternal already knows It's Eternal. So, It's not saying those kinds of things. There are a lot of tricky things that go on in the beginning when you begin to approach your, what you call Awakening or what I call Remembering. [3]

So, lots of tricky things go on in the mind. Considering the fact that you made up this world in its entirety, you can certainly make up all kinds of light experiences, all kinds of love experiences and all kinds of pain experiences. You can make up all kinds of stuff. Your mind is really fascinating, but

---

[3] *Rananda calls it Remembering because we are already in the Presence of God. We only choose to forget that and Remembering it will restore our experience and Awareness of it.*

more fascinating than what you're doing with your mind is the Creator of your mind. When you go for That, then you're going for the goal, as they say. Is that helpful? OK. That's three now. This is really a successful evening. Next thing you know we're all going to disappear and you go, "Wow, dude."

Q: I experience God as the most refined substance, the expression of God is the most refined, beyond nothingness. It's the first manifestation out of nothingness that's all and that's beyond. Personally speaking I'm experiencing it as all-consuming.

R: If you want to try to compare, which is what the illusion is, you will fail. You cannot compare Everything to nothing; there's nothing to compare with.

Q: Conveying any kind of knowledge in the crude way of language is always imperfect, because language is based on comparison.

R: Yes, that's the problem with it. So, don't do that.

Q: Apparently you can't talk about God.

R: You can, but you'd always be wrong.

Q: That's right!

R: Right. God is not what you say. Neither is the illusion. Thank God! Did you get that? No! Oh. Come sit-up here in the front, that's where you really get it. Read my book, when it comes out. Hey!!! It's good not to be so serious trying to wake yourself up. At first you were so serious about trying to be separate from Everything, so you could be you, right? Isn't that important, to be you? Haven't you been trying to be not like everybody else? Hasn't it been important to you to have your hair in a certain way? Well, for some of us it has been important to have hair! So, that's basically what you've been doing and you call that life? That's life. I did it my way. And failed. But at least I tried!

Things can change when you begin to allow The Light, or Spirit, or whatever label you like to put on That, to guide you from moment to moment. I know that the only reason you really don't do that is because you think Spirit is not smart enough to take care of you. I mean you know a lot better than Spirit does. You have lots of experiences. Spirit doesn't have any experiences. How can you trust that? "It probably wants me to walk around loving everybody." You can't just do that, it might hurt you. Right? It's not wise to just love everybody. Right? You have to pick and choose. Right? Very carefully. Based on everything that happened in my past. And man, every time I carefully look at my past, oh my God, I hardly learned anything. I didn't learn to carefully look at my past – the only thing that really would have helped me. Because, then I could be here now, letting The Eternal guide me, which is the path. If there is a path, that's it. You let The Light, The Eternal guide you. You stop telling It what you want, how to do it. Instead it's like, "Into Thy Hands, show me, help me to see. When I'm weak help me find Your Strength. When I'm strong, help me to follow your Will. When I'm following Your Will, let me stay free from the temptation to return to my own ideas."

* * *

So, what's happening here tonight is that you're being stimulated to carefully look at your own mind, at your own thoughts and what it is you want. How true you have really been or not been to the answers that you get when you ask yourself what it is that you really want. "What is it what I'm really doing?" And then you carefully look at the idea that you're not getting what you want. You'll know why. And, you stop blaming your neighbor when you're trying to meditate, because he's making all that noise. Did I get that alright?

Q: It's helpful that we have not arrived yet.

R: See, that's the kind of stuff that keeps you from knowing You're Eternal!

Q: Yes, OK.

R: When you say, "I haven't arrived yet," let me ask you a question. What are you using to prove you haven't arrived?

Q: I can sit and think.

R: That's good.

Q: I try to have the feeling of being eternal, the experience, the idea that I'm dead, but then it seems I am in the illusionary world.

R: OK. So, wait right there. "I'm in the illusionary world!" That's what you're using to deny You're Eternal.

Q: I'm also the body-mind. I experience that also.

R: You're whatever you say you are!

Q: Yes, yes.

R: Yes, yes.

Q: That's the problem!

R: That would be a problem if you weren't saying You're Eternal!

Q: Yes, sometimes I can...

R: OK. I get it. I see where the problem is. Thank you.[4] It

---

[4] *When Rananda teaches, he is in direct contact with The Divine and sometimes this plays out in little conversations with Whomever is inspiring him, like the "thank you" in this instance.*

works like this. You can't make yourself Eternal, because You already are. So stop trying and let What can show you that You're Eternal do Its job. What shows you that You are Eternal is The Eternal Self! OK? So, it's OK to want to know The Eternal, it's OK to want to communicate with The Eternal, it's OK to want to be Eternal, but it's not OK to try to make yourself that, because the thing that tries to make itself that is the illusionary self that you made to believe in the illusion. OK? So, all those efforts are actually getting in the way. That's why we have the word surrender, and into Thy Hands. Whose Hands? "Not to get me to surrender into somebody's hands. That's how I got into trouble last time." That can be funny sometimes, can't it? Right? I didn't pick on you at all. See how good you're doing?

Q: Can I ask something? How does knowing or realizing The Eternal stop this from happening?

R: It stops the suffering, because there is no suffering in The Eternal. Now, what I think your question really is...

Q: I think your answer will be, "Now."

R: Yes, actually, my answer, when people say when, is, "That's none of your business." Because the one that wants to know when, is the one that doesn't know that He's already Home in Heaven and so he can expect those kinds of thoughts to come into his mind: when and how?

Q: So, if I tell myself every day a 1000 times, "I am Eternal", would that be a way?

R: No, that's more like the way magic works, OK? And, what I teach is not magic!

Q: So, is there anything we can do?

R: No, see, it's just relentless, isn't it?

Q: Yes.

R: You follow what I'm saying? The reason that this keeps happening is because you think that you're a problem solver. So you constantly think, "Now I have a problem to solve. How come I don't know who I am? You're telling me I'm Home and I don't know?" I don't know why you keep doing that! I ask you to look at what you keep doing to not know You're Eternal. And, as you look at what you're doing... you know... don't do that! When you see in your mind what you're doing to not know You're Eternal, don't do that!

Q: How can you not do what you're doing?

R: Why don't you just accept that you could do it, because I told you to? Why? Why did you reject it?

Q: I was just asking.

R: I know you're just asking, but I'm asking, "Why reject that?" I told you exactly what to do. Why would you reject it? Why wouldn't you just go, "Oh, good, now I know what to do. Every time I see what I'm doing, I'm just not going to do it!" I mean, now do you understand what I'm saying? The illusionary self that you made for yourself is asking these questions, because it has no intention to disappear. Its whole purpose is to be a part of the illusion. And so it says, "How can I do that?" You can't do anything. Didn't you hear me say you can't do anything? "Yes, I know, how can I not do that?" See, you just say, "No, Rananda, it was an innocent question." No, there was no innocence in that question at all. There was a complete denial made to seem to be innocent. See, this is what we are tempted to struggle with on our spiritual path, because we are very slippery. You know why? Because we keep doing it and we don't even know why any longer. It was set in motion in the idea of time so long ago that no one even knows and everybody makes up these amazing stories. You know which I like the best? "God doesn't know Who He is! So, I'm here doing al these things so He can remember who He is." I figure that God must have Alzheimer's. Ha. I'm absolutely convinced that when people talk to me that way, their God has Alzheimer's! He forgot Who He is! And, He sent you into a world of pain, suffering and death, because He doesn't know! Now, you have to have Alzheimer's to do that to something you love. If it were possible, mind you. I'm getting on here. You follow me?

Q: Yes, the next question is already coming.

R: That's OK. See, the mind is a place where thoughts are allowed. But, it also is a decision maker. It believes it has choices. It doesn't, but it believes it does! So, while it believes that it does, it experiences choices. OK? At some point it's going to recognize, because there is only The Eternal, that the only choice it has is, what comes from The Eternal. But you can't make yourself be a part of The Eternal, because You already are. And you can't make yourself wake up to it because you're the dummy who is asleep. So, all you can do is want to wake up! Stay with that wanting and allow Perfection to do the work for you. Let The Light do the work for you. The Light does all the work! You just get in the way. When The Light is doing Its work, you disappear! You disappear into the Knowing of Oneness and the joining with one another. And you know what? Sometimes I hear people saying things like: "I joined with you." Let me only give you a clue about joining. When you join, Everything that joins, knows it! So, sometimes I have no idea what you are joining with. No idea! Because you're making up stuff in your own mind. Because you don't like the world that is of your own making. The one of pain, suffering and death. But I guarantee you, when you hit a moment of sincerity and willingness to remember that Everything argues for your remembering, Everything That Is argues for you to be in the remembering of You that is Eternal. And there the joining happens and Everything knows the joining; everything knows the joining! There are no people doing something to you. There's just You as a You that's not located, because it's Everywhere, because it's not limited! So, you have a wonderful future.

Good news. Is this good news? Is that helpful? Yes? So, as you pay attention to your mind, you see these thoughts come up. And when they show up, you just go, "Oh, that's what Rananda was talking about; yes, look." It seems like an innocent thing. It seems natural to a world that denies everything. But, I get that it denies I'm Eternal already. Why would I want to have anything to do with that? That's not what I want. So, if you don't remember what you want, you get involved in what I call "the story". OK? "The dream", "the illusion"; you get involved in it and you try to do the best you can to be happy in it. And you will fail, because you're looking for happiness where it's not! You can only find happiness where it is! Just like The Eternal, you can only find The Eternal where It is! If you keep looking where It's not and wondering why you don't succeed, you're only doing it to yourself.

Q: So It is in you?

R: No, It's in You! Is that helpful?

Q: Would you recommend altering those thoughts always? That seems like quite a job.

R: No, I'm not asking you to monitor your thoughts all day long, because then you wouldn't know The Eternal.

Q: Yes, but all day long we've thoughts going.

R: We do?

Q: I'm sorry. Pfffffff.

R: Thought I was missing something there for a minute. Yes, all day long thoughts come into the mind and they come from more than one source.[5]

Q: What do you mean by that? An external source?

R: External? To what? Thoughts come into your mind. There are no thoughts external to your mind if they come into your mind. They're already in there. They just come to your awareness. Right? You're aware of a thought or you choose not to be aware, but it's there anyway, isn't it? You call it unconscious or subconscious or wherever they come from. But they were there. Hey, it's just BOINK. Don't you hate it when you get some of those thoughts that just boink and you go, "Oh no, I'm spiritual. Where did that come from?" Well, don't you hate it when that happens? It just blows your image of you right to pieces. "Get out of here," you know, mmm. You try to do your magical thing. Straighten yourself up, make sure you get your white clothes on. See, mine are not all white. See, if you try to monitor yourself all day long, that's what you will be. You'll be a monitor.

Q: So have fun?

R: It's really important that you hear the most important part about your Awakening! What I've said tonight! And to me the most important part of what I said about your Awakening tonight is that you cannot wake yourself up. So, the idea of monitoring your thoughts all day long as a way in which you can wake yourself up, is just the rejection of what

---

[5] *Our mind has input from two sources of thought. One is Spirit, the other ego. Spirit's Thoughts are the Thoughts we share with God, our Creator, and they always speak of Perfection, Love, Wholeness. The other is ego and ego's thoughts speak of conflict, separation, imperfection. And all day long we choose which thoughts we value, and experience the consequences of our choices.*

I've said. OK? What I am saying, however, is that as you look at ideas that come into your mind and you're doing that all day long, there are lots of ideas that come into your mind that you just accept and you don't look at them.

There's also a whole system of thought that you accept without even realizing you're accepting a whole system of thought. OK? For instance, when you get up in the morning and you decide to get out of bed, you don't go, "GRAVITY!!! Oh, I'm so glad there's gravity. Pfff. I almost just flew off!" You don't do that. You follow what I'm saying? There's a whole system of thought that you just have a deep acceptance of, so that you don't need to have the thoughts that come into your mind to be a part of your activity. Because it's a part of a whole bigger thing! So, the idea to try to monitor every thought wouldn't make sense. Right? Because, how would you get to gravity? For instance, if you are not even letting that be a part of your awareness. OK?

What you can want, however, is to want The Truth to reveal Itself to you. OK? As you want more and more The Truth to reveal Itself to you, It will. Because, the only reason that you think It's not revealing Itself to you is because you're saying, "It hasn't." Truth is... is It Eternal? Is that word OK for Truth? So, when will you decide to let The Truth reveal Itself to you? In what moment will It not be available to you? It's Eternal. So, the problem is not one of The Eternal not being there for you. It's you not being willing to let The Eternal reveal Itself to you, because you focus on the illusion for what you want. Even to the point of saying, "Oh yes, but you just can't stop. You just can't do that, don't even try to make me look at that. I'm not nuts, you know!" And, I'm telling you, "Yes, you can!"

Time is not a requirement for your Awakening. It has nothing to do with time. You can sit and meditate until your cows come home. And for what I've seen they're still out there. And you're still meditating! I mean... do you understand why I'm saying that? Because, meditation has a beginning and then an activity and hopefully desired results which you never get to, because you get up and go to work. Or, you decided to go to sleep or whatever. But the idea itself has a beginning, an activity and an ending! That's what time is! So, you cannot take a part of the illusion and cause the illusion to end! Hello? There is no part of an illusion that can cause an illusion to end! I hate to tell meditators this. Believe me, it's just like they either get really mad at me or their world just crumbles. Sccccccscscscscs. Because I was just extremely reasonable and you had to accept it. But, you decided to be upset over it. Which has nothing to do with accepting; it has to do with rejecting. What you reject you are separated from. And your intent to be separate does not allow you to have access to Oneness. Now, ask me, "Why isn't meditation helpful?"

Q: Yes!??

R: And I say, of course it will be helpful to you! It's better than going out and killing your neighbors. But who has to meditate in Reality? Wow, mmmmmmmm. Ohhh. Something that knows Who and What It is? Yes, that's You! There's nothing that knows What It is other than You. "Well, I don't know." Why not? Why don't you know? And then you get that incredible answer all over the world, the same exact answer, only in different languages, "I don't know." It's the most heard response in every spiritual community. Why do you do that? Did you ever say it? Are you guilty? Are you guilty of being one who has said that? Perhaps more than once?

Q: No!

R: No? You're not one of those?

Q: No!

R: No, that's OK. Is everybody having fun now?

* * *

Q: Does meditation connect you to The Light?

R: Does it, or does The Light connect you to the meditation?

Q: When I meditate I really feel connected to The Light. It is as if I am The Light.

R: Oh, really?

Q: I think so.

R: You think so?

Q: You said a moment ago The Light does the work!

R: That's great, so then you don't have to meditate on The Light, do you?

Q: Oh no, I don't meditate.

R: The Light does the work!

Q: I open the door to The Light.

R: Oh, you're going to do that? You're not going to let The Light open the door? See, this is what I was saying. You see how fast, how easy those thoughts just slide in there? They seem so reasonable and so innocent.

Q: Opening the door means giving up the illusion, not The Light.

R: You're not going to do that! It's going to disappear, because of the nature of Light! The Light is going to do it!

Q: Some time ago you asked me what I am doing in order to avoid The Light.

R: That's a good thing, a good question. I didn't hear a lot of answers, by the way. I like to remind you. You can check your path there. You didn't give me a lot of answers to that. Go ahead, I'm sorry, I did interrupt you.

Q: I would like to link this with what you said about the other source of thought. So, apparently there are at least two sources of thought, and you also said you can communicate with The Eternal. Is that communication verbal?

R: It's a language of Light.

Q: Language of Light?

R: Yes.

Q: That's very beautiful!

R: O, it is. I can't wait for you to remember, and you can begin to communicate with me through balls of energy. Complete, complete. No, no, no, complete! Right, not linear. Not like this and then you turn around, look back and go, "Ohhhh, I forgot that, mmmm." No, it's complete. BOEMMM, OHHHHH!!! It's like getting the whole book in your head, instead of going page, by page, by page. That's linear, you read the lines. "Oh, I'm a fast reader, ssss, ssss." Yes, but faster than that! Plunk, and you got the whole thing! Yes, instantaneous! Because it's not bound by the limitations of the speed of what you call light. Everything of the illusion is at the speed of light. Everything is at the speed of light! Everything in the illusion, one last time, is at the speed of light!

2

THE REAL YOU

Time / Help / The Real You / Forgiveness / Willingness / Enlightenment / Golden Energy

Q: Why did we take 2000 years to discover this Light, this Oneness?

R: 2000 years? Because you wanted it to.

Q: ... it's like playing and now...

R: Are you serious?

Q: We are tired of playing now.

R: Are you serious now?

Q: Eh, yeah, well, for 90 percent.

R: Oh, 90 percent, OK.

Q: Yes, yes, yes, and that's heavy, heavier than this little 10 percent. Yeah, yeah. [Laughs.]. I don't know what about you...

R: 10 percent won't really let her look at me. We could take care of that 10 percent right now, do you know that?

Q: OK.

R: But, there's a little fear in there. That's what the 10 percent is. So, if you were to look at that, that 10 percent represents something to you that you value. Yes?

Q: Mmmm.

R: OK. So, that also means that you have to find no value in that 10 percent for it to be released or converted. Right? But, up until this very moment you have valued that 10 percent.

Q: Yes, well, there was a little confusion...

R: That's what 210 percent is, confusion.

Q: Yes, because I have some definition about me and this all changed very, very fast. Every week I think I have a new perception about myself.

R: That's the 10 percent, yes.

Q: ... and then two years ago something started for me...

R: That's 10 percent.

Q: ... like a plant, and now the plant is growing, growing, you know? I had a little seed and it's becoming a plant and I wanted to have the fruit of this plant.

R: I love mango's.

Q: But, you know, finally something comes out and now I don't have the taste anymore for what I liked two years or two months ago. My taste is changing so much and this is confusing...

R: Mmmm, that's 10 percent.

Q: Yeah. [Laughs.] Yeah.

R: Yeah. So, are you ready to give up your 10 percent or do you still think it has lots of value for you?

Q: Well, I don't think I have a lot of choice. There is no me that can choose anymore, really.

R: Really? Who's saying that?

Q: Me.

R: That's the 10 percent.

Q: No, no, it's a feeling that there's no me, because I'm already in this boat and this boat is going, so...

R: It is inevitable! It is inevitable. But, you know, a lot of people get on those bicycles that don't go anywhere. They can alter the resistance, but they don't go anywhere.

[Audience laughing.]

R: That's the 10 percent.

Q: Well, maybe they want to lose 10 percent of fat, eh…

[Audience laughing.]

R: Don't wait. Use time wisely! It is possible, even though time has no Reality to it, to waste it.

Q: Could you repeat that please?

R: Even though time has no Reality to it, you can waste it! I'm encouraging you, don't waste time. Because, time is what pain and suffering is! If you waste it, that means you are willing to have more pain and suffering. If you use it wisely, you'll use it to bring Love, healing and goodness. Then, what you say you want, this plant that you're working on, it will bloom and it will have this sweet fruit. Everything will be OK. God will come along and pick you up. But not while you're hanging there onto your 10 percent. Would you want God to pick you when you had 10 percent sourness? And, He goes, "Gggg, blah, bah." Something like that, you know. Or, do you want Him to go, "Gggg, oh, this is great!"

OK? Don't waste time! You have a lot to give. See, now all that stuff has gone. All that shield that you have to hide yourself, it's all gone, it's just you there now. That's the Real You. OK?

Q: Thank you.

R: So, ask yourself, do I want to hear what God has to say to me or am I too afraid that He might tell me something I don't want to hear?

Q: Does God have anything to say to me that I don't want to hear?

R: That would be up to you, wouldn't it?

Q: [Deep sigh.] I don't know. Maybe I know. I feel like I'm not strong enough to hear the message. Can that be?

R: No, you're never given something that you cannot complete. Never. From Spirit, you're never given anything that you cannot handle.

Q: Can you say no to Spirit?

R: Well, I think that's what the illusion is!

Q: Actually, I don't want to do anything at all. I already exist but I don't know what to do with myself.

R: Aha! Whom have you been asking for help?

Q: Yes, I think I need help.

R: Yes, whom have you been asking for help?

Q: God.

R: Well, then you should be getting it, don't you think? Don't you think if you ask God for help that you get it?

[Audience.] For sure!

R: For sure! Wow, did you hear that?

Q: But sometimes we don't see the message because sometimes we ask God, "Please help me," and then He comes and brings someone that is knocking on our door and that person says something that really would help us, but we are sometimes listening too high and sometimes we miss the point that God is talking through people and through everything in life.

R: Is that your choice?

Q: What is my choice?

R: What you're talking about.

Q: No. I know some people who are saying, "I would like God to help me."

R: Yes. Is that their choice?

Q: Asking God for help? If you ask God if He wants to help you, then that is your choice?

R: Yes, that's what I asked. Is it your choice?

Q: Yes.

R: OK, so you can choose differently then. A choice means you have more than one option, doesn't it?

Q: Yes.

R: OK, so you can change your mind. Isn't that good news? You're not stuck! You know stuck? Yeah. Hallelujah! [Rananda sings.] Hallelujah, hallelujah...

Q: Yes, I want to change my mind...

R: Ahaaaa.

[Applause and cheers and audience laughing.]

Q: I want to change myself constantly, even when I'm happy, I want to change. I don't know why.

R: Yes, well, how about if we could help you find Something that's Eternal and Immortal, so It never changes.

Q: Eternal...

R: Yes. And Immortal.

Q: I like the idea.

R: OK, now, here's a secret. Can I tell you a secret?

Q: Yes, of course.

R: It won't be anything like the you that you think that you know right now. Are you OK with that?

Q: Absolutely.

R: OK. There you go, see, he's made a different choice.

Q: [Deep sigh.] I know one thing for sure, I want a peaceful life.

R: Oh, oh.

Q: A peaceful life. Harmony.

R: Oooh.

[From the audience.] That sounds boring.

Q: Boring.

R: No, I wouldn't say boring. It's just when you're dealing with an illusion, peaceful doesn't make a lot of sense, because the illusion needs to disappear. Then the peace follows! But, the illusion is the idea of opposition to Perfection. So, to think that it's going to be a dance in the park kind of thing, you know, it's not like that. What's required is looking at those ideas that are not yours, and not finding value there any longer and then they just get removed. See, believing that you are you and that an illusion is reality is much more difficult than ending that. However, if I ask people who still are caught in this duality, they will say, "No, it's really hard to wake up." And, teachers even teach that, too. "Lots of lifetimes before you're going to wake up, it's really hard."

Q: Yeah, I read about it.

R: But, it's just the opposite. Actually, it's very easy! How hard can it be to be What You already are? You're Eternal! How hard can it be to be Eternal, if You're Eternal? It's got to be the easiest thing going. But, there is this thought system that says, "No, no, no, no, no, no, no, no, no, you'd better work on this, dude, you've been so bad at working on yourself." And, then it wants to kick you in the butt. Right?

But, it's really easy because all you have to do is surrender to the help that's coming to you from The Eternal.

Q: I want to surrender.

R: Yes, and all that you can do is want to, because you can't make yourself surrender! But, you can want to, and in that wanting The Eternal will make it happen for you. But, you have to stay consistent in the wanting. You can't let go and go back and try to find all kinds of value in the illusion and then complain that you're not getting the results that you want, which requires you to maintain awareness of the wanting. So, in that sense, it might take practice.

Q: How can you practise?

R: What do you do not to practise?

Q: I'm being blocked.

R: OK, don't be blocked.

Q: Don't be blocked?

R: Right. Before you said, "I'm me." And I said, "Don't, don't, don't be you." Let yourself be shown who the Real You is. The Real You is not blocked! So, you'll always come back to your own ideas of yourself.

Q: I think I have tried sometimes before, but I don't want to. I don't want to experience to not be successful in letting myself go anymore. I'm tired of being blocked, I think.

R: If you're on your own it's very easy to fail because that's what being on your own is.

Q: How can you not be on your own?

R: Aha! What do you do to believe you're on your own?

Q: What do you do? I think I reject it often.

R: OK, don't do that!

Q: Don't do that?

R: Right. Anything else?

Q: How can you call on a master?

R: Oh, easy! [Rananda shouts] MASTER!

Q: Master!

R: How hard can that be? See, the calling is not difficult, is it?

Q: No.

R: Right, it's not! It's wanting to call that you find difficulty with because you hear all these other thoughts in your mind that say, "Oh well, I tried this before, I failed," or whatever. You tell yourself a story, but if you'll just sincerely, from the recognition of the pain and the suffering that you're experiencing, call from there for help, you'll always have the help. Always! So, you'll have to get yourself to the point where you're willing to call for help.

Q: Can you not make some Master to help you? To help me...

R: Yes, sure, Masters are here to help.

Q: [Laughs.] OK.

R: Are you getting any help tonight?

Q: Absolutely!

R: Yeah, well, then, there you have it.

Q: Yes. Thank you very much.

* * *

Q: You talked about mistakes. To accept my mistakes. Then I will change. But the problem is the mistakes of some other people in my life who abused me and misused me. I see that somehow it was useful for my soul, so I can forgive them on that level, but please help me to solve this problem.

R: Well, how about if we looked at the lifetime of Jesus Christ of Nazareth?

Q: "Forgive them, because they don't know better?"

R: Well, that's not actually what he said. It's close, but it's not actually what he said. He said, "Forgive them Father for they know not what they do." What do God's Children do?

Q: This was not loving. [Laughs.]

R: No, no, no, you're not answering my question.

Q: I'm trying to see that it was loving, what they did.

R: Yes, but you're not looking at my question. My question is, "What do God's Children do?"

Q: Living their life. Doing.

R: Well, where are God's Children?

Q: Everywhere!

R: Oh, this is an illusion. They're everywhere in an illusion? Or they're Everywhere in Heaven? Which is it?

Q: You always say, "You're already Home in Heaven," so I guess that's the answer.

R: Yes, so what do you think he was saying? What do you really think his communication with his Father was, when he said, "Forgive them, they know not what they do." You think he was saying, "Forgive them, they don't know they're Home in Heaven with You?" Or do you think he believed they were really doing something and therefore he wasn't enlightened because he thought they were doing something while it's an illusion? If Jesus was enlightened, he knows this is an illusion. Yes? If he was enlightened and if he resurrected and ascended — I think he was probably enlightened first — so I think it's OK to accept the premise that Jesus was enlightened. Can we do that?

Q: Yes, yes.

R: OK. So, let's accept he became enlightened at some point. From a point of enlightenment he knew this was an illusion. OK?

Q: Yes.

R: If you're enlightened and you look at things in an illusion, do you really think they're real, or do you think they are part of an illusion?

Q: Both.

R: Nooooo. That would be a split mind.

[Audience: it's maybe not possible to answer if you're not enlightened.]

R: He's enlightened! He sees this is an illusion! That's what Enlightenment is. Yes? So, now he sees something going on in the illusion. Does he think it's real, or an illusion?

Q: Illusion!

R: Illusion! Now, if he was seeing all the things that were going on are an illusion, would he say, "Forgive them for what they're doing?" as if it was real, or was he saying, "Forgive them because they don't know it's an illusion and they don't know what they do because what they're doing is being Home in Heaven with you."

Q: I think I'm not up to it to answer. Because...

R: Because those ten percent are hanging out in there...

[Audience laughing.]

R: See?

Q: Yes. You see I need help.

R: Well, I'm helping you, though. I'm trying to help you see you're having a difficulty with healing a grievance, and once it's real, it's extremely hard to heal any grievance. If it's real, how could you ever, in fact, forgive?[6] Because it happened! That's why. If you make it real, it happened.

Q: Yes.

R: Now, it's impossible to forgive it, if it happened! But, forgiveness is actually, it was part of an illusion and has nothing to do with Reality. So, I can forgive it, because I want Reality. I don't want to be bound by the illusion. If I treat it as if it's real, then I'll never know What is Real and my grievances bind me to the illusion. My Joy and Happiness set me free from the illusion. And, what you're learning is that your Joy and Happiness are self-effulgent, which means they come from within and are not based on anything that happens outside of you. Because, the idea that there is an outside of you is what the illusion is.

_____

[6] *Forgiveness needs to be understood in the way it is explained in 'A Course In Miracles': "The world we see merely reflects our own internal frame of reference – the dominant ideas, wishes and emotions in our minds. 'Projection makes perception'. We look inside first, decide the kind of world we want to see and then project that world outside, making it The Truth as we see it. We make it true by our interpretations of what it is we are seeing. If we are using perception to justify our own mistakes – our anger, our impulses to attack, our lack of love in whatever form it may take – we will see a world of evil, destruction, malice, envy and despair. All this we must learn to forgive, not because we are being 'good' and 'charitable', but because what we are seeing is not true. We have distorted the world by our twisted defenses, and are therefore seeing what is not there. As we learn to recognize our perceptual errors, we also learn to look past them or 'forgive'. At the same time we are forgiving ourselves, looking past our distorted self-concepts to the Self That God created in us and as us." (From A Preface to 'A Course in Miracles'.)*

Quotes from 'A Course In Miracles' in this book are from the second edition. ISBN 0-9606388-8-1, 1996.

Q: Mmmm.

R: So, there are many what we call, "terrible things", that happen in this illusion. But, it is an illusion! We still feel the pain and everything because of the ideas that we have about a self that's a part of that illusion. I understand that. Of course, that's the way it would be. That's why forgiveness is also the answer! It could be the only possible answer to an illusion! If not, God's not Love, is He? Because, He made You and He is giving You a hard time. What kind of a God would that be? Certainly not a loving One! You really think a loving God would let You suffer and have pain? I mean, did you ever love anybody? You did? Have you ever wanted them to suffer while you were loving them?

Q: No.

R: No, see, God's not like that either. God doesn't like You to suffer. But, you know a self that has suffered and has experienced pain. That's why it's an illusion! But, if you don't forgive yourself and forgive everyone else the belief that the illusion is Reality, then you'll never be released and you'll never release!

Now, I'm not saying that you might not experience that as quite difficult because you have the energy associated with the ideas in perception that it actually did happen. So, the best that you could possibly do, is to want to know it only happened in an illusion. And, because you want to be what God created, which is Love Itself, you want to be That, you'll just go forward with as much Love as you can, moment by moment by moment, and want it to be healed. You can't make it heal.

Q: Only wanting and being willing.

R: You've got to, you've got to want it though, you can't get away from the wanting. The willingness will come. It's right in with the wanting. But, grace is what makes it happen. Believe me, I've had a lot of people ask me what kind of techniques I worked on, that brought about my Awakening. And, I can tell you that I spent many years with different techniques, meditation, many, many different things. But, none of it had anything to do with my Awakening! I was reading a book when it happened.

Q: Which one?

R: I think it was The Wizard of Oz.

[Audience laughing.]

R: "Click your heels three times. There is no place like home". [Rananda makes three clicking sounds.]

Q: Yes, Dorothy.

R: But, can you hear what it is that I'm saying?

Q: Yes.

R: Yes. So, you know, sometimes you fall, but pick yourself back up again. And, if you fall again, pick yourself back up again and just stay on the path of wanting. It will hurt and it will be OK and it will hurt and it will be OK and it will hurt and it will be OK, but just stay with it, because you don't know when the last moment of hurting and being OK is. You know what I'm saying? You can't see ahead. You don't know when that last one comes. But, you can just stay with it, because, once you're on the path, to go off doesn't make sense. Because, it might be just the next one, you don't actually know! All your failures are behind you and you know that your success is built upon your failures. No one reaches success without failure. Everybody is so disappointed with their failures. I reached a point where I was excited, [Rananda shouts.] YES, I FAILED AGAIN. YES!

[Audience laughing.]

Q: I must be close...

R: And, I'm not giving up! You see? That's the thing and it's just like, that's one failure that's not in front of me.

Q: That's positive thinking...

R: Yes, well, you see, you can call it that way. I never looked at it that way! I looked at it as I know The Truth. I know The Truth is, I'm not going to know when, but I'm certain of it! Because, if there's no Perfection, I might as well just die. But, if there is Perfection, then the certainty of the inevitability of my Awakening, my Enlightenment and eventually my Resurrection and my Ascension is guaranteed.

Q: Sure, I know.

R: Yes, yes.

Q: It takes some time!

R: No. It doesn't take time! It takes your...

Q: Willingness and wanting.

R: Willingness and wanting! That's what it takes.

Q: Yes.

R: It doesn't take time!

Q: Well, you said, you know, you get up and...

R: I said if...

Q: ... you fall and...

R: ... If you fall, get up! I didn't say you're going to fall! You're the one that put that in there! I don't want you to fall. I want you to succeed. Now! In fact, I will go so far as to say you've already succeeded. See, this is called mercy. Do you understand mercy? Mercy in this instance would be me willing to see you further along than what you think you are. And, if you join me in that then we've collapsed time. Time is not what is required. The willingness to join where you were not willing to join, which is what forgiveness is, is what allows the Awakening!

Q: Mm, mm. I am willing, that's why I asked you.

R: Just be with it, then. That's all that I'm saying. I don't have magical wands or anything like that. All I have is the Love of God! I know that God loves Me and in that I know that You love God and God loves You! I have no doubts at all in my mind with anybody that I meet, that That is The Truth of Them! When they tell me that That is not The Truth of Them, then the mercy comes forth. Because, I'm not willing to see Them any other way. So, they either join me in that or they reject me. Their rejection is the willingness for more pain and suffering; the joining is the willingness to know The Truth!

Q: But how can somebody be willing to suffer?

R: You have a whole planet full of them. I don't know! How do they do that? It doesn't make sense. I agree with you on that. It doesn't make sense, but this is a planet that doesn't make sense, is it not? It's not here to make sense. Right?

Q: You are right. I don't want to suffer anymore.

R: See, once you become a part of the solution rather than being a part of the problem, things really begin to move quickly. And, that is a decision! It is a choice to be a part of the solution rather than the problem. The way that you successfully become a part of the solution, is for you to choose for God. You choose to share Thoughts that God would share with You. And, then you begin to find that you're being led. In fact, you then come to realize you've always been led. But, there's been two guides. Then you begin to see, "Oh, when I listen to these thoughts and I make them mine and I start to follow them, I always get in trouble." And then, using choice, you say, "OK, I'm just not willing to do that anymore. My willingness is now going to enjoy the Thoughts that I can share with God." Then that will lead you. To what? Thoughts that you can share with God. What would that be like if you were sharing Thoughts with God?

Q: Loving Thoughts.

R: Because you're talking about The Eternal, you're getting Guidance from The Eternal, from The Divine. OK?

Q: So, why deeksha?[7]

R: So, why not? Whys? Whys? I've never understood whys. Because some wise guy always says why not. See, for me it wasn't deeksha. In 1984, what happened with me, Jesus showed me. When I reached that point where I couldn't handle The Love anymore, and I began to realize that the Golden Energy was completely taking over my body and my awareness, I didn't know how to deal with It! I tried doing the kundalini thing, I tried all my practices, all the techniques to try to handle this thing that was happening with me that I, as far as I knew, didn't ask to have happen. I was just lying in bed reading a book. It had nothing to do with self help in any way whatsoever. And, it started happening and I couldn't handle it in any way whatsoever. And, then, when I reached the point where I was really sure I was going to die if this thing didn't stop, Jesus...

Q: Did you think that you would die?

R: Have you ever thought that you might die? Ever?

Q: Yes.

---

[7] *Deeksha is the transference of Divine Energy by laying on hands, inspired by Bhagavan and Amma from India.*

R: Well, then use your own experience. Listen, when this energy completely takes over the dissolving of your body, and that idea was not even a part of your working mind, it's a little bit of a shock! And, when it's happening, it's even more of a shock! It's not like, you're sitting there and you're going, "Well, let me think about this. Would I like to have that happen, or not?" No, it is happening, babe!

Q: And, how long did it take? Was it for days or hours or...?

R: Well, I wasn't looking at the clock...

[Audience laughing.]

R: As far as I know it happened in one evening, but the effects of it last till right now. The point I wanted to make was this, it started with awareness of Love. I was receiving waves of Love through my whole being. I mean, people say, "Oh, when Love gets in your heart..." But listen, I want to tell you, Love gets to more than your physical heart! It gets to every cell of what you believe is you. And, It begins to release everything that makes up the illusion. That's what happened with me. The waves of Love happened and It went into the cellular structure to every part of my body and It began to release the Golden Energy. I had never had that happen to me. It was like dying! It wasn't wonderful! I wasn't ready to write home to mom.

[Audience laughing.]

R: "Guess what happened to me, mom, you'll never believe it? Wow, boy, it was so nice I wanted to get up and dance." No, it wasn't like that! It was a threat to everything that I believed in! Then right at the point where, as far as I was concerned, I was about to die and had tried all these different techniques that I had practised, [Rananda takes a deep breath], all the different techniques that come out of India that I had worked with, and I tried everything, the more I tried, the worse it got, meaning the more Love there was. Then, finally, it was like I was willing to die rather than have more of this intensity. The intensity was just there, because I was resisting! But, I didn't know that then!

So, I was in the feeling I'm going to die and right at that point, where I was ready to surrender into dying, Jesus said to me, "Let it be released from every cell." And, as soon as he said the last word my whole body, everything, my awareness, everything became Golden Light, even the person that was in the room with me. The Light in the room was not just a little lamp, the whole room lit up in Golden Energy. And, she said at the same time that I did, "It's the Golden Energy." Of course, by then I didn't need anybody to tell me that, and neither did she at that point. [Rananda laughs.] And then, from there, it went into what you here tend to call Oneness!

Q: So, the intensity that you experienced was due to resistance…

R: I was resistant, yes.

Q: …and when you let go of the resistance, then was it softer, or…?

R: No, I wouldn't say softer, but it had its way with me. You *are* the Golden Energy. It's trying to reveal Itself as You. But you've got your hair done the way you do and you wear glasses and you put clothing on your body. See, we have these ideas and those ideas of self are what is in the way. That's what I'm saying, it was difficult for me. I had a whole thought system of who and what I am and what Masters are and what they're called and who are the ones working with me.

So, everybody has their story! Your story is what's in the way! So, your whole story has to be removed from your mind for you, for you to know what is there when your story is not there. OK? That's what was happening to me and it wasn't like I was in deep meditation and went into this great beautiful, you know, oh, yeah, Buddha-land, wow, cool! It wasn't like that at all. I was literally reading a book when this whole thing happened to me. It was sort of like I was plucked and it happened. I had no one to tell me how to deal with it!

Q: So, you went through it alone...

R: Basically.

Q: ...you didn't have a teacher...

R: No, not at that time. My teachers were not in human form.

Q: So, you are aware having contact all the time with eh...

R: No, no, no, I wasn't. They would bother me too much if I did that. They don't want to do that. They want you to get on with what you're here for. They are guides. They guide you so that when you come to those moments where things are difficult for you, they're there as guidance. Masters don't want to take away from you. They want you to recognize what is already there so that you'll begin joining with that, sharing it. That was the beginning. From there I made a lot of mistakes and shared a lot of Love and everything began to unfold in the way in which things unfold. As long as you're in association with an ego there are still things that need to be healed and when that's finished then you are finished. Until then, you be about your healing. You do the best you can and when you make a mistake, you pick yourself up, practise forgiveness and move on along the path of Love as best as you can, knowing that there's guidance there for you if you'll just keep staying on the path. You're not bound by your past unless you bind yourself! Your brother is not bound by his past unless you bind him to it!

Q: Is forgiveness, what you talk about, is that higher than karma?

R: It's a karma breaker!

Q: Is karma washed out by this Christ Consciousness?

R: Yes, there is no such thing as karma, in fact! Karma means nothing more than you get the results of your thoughts! If you make it into a system, a law, then you have laws of an illusion! Well, what is more valuable than laws of an illusion are God's Laws! God's Laws are, "You're My Son, you're Perfect and Pure and Whole and I'm well pleased with You." That will break the laws of the illusion! The question is, do you want karma to be broken or do you want to be bound by it?

Q: That's a good question!

R: Yes, and while those thoughts are there and valued, you will have karma and that will happen. And, you will be bound and come around again. Why? Because of your own thoughts, which is the way it works!

3

YOU CANNOT WAKE YOURSELF UP

Enlightenment / Separation /
The Light Does All the Work / Spirit versus Ego /
Creation / Imagination / Judgment / Heart-Mind

Q: You said that the undoing of the dream can occur in an instant.

R: In fact, it does!

Q: What is the ending of the dream then?

R: The moment where there is no dream. The dream is of time. It's a dream of time and space. If the dream ends, where is time and space?

Q: Nowhere.

R: So, there is a nowhere? Hello?

Q: Yes.

R: Yes what?

Q: There is a nowhere.

R: There is a nowhere! See, that's the intent to make it real and then overcome it. It will never work that way. Here's the way it works. You have no idea. Why? Because the ideas of the illusion have been removed from your mind for you by The Light. So, you have no idea! The best you can say about it is, "Wow, Everything is beautiful." And, you're talking about Everything because there is no idea in there about an illusion. Not even one that is gone. The ideas are gone. It's not there. The only thing that's in there is the Source of thought that is with Everything. With Oneness. The illusion literally disappears. Now, when it disappears there will be a moment when it goes from your awareness of it to no awareness of it. That's what we call quantum.

Q: Is there any transforming experience in the body when you are in the process of Awakening?

R: Yes.

Q: I mean Enlightenment.

R: Just for a moment. Enlightenment occurs when you're not aware of a body any longer. So, there is a moment where that transmission takes place. And part of the transmission that takes place is because you have not only the idea of a body, but the purpose of the body is also in the mind. And the purpose of the body is to prove separation from Oneness. So, there has to be a moment where you are literally recognizing the pain and the suffering of its existence, simply because it keeps you from Love Itself.

So, its existence alone is pain and suffering. However, it's not usually recognized. You follow what I'm saying? I'm literally telling you that everybody who thinks they're in this illusion, that their pain and suffering is constant. And people deny that. But, their denial has a purpose. And, my declaration that every moment of it is painful, has a purpose.

If you are that that has a choice and you can see that every moment is painful, then you will not choose this illusion, because nobody in their right mind wants pain and suffering and death. Nobody in their right mind wants that. Only us insane guys that run around this planet think it's OK to die, grow old, kill one another, wipe species off the planet, pollute the air and wipe out forests. Only insane minds do things like that. Like the human species.

Q: Isn't that all an illusion?

R: Yes, it's an illusion. Yep, yep, it's an illusion... And you're suffering in it...

Q: How come that some people are stuck in the body?

R: It appears that way because there is a belief that that is true. There is a desire for that to be true. You know, if you think of the illustrious teacher of 2500 years ago whom they called Buddha... He told you that what gets you in your deep brown stuff are your desires. Right? Hello? Your inability to satisfy your desires. So, you are here because of what you desire. And people don't like to admit that, do they? Do you like to admit that you want to be where there is pain and suffering so you can get some of it? You want to get your fair share of the pain and suffering?

Anybody here want to admit that?

Q: I want to be here, I like it here!

R: Yes, see. There you go. He likes his pain and suffering. And, everybody who is here does the same thing, but no one – except for this young man over here – likes to admit it. But it's a necessary part of your Awakening to admit that it's your choice. And then, when the body gets ill, you get angry at it. "Grrr, why can't you be a good body?" Look what you've been doing to it. "Me? No! What's wrong with smoking cigarettes every day, and drinking alcohol and staying up all night long and eating terrible food? Everybody has got to go sometime. What's your problem, boy?"

Q: So why do we want separation?

R: No one knows. It's one of the things no one knows, because it's insane. No right mind can understand it. As a matter of fact, when you start making progress... Do you know how you're going to know you're making progress? It doesn't make sense to you here anymore. And then your favorite word is going to be... whoops. Do you know that word, whoops? You have any idea what it means? It's the same word in Dutch, only it has a Dutch accent to it. I've noticed that that word is not really well-known in Holland... because I hardly hear anybody say whoops.

Q: We don't like surprises.

R: Well, whoops is not necessarily a surprise; it's admitting that's what they don't like. They don't like to admit they made a mistake. That's why they don't say whoops. Otherwise, if whoops was: I made a mistake so it can be corrected, you would be going whoops all the time.

[Audience laughing.]

R: "But no, this is serious stuff we're in here, boy. I'm spiritual, man, come on. Don't make me look at things I don't want to look at. We're all doing fine, aren't we?"

[Audience laughing.]

Q: How can we still want to suffer then? Or, is it only a matter of time before the suffering ends?

R: What is going to end it?

Q: Not me, but...

R: I bet it's not you. Unless you are talking about the You that You really are, which is The Light![8]

Q: Who is the obstruction?

R: Nothing is obstructing The Light! The Light is Eternal! Nothing is obstructing It! That's where your healing is.

Q: So, this suffering isn't real?

---

[8] *Rananda makes a distinction between the illusory you and the Real You. The illusory you is called the ego in 'A Course In Miracles' and is nothing but an idea of a false self in the mind. The Real You is in constant communication with God or our Source.*

R: You're giving it the belief that it's real. You want it to be real.

Q: So, how can I stop wanting it to be real?

R: Who does all the work?

Q: It only means that I can't do anything?

R: YES, THAT'S WHAT I'M TEACHING!!!

Q: So, my suffering must go.

R: No, The Light does all the work!!!

Q: When?

R: Aha. It's a time thing. Listen, "Where the hell have you been all my life anyway? Haven't you heard me complaining? What kind of light are you? You probably forgot to pay the bill."

[Audience laughing.]

R: You can't wake yourself up. The Light does the work! The Light does the work because It will get you in touch with the longing that Perfection put within you when You were created. You have a longing. Love longs to be Love.

Q: But that's a desire?

R: No, humans have desires. The Eternal You does not desire anything. It is Everything already.

Q: Yeah, but what do I have?

R: But? Wait a minute! I just told you that You are Everything and you say but?

[Audience laughing.]

R: Boy, I can't wait till you're up here, teaching everybody. "You know, I had this guy, Rananda, who did his absolute best to help me, and you know, I just couldn't hear it." When you can't hear it, you can't hear. You know what I'm saying?

And then you go home and you say, "What the hell was he talking about?" And then you go to somebody else, "Do you know what he was talking about?" And they go, "No, I don't know what he was talking about. Something about, 'We're Perfect.'" "We're Perfect? He couldn't... he can't know what I do every day." "Yeah, that's what he was saying, what you do every day so that you don't know You're Perfect." Do you see what you do, not to know You're Perfect? Because when you do, you'll stop. How? The Light will show you the way.

Q: So, what's the use of talking? This talking?

R: Because you're getting help.

Q: How?

R: You listen, I talk, you get help.

Q: That's what you say.

R: That's what I said, yes. So if you reject what I say, no help! That's how it works! Hey boy, are we having fun?

Q: Can I make a confession?

R: A confession?

[Audience laughing and cheering.]

R: [To the hostess.] Did you bring my holy water? Wait a minute. Oh, yes, the holiest water on your planet. Come here. Come here.

Q: For about two or three years I have been listening to you.

R: That's only the couple of years that you could remember that you have listened. We've been at this a long time, brother. More than one lifetime, I'd like you to know.

Q: What I want to convey is, that all this time I was thinking of the other source of thinking, and many times I saw myself negatively thinking of myself. And I said to myself, "You don't deserve that."

R: Oh.

Q: That's my confession.

R: OK. Does that mean I have to come around again in another three years?

[Audience laughing.]

Q: No.

R: I get to see you every three years now? That's it?

Q: So, I have to choose between two systems of thought?

R: Yes, absolutely. Spirit or The Eternal always encourages you to share the Thoughts that God would share with You, that Perfection would share with You. That's all It ever does. This other devious thought system always wants you to get involved in something in the story that lets you believe it's really going on. Sorry, but that's the way it is.

Ego speaks with certainty and you come up with the doubts. It is certain it can convince you to have doubts. It is certain you're separate from God. It is absolutely certain that you're not awake to The Truth of You, and it knows that's a fact, because you are listening to it. It's very certain within its own closed thought system and Spirit is completely certain in Its closed thought system, because Spirit doesn't know about the thought system of the ego. It's too busy having fun with God, sharing The Light, The Love. It doesn't share this thought system and this thought system does not share the Thoughts of The Light and they're both completely certain. And you, the mind, you sit there going, "Mm, mm, I wonder which one I should choose? Let me see, this one is nothing in certain death and This is Everything in certain life. Mm? I don't know!" But that doesn't mean that the intent of Spirit talking to you is to cause confusion.

Q: But it doesn't argue with it?

R: Who argues?

Q: Ego argues.

R: Yeah, but what would Spirit argue with?

Q: It just presents Its Thoughts.

R: Yes, to your mind. But ego, what you call ego, that thought system also presents thoughts to your mind. You can't try to tell them they're working differently in your mind. They work exactly the same, because your mind only works one way. But it has different thoughts that come into the mind with a different purpose. And then you, the mind, chooses. Because one of the thoughts of you is that you have choice. Do you think God created You with choice as to be What God created You to be? There is God, All-Knowing, All-Powerful, Everywhere, creates You and goes. "Oh, gee, I don't know what to do with You. Just go play. Do whatever You want." Do you think that's what God did? "Get out of here, I'm busy creating."

[Long silence.]

R: "This is my Son in whom I am well pleased."

[Audience laughing.]

Q: So, there's no Creation?

R: Yes, there is only Creation! That's what's Eternal!

Q: Yes, but Creation involves...

R: God and You! It's Everything that there is extending Itself so there is more of Itself. And that extension is what you call Creation.

Q: Is that like the Son of God who is also called the word?

R: Yes, there is a lot of things being said, except for in Heaven. There is not a lot of things being said there.

Q: That's Creation and that's the word.

R: Yes, what word? What is that word? Yabadabado? Yahweh?

Q: I'm referring to what the book of Genesis said.

R: OK, Genesis. Is that the word?

Q: No, I'm not saying that...

R: No, I'm asking. What is the word? Is it Dutch or English?

Q: No it's pre... It is not linguistic.

R: Then why do we call it a word?

Q: Because it is pre-English. All languages arise from the word.

R: Right. All languages are an illusion. Aha. In the beginning was The Inner Word. And, that was with God and still is, and is God!

Q: Yes, but It is also eternally expressed by God.

R: Yes, as You! And you have been trying to do this other thing. That's why you don't know The Word.

Q: So, you said, "God speaks The Word." Could we not say...

R: God doesn't speak The Word.

Q: Expresses God.

R: God *is* The Word! So are You! You are an extension of God as God's Creation! Your mind was created by God. By God's Light.

Q: Well, thank you, because I cannot imagine something higher.

R: That's great that you can't image it. It's really good that you can't image it. But, can you want to know or let yourself want to know? Because you can do that. What would you want imagination for, when Reality is Everything? I think imagination is really overvalued. Something here that has imagination, what do you call that? Humans? You don't go around saying, "Man, that dog has the greatest imagination. Cats now have imagination. But dogs? Man, they're so..." Daaaaaaah, give me that, eh... [Pants]. Thank you. Cats are like, "Excuse me, I'm sleeping now." You know, and they're off in their imagination. And cats are really big on that. But if cats had a greater imagination than people did – just if, OK? – there would still be something greater, because what makes cats? And people? And trees and all the greater stuff? Now, being in touch with that would be just a little exciting, I would think. It's better than talking with David Bohm, mister quantum physics himself. It would be better than Einstein, who said you can't go faster than the speed of light or you're going to die.

Q: Einstein was wrong?

R: Well, no, considering what he thought he was, he was absolutely right. But considering what God knows Him to be, he was a little off. See, you're always going to get the results of the way you want to think about yourself and that's my whole point. Be careful the way you want to think about yourself, because you're going to get the result of that.

* * *

Q: I catch myself judging somebody and at that moment I'm very much saying to myself, "You shouldn't do that and that person is entitled to his own process."

R: Yes, don't worry about it.

[Audience laughing.]

Q: OK. Is that the answer to any question? Always right. No worries, mate. Don't worry about it?

R: Well, kind of, but worrying never helped anybody. So, you know, specifically, when you say, "Is that the answer to any question about worry?" Yes, that would be true. But, it might be helpful to have a clear understanding of the nature of what it is that you're looking at. But when you're actually just talking about worrying, if you're asking me, you know, flat-out about worrying, it never helped. It has never helped anybody in any moment of time.

Q: I found myself listening when you were talking to the gentleman and I have ideas about it, judgments about it, and I'm trying not to be judgmental and to think he's entitled to his own process.

R: Yes. And my answer was?

Q: Whoops.

R: No, I didn't say whoops, I said what?

Q: Don't worry about it.

R: I said, "Don't worry about it. Let The Light do the work."

Q: Yes.

R: So, when The Light makes it clear to you what's going on, you've to let it show you what the correct or the wise or the spiritual, or whatever words you want to use, answer is. But where is The Love? How do you think that you recognized that you were judging in that moment? Do you think The Light had anything to do with you recognizing that?

Q: This doesn't feel right to me.

R: Well, of course it doesn't. How can judging yourself make you feel good? There's no Love in that. No, no, no. So, don't do that!

Q: But how do I stop it? I do it, so...

R: Don't do that! There is something I don't understand. How come, when someone like me says, "Don't do that," you always have a hard time with that? Why don't you just go, "Yeah, that's right. Hey, I don't do that anymore. Yeah, wow, wow, wow!!! [Cheering.] It's gone, it's gone. It's gone. Yeahhhh, yeahhhh. Party!!! Call out the neighbors. I don't do that shit anymore. What an exciting moment!!!" No, instead it's like, "Uh, pooh, well…, uh, how, how do I don't do that anymore?"

Q: Can I say something? The problem is, if you say, "Don't do that," to yourself, your subconscious cannot understand the word "not", so it's saying to itself, "Do that." That's the whole problem. So…

R: Pooh. You think, do you really think you're going to talk to me like that, and I'm going to go, "Oh yes, I forgot, the ego." Do you, I mean, really, do you think I'm going to do that? Do you think I would do that?

"Rananda, don't you know how strong the ego is?" Let me see: that thing that doesn't exist. Mmm. You want me to be concerned about that? You really think it works that way? You've convinced yourself that that's the way it's OK for your mind to work. And I'm saying, "Don't do that!" And I'm telling you, "Listen to me!" Are you going to reject that?

Q: But, what he's saying is…

R: I know exactly what he's saying. Does anybody want to know what I'm saying?

[Audience laughing.]

R: Oh, I'll calm down. I'm in Holland now… I forgot. One final time here, OK? Spirit shares Everything with God. God doesn't know "not". Not is a word that comes from the thing that you call an ego. OK? Got it? Simple. Spirit always represents God, Perfection, It's Eternal, All-Powerful. All-Powerful! When somebody says to you, "Don't do that," I'm directing that right to the All-Powerful part of You. If you go there with me, if you enter in there with me, you'll never do that again. I guarantee you and I promise you that's The Truth!

Q: Oh, can you say it once more then?

R: I don't know what I just said.

Q: Don't do that!

R: OK. Don't do that!

[Audience laughing.]

R: That was the most important part. See, you've trained yourself to think that all these other powers, and all these other thoughts, and all these other ways in which you think that you've divided your mind up – subconscious, unconscious – is Reality. You're nuts! You're absolutely nuts! You're insane! What do you tell yourself, and what have you convinced yourself of? You're nuts! You're Eternal! You are Eternal! You are what Love is! Please, just let go of what you prove to yourself in this illusion. Let go. And believe me, I'm telling you, because It is Eternal, It's that way right now. And I'm telling you, like it or not, You're always going to be Eternal, because that's what Eternal means. And, You're that right now! That's certain. You want to talk about certainty? That's certainty. But, that is something you verify not with your reasoning. That's something you verify because you recognize it in your own heart. And where is your heart, if not in your mind?

Q: It's not in your mind?

R: It is in your mind. Everything is in your mind because God created your mind to know everything. And it is true, there is a Heart. And it is true that the Heart receives direct communication from The Divine. But it is in your mind. God creates through God's Mind. Mind is not the bogeyman that the eastern teachers teach you that it is. It's The Light of

God! And you've abused it by believing in these thought systems that bring you experiences less than Love. The Heart is in your mind. It's the most beautiful part of your mind, but It's not separate from your Mind. If It was separate from your Mind there would be no such thing as Oneness. Oneness is Oneness. One thing. Not lots of energies. One. Not lots of lights. One. Not lots of colored light. One energy. Love Itself. Let's get over it. You know what I'm saying? All the crap from all the teachers from all the religions. Let's be done with it and let's go, "Show me. Show me." And then let yourself be shown.

* * *

Q: Aren't we conditioned?

R: Who conditioned you?

Q: I don't know. I came here...

R: Where?

Q: Here.

R: In your mind?

Q: In my mind.

R: OK, then who conditioned you?

Q: I don't know about the beginning...

R: AHHHH!

Q: I can't remember that I was thinking, "I'm Eternal." I was thinking, "I'm me. I'm something..."

R: I'm conditioned.

Q: Yes.

R: Yes. You're not. You're Eternal. If you think you're conditioned, who do you think conditioned you to think that? Who makes the choices?

Q: In all these years?

R: Yes, yes...

Q: It's not easy...

R: Experiences. Your choices?

Q: That's why we ask sometimes, "How can we follow a path...?"

R: You can't!

Q: No, but then you have to say, "OK, I'm Eternal, I'll wait for grace."

R: No, no, you have to hear me. You have to hear me that it can be right now!

Q: I can't say whoops?

R: You have to get so excited that it can happen right now! And then there's a little passion. You know, the Dutch don't like to be passionate. And I should be more like the eastern teachers. I should sit here, you know, I should have flowers around me and I should just be really, really gentle with you. But, I'm not like that! I'm alive! You know what I'm saying? I'm alive with an energy and a passion and a spirit that's moving and wants to communicate with you about how incredible You are. And you want to sit there and keep telling me, "Oh, no, I'm not. No, I'm not." So, you're seeing the "No, I'm not", and I'm seeing the True You, because I've awakened to the True You. And you keep on doing everything you can to try to get me to accept that crap that you believe in. And I'm doing everything *I* can. Things that you can see and things that you can't see. Because you haven't let your eye be opened up yet, to help you. And, if that's not Love in the face of your rejection, I don't know what it is. But that's all that I have to share with you, my help. Having been shown the way to bring it to you and tell

- 55 -

you, "Look it's not a big deal." It might be the only deal, but it's not a big one, because You're already Perfect. And all it's waiting for is for you to accept it, to want it and stop telling me this other story. You're telling the other story. You can stop! "Yes, but I had years and years and years and years and lifetimes of telling the story." So what! What does that mean? What does time mean when it's an illusion? "Well that's fine, but I don't believe that." Well, then you'll get the result of not being willing to believe. What do you want me to do? All I can do is present The Truth to you. You're going to do with that whatever you want. I know that. I know I can't make you experience the True You. However, I know that I can experience bringing you the frequency and the energy that allows you to make an instantaneous shift in your mind that is a holy instant where you join and You know the Real You. I know that that is not only possible and – you're not going to like this – it is inevitable!

Q: What?

R: Inevitable! That means you don't have a choice, dude!

[Audience laughing.]

R: I can get you now, or I can get you now! Right? Because it's an Eternal Now!

Q: It is the choice just to be passionate?

R: Yes.

Q: As you are?

R: Yes.

Q: That is so funny.

R: Yes.

Q: All around you passion, passion, passion. Everybody passionate, passionate, passionate. That's where all the energy comes from, you know. And The Truth is there before you start thinking. Wow. Being here… My goodness! That's the illusion too, right? Yes?

R: That's right. But it's the part of the illusion that ends the illusion! That's why it's important. It's just not a part of the illusion. It's how the illusion ends! And that's the most important part, because you got stuck in the beginning. And you didn't even think there's an end that didn't include death. So, it is important. Yeah, certainly this is all a part of the illusion, but it doesn't come from the illusion because its purpose is not to maintain it. It's to end it! And that's why it is valuable. The only value it has is that it will end the illusion with you.

In the end we've always said, Love is the answer! And that's because Love is the answer! And we've always said - what? God is Love! And so, therefore, whatever God creates is also Love. And, if you don't share those thoughts about You, then you want to separate yourself from God and what God creates. And, that's what the nature of the problem is. The answer is, there is no such problem because your idea of separating and not being Love has not succeeded. They are thoughts that have entered into your mind, but they have not been a part of Reality. That's the saving grace.

If you hear that, then all that remains is to accept it. And acceptance doesn't take time. It just takes willingness. If you reject it, then you will say, "I want more time," and nothing will stop you from having more time. But don't tell me that time is needed to accept it because that's not true. Willingness is needed to accept it and that's all. Time is needed when you reject that. God is Love and You are Love. Because the rejection of that is what time and space is. OK?

Q: And there is no time because it's an illusion. How is that?

R: That's right! But, if you're stuck in it and you're saying that, it's not helpful for you to get out. It's OK to start there, you know what I'm saying, so that you understand it as a concept and then you go, "Oh, because I understand that concept, that must mean this and this," which leads you to recognize it must not actually be that. "But, this is going on in my mind, so I must be doing something to keep it going on in my mind. So, if I don't do that, it will stop." Now, if you have a thought in there that says, "I can't stop it," then you won't. But if it comes in there and you go, "Oh, I see, this is what I do to keep it going," and when you don't do that, it will stop. So, if you don't find the strength to do that, then that's when you pray and call for the help to experience the strength. So, when it shows up, you'll be true because you want to share the Thoughts of Perfection. You want your heart to be on fire for God because that's when you're really You.

You don't know what to do with yourself and that's when you'd better be listening to Spirit because you can also take that same passion and energy and dump it into this world. And you'll be sorry for doing that. More pain and more suffering with all that passion. But, when you turn it to Love and when you turn it to Life, you begin to have everything to disappear. In fact, the first thing that happens, is you begin to have a portal of Light, a rip or a tear in space and time and it will begin to allow, out!

And, that's what we do. We come together; we experience the judgments and the release of that through forgiveness. The Love begins to show up and in that Love we begin to recognize the joining that takes place. And, as you join you begin to make a rip and tear in space and time – in the illusion. And, in that rip and tear of time and space you can access Oneness. And, as you access It, you will find that you prefer It. And, when you prefer It, you'll be willing to join, over and over and often and often until there is no time. OK?

4

LOVE IS WHAT SUSTAINS YOU

Obstacles to Oneness / Dream-Reality / Knowing / Creation

Q: You say that what counts is Oneness and that we raise obstacles to Oneness.

R: It looks that way.

Q: Is it really me who raises the obstacles?

R: It looks that way.

Q: I can imagine many situations where the obstacles come from – I hardly dare to say the word – karma, your neighbor or whatever.

R: It looks that way, doesn't it?

Q: Sometimes it looks like the obstacle comes from the other.

R: Do you understand the difference between it *looks* that way and it *is* that way?

Q: I think so.

R: OK. Then you wouldn't have any problems. You are not concerned with what it looks like but you're concerned with what is. When you sleep, do you ever have a dream?

Q: Yes.

R: Did you ever have a dream that you thought was real while you were dreaming?

Q: Yes.

R: And then you say you woke up?

Q: Yes.

R: And then you remembered the dream?

Q: Yes.

R: While you were dreaming it was real for you. It's kind of like that. Does that help?

Q: Yes.

R: Your Awakening is actually really no different than you recognizing what you call awaking is actually part of the dream, too. In other words, that idea of shifting through different consciousnesses, what you call consciousness or awareness, you begin to realize that there is a single You behind each and every one of those movements. Not a different you! And, then you recognize that the one that's aware of this, what you call reality here, is the same one and it's not actually reality, it's just another dream! But, it has different parameters. The laws are a little bit different. But it is still a dream. Isn't that good news?

Q: This world that I experience with my senses seems so real!

R: It seems that way. But what is it? Have you ever noticed wherever you look that you can't see everything? Have you ever noticed that if you listen you can't hear everything? So, it seems that way. But, if you knew that neither your hearing nor your seeing was giving you the whole picture, why would you trust it to give you the whole picture? Why would you trust it if you knew it doesn't give you Everything?

Q: That's a good question.

R: I have lots of really good questions that are not only worthy to be asked but also worthy to find the answer to.

Q: This single you, behind all the experiences, is that close to God? Or the closest that you can come to God?

R: That's a tricky question. You see, the maker of experiences is an illusion. The Creator of Reality is the only Reality there is! That's why you call It Oneness! If It's Oneness, there are no parts to It. And, you want to know what's behind something. Well, that's what twoness or more than twoness is. It's not Oneness. There is nothing behind Oneness. Unless you want to call that God. But once again, when you do that, the risk you run is that you think there is two. There is a Creation and then there is God. And you think there are two. You don't think they are the same thing. And that's basically what this illusion is, the idea that this is not God.

Q: So, even the giving of the name is creating a division?

R: Yes.

Q: That's why language always divides.

R: That's right. It wasn't created to join. Language was not made in your mind in order to join. It was made in your mind in order to divide. And you know that's true because you have more than one language.

Q: The Bible speaks about the language of The Word inside which is true for all of us and which precedes all languages. I compare this to the apostles. At Pentecost they spoke in tongues and everybody could understand it.

R: Hm, no, we didn't all speak in tongues. Some of us just sat and listened.

Q: OK, but, this has been elaborated by Saint Augustine. He says that before all language there is the word, which is received from the Father, which is not in any kind of language.

R: Actually it is, but it is not in a spoken language. We call it a language of Light. Everyone is already communicating without a language, and not only what you call psychic people. If you think you don't have that kind of a capability, then you think those are special people. But the closer you come to the True You, the more that you allow your mind into the Awakening of what It is You have been created to be. Everything, Oneness, is in communication. All of Oneness is an activity of Knowing, a Beingness. It is What You are! It's not something you experience! As if there is you and an experience. It is What You are! It is being You! Isn't that good news? We have lots of good news here tonight.

Q: Great! It is very beautiful.

R: Good news is beautiful too, absolutely. So, the idea is to allow yourself to be inspired and be brought into the Remembering of The Truth of You. Would that work?

Q: Isn't that the experience we need, to come to the True You?

R: It kind of looks that way. But, if you look at the way things have actually been reduced from Singularity, the reason you had experiences was to prove that You are not singular. Because it is impossible to say that Oneness has experiences. Oneness just is, It doesn't have experiences. It just is! But you who think that you are something separate from Everything have experiences. And then you believe you can describe them. And the words and your ideas of what those experiences are, are set apart in your mind from other words and other ideas of experiences or what you tend to call, what? Situations? Circumstances?

So, when you say, "I am in a situation," you're talking about a you that you define as you and other things that are in relationship to that, right? So, there is no Oneness in that. Every time you talk about an experience that is in association in your own mind with the idea of a situation, you already define a self as being separate and therefore experiences are actually of an illusion.

Knowing, on the other hand, has no experience to It. It's being what It is. Now, that might sound like I am splitting hair, you know, things that really aren't important and trying to give them importance. But, I can guarantee you that there is a number of these ideas that are in your mind that are used to confuse you and that do not allow you to have a clear picture of Reality. You do it with the idea of forgiveness. You do it when you use the word consciousness. You do it when you use the word Reality. There is a number of words that are really important and if you don't understand the Purity that goes with those words, you will abuse them by applying them to the illusion. It is really important to be able to discriminate between what is illusion and what is Reality. And, that's what the idea of your Awakening or Enlightenment is all about.

If you only had so much time, or maybe I can put it into money. People seem to relate to money. Whether they have it or not, they seem to relate to it. If you had so much, if you had a certain amount of time or money, it would have a value for you. And, that would be more or less. You have more or less money or more or less time. Yes? And so, if it was valuable to you, you would want to use it wisely. Because time passes and then it's gone and you won't have it any longer. And, the same with money! If you use it, there will be a point that you won't have it any longer. So, you want to use it wisely.

If you knew the nature of You, you would use it wisely. And the way to use that wisely would be to discover the Real You and stop trying to fix the one that you think you already know. Because, if there is a you that you can fix, that's not the You I am talking about. Perfection doesn't need to be fixed. The Eternal does not need to be fixed. It's not broken, there is nothing wrong with It. But you keep on thinking of a you that needs help, that has problems, that needs to be fixed. That can't be the True You! And, you say you want to do that so that you can be Perfect, know The Eternal. But, wouldn't it just be as simple as recognizing that that's not the True You? Wouldn't it be as simple as not telling the story of all your problems? Perhaps?

Q: I'm very practical and...

R: So, now you are going to tell me you are Home in Heaven, right? That's being practical. Yes.

Q: That's the thing. We've just been away on a trip and it was lovely. I come back and see my bank account and I freak out.

R: That's fun. Then you learn something about yourself, when you freak out, don't you?

Q: Hm. Yes. Lousy habit, but it tends to get me off the hook or on the hook. I don't know.

R: If you let go of your judgments and just learn to stop beating yourself up, I might be a little helpful to you. But, learn, that is the key there. So, that you don't have to keep making the same mistake over and over again. And, making judgments is what making the mistake is. How about if you would have returned and the bank made a mistake on your account and it had a whole bunch of zeros behind a number? Then you would decide to be happy? So, your happiness depends upon numbers?

Q: Well, money can't buy me Love, I heard on the radio.

R: Yes, and everything we hear on the radio must be true!

Q: So, you are saying that we should stop judging, right?

R: I am not telling you what you should do! I am telling you what result you'll get when you tell me what it is that you do.

Q: OK. Isn't it essential to judge in this world? I mean, from the beginning when people just came to this earth, they had to judge that they could eat certain berries and could not eat others. That was the way to keep themselves alive, wasn't it? So ....

R: No. No. Love is What sustains You, not food. There are many things that man has forgotten and many that he is about to remember. Where those questions that you're asking would lead me – I don't know where they lead you – but they would lead me to ask, "Why did I come here to begin with?"

Q: I was interested in what you were going to tell us.

R: Why would you ask me? I think you are asking the wrong person why you are here. I think you ought to be asking yourself why you're here. Do you understand what I am saying?

Q: No.

R: Well, how many people are there in this world? Just an estimate.

Q: You tell me.

R: So, you are going to do it again, are you? Just make an estimate, who cares, it doesn't have to be right or wrong. We're just talking so that we can see how our mind works.

Q: Five billion.

R: Five billion. OK. So, you have five billion people in the world, and you're one of them? And, you don't know why you're here. Right? And, you can go to anyone of those five billion people and ask them. Couldn't you?

Q: Yes.

R: As long as you could reach them, I mean. Have you tried anything like that? Have you gone around and asked people why you're here or why they're here?

Q: No, I haven't.

R: So, this is the first time you've asked?

Q: Well, I have not really travelled around to ask people why they're there, but this is not the first time I have asked somebody.

R: So, the last time you asked, what did they say?

Q: I don't really remember.

R: Whatever it was, it was not accepted as the answer by you, because you don't remember, right? I mean, if it was really the real answer there would be a whole thing that went along with that. My point is this, there are billions of people on this planet and everybody makes up their mind about what they think is going on. All of them do. And, everybody is asking everybody else. Do you know? Do you know? Do you know? Do you know? Do you know? They're all asking each other. Do you know? Do you know the secret? Do you know what is really going on? And then some people have been decided by some people to know more. They've decided that. They've decided that one knows more. For whatever reason they've decided to make that conclusion. But, see, that is not something that anybody can tell you. And, even if I did... you could either accept it or reject it, couldn't you?

Q: Yes, of course.

R: And, how would you know whether you should accept it or reject it? What would you use to make that decision?

Q: My mind.

R: Yes, but do you see what I am looking at?

Q: Not really.

R: How would you know? How would you know if I said something or this gentleman or this lady? How would you know? Yes, how would you know? That's what I am asking you. How would you know if he said something different than me and she said something different than me. How would you know? If it were just words, you know, just an answer to the question. See. So, what you really want is to know. You don't want to understand, you want to know.

Q: Yes, I don't want to trust my senses or experiences.

R: Yes, but you want to go beyond experiences because we talked about experiences a moment ago. See, you want to know. And, words are not Knowing. But, the words that I use can indicate to you how you can find the Knowing. That's what I do. I don't give you an answer. I help you find the answer within you. That's not a problem. That is actually very easy!

Q: Finding the answer is easy, you say?

R: It certainly is. Where is it hiding?

Q: I don't know, because I don't know what the answer is.

R: Isn't it in your mind? How could you not find it? Whose mind is it that's hiding in?

Q: Yes, but then I trust that the answer is in my mind.

R: Yes, I would trust that. It would have to be in your mind. Whose mind is it? "What do you mean, how would I know? I don't get it." How would you not know? What are you doing not to know?

* * *

Q: Is there a point of us being here? Even if you tell me or not. Is there a point? I am so confused...

R: That's a good place to be. Finally!

Q: Yesterday you told us, "Everything that I see is an illusion." So, today I am looking at the world and I'm looking at the news and I'm shopping and everything is an illusion.

R: Isn't that cool?

Q: No.

R: I could have sworn I was being helpful when I said that. It really seemed like it at the time when I said that everything you see is an illusion. I really thought that was being helpful. Really!

Q: Maybe I am mistaken.

R: OK. So, everything you know is in your mind. It's not in your elbow. It's not in your big toe. It's in your mind. Everything that you know. So, where are you going to find the answers to the questions that are also in your mind? Good, you don't have to be a rocket scientist to answer that question. Where? Where?

Q: Yes, but maybe I don't trust my mind.

R: Don't then, but where are you going to find the answer?

Q: In my mind.

R: OK, then that's where you should be looking for your answers. In your mind. Because, that's where your answers are. And you can choose not to be aware of what you know. That's what an illusion is. So, the job, should you choose to accept it, is to pay attention to what's going on in your mind, rather than avoiding it! Because it seems like it's a huge junkyard. You know what a junkyard is? It's what your current mind is like. A lot of decaying things.

Q: How can you know if the stuff you are thinking is true thinking or false thinking?

R: It is so easy. There is nothing like Reality. It's Singular. There is nothing like It. Singular, Single. Kind of like you were before you got married. Singular. So, you know when you experience Reality. You know it! You don't debate it! O, let me see, do I want that to be Reality or not? No, it is so obvious! Isn't that good news? Reality is obvious! Who would think It is not obvious?

Q: The one who is thinking doesn't know.

R: The one who doesn't *want* to know. Right? That makes sense, doesn't it? If you didn't want to know you wouldn't know. It's your mind. You're doing with it what you want to do with it. You're the one making the decisions of what you want to do. Like somewhere today you made the decision to be here. And then you came. So, if I say you get the results of your thoughts, you don't question that, do you? You thought to come here and you did. I mean, how hard is that to understand? You get the results of your thoughts.

Q: Yesterday you were saying you are thinking all the time all over again and there is just one mind. So, where are the thoughts coming from? You can think whatever, but where, how can you get the real thinking? Is that just the machine of repeating stuff and...

R: OK, so what you're asking is, do I get the results of what I want?

Q: No.

R: No, no, no. You asked me a question. Now you follow me and I can help you!

Q: OK.

R: You're asking, "How do I know? And I said, "You get the

results of what you want." And now you're asking me how do I know what I want? You're getting the results of what you wanted. Are you asking me how do I know what you should want? That's your choice. Now, is there more than one source of thought? Therefore, I have an option as to what I want. Well, the way you describe yourself you do have an option, don't you? You can make choices. OK. So, if that is true or while that is true to you, then you do have options. Because, you get the results of your thinking! So, if you have options, you are talking about at least two. When you are talking about sources of thought, there is only two sources of thought. That that is of Singularity, Spirit, God, whatever words you want to use, Perfection. And, the thought system that includes duality, multiple, OK? So, how do you know which is which?

Well, one of them is shared by Singularity and one of them is shared by duality. It's not hard is it? When you really look at it you go, "Oh. So, if I use the word God, this is a thought that God would share with me, because it wouldn't be about multiplicity. It would be about Perfection, Beauty, Love. Not about this world in any way whatsoever. And, anything that has to do with this world comes from the other source. Because Spirit only wants me to know that I can share everything with God.[9] In fact, I don't have a choice about

---

[9] In 'A Course In Miracles' Spirit or the Holy Spirit is described as: "the remaining communication link between God and His separated Sons. [...] He knows because He is part of God; He perceives because He was sent to save humanity. He is the great correction principle; the bringer of true perception, the inherent power of the vision of Christ. He is the light in which the forgiven world is perceived; in which the face of Christ alone is seen. He never forgets the Creator or His creation. He never forgets the Son of God. He never forgets you. And He brings the Love of your Father to you in an eternal shining that will never be obliterated because God has put it there."

that. God didn't give me a choice! God created me like God! Perfect, Pure, Whole as a Spirit." OK? Those thoughts have that Source. When you start talking about an illusion, that is not coming from Spirit.

Q: And free will is part of the illusion?

R: Yes, there is only One Will. It was freely given. But, It has nothing to do with choice. Will has to do with creating! The Will of God is to create! The Will of God created You just like That. So, you are created with the Will to create.[10]

Q: So, the only thing you need to do is let God create through You. You don't have to think about it?

R: Well, you can look at it that way if you want to, but You can just create! However, you're not going to do that here in an illusion. There is no creating going on in an illusion! Creating is what Reality is!

Now, if you listen to what I just said, I just gave you a clue so that even the Dutch should get excited. Because I gave you a clue that in Reality You have been creating before You believed You were separate and in an illusion. No, I am telling you, You have creations in Reality that You are responsible for. These extended forth from You as a loving expression of You. And you don't even remember them. But because Reality is Eternal it's still there. All that You have created, just like You, is still in Reality, while you're in this nightmare of time and space. Everything is still there, Beautiful, Perfect and Whole and Loving. Isn't that good

---

[10] In the illusion free will is seen as being free to do as you please. 'A Course In Miracles' opens with a different perspective on free will: "This is a course in miracles. It is a required course. Only the time you take it is voluntary. Free will does not mean that you can establish the curriculum. It means only that you can elect what you want to take at a given time.' (From the Introduction of 'A Course In Miracles'.)

news? So, when you're done playing around, trying to figure out Who You are and you are just willing to accept The Truth of You, you will be able to return to The Truth of You and continue to create. Because that's What You are. But as long as you are having fun in your illusion you won't let it go. And if you don't let it go, you will get the results of your thoughts. So, we're right back to cause and effect, aren't we? You get the results of your thoughts and I was using a very simple example, wasn't I? Somewhere tonight you thought about coming and you did. You get the results of your thoughts.

I'm telling you everything that you believe, everything that you experience – and there you can use experience – is a result of what you're thinking and what you want. You want to be in an illusion and that's why you're here. Don't ask me why! It doesn't make sense. I know it doesn't make sense. So, don't ask me why you're doing it. You should ask yourself why you're doing it.

Q: I've been wondering about this this afternoon. I knew I would be coming here. I was certain. And then I started thinking, why should I go there? Whatever thought I came up with couldn't resist or demolish the statement that I should be here. It makes no sense trying to make this situation understandable to yourself. In fact, it is dust.

R: Well, I'll speak to you specifically, do you mind?

Q: No. Go ahead.

R: Love is attracted to Love! That's why you're here. Regardless of what words run through your head. Isn't that good news? I am so full of good news tonight. I feel so good. I really feel good tonight. There is so much good news coming through here.

Q: Love is from Oneness?

R: It is what Oneness is.

Q: And what about Trinity? And Holy Spirit. How do they relate to Oneness?

R: How do you want it to be?

Q: Loving.

R: OK, then let the idea of a Trinity be loving. Wouldn't that be enough? As far as I am concerned – you're not going to like what I have to say, but I'm going to tell you anyway – there is only God! There is not God and you and somebody else. And there is not a whole bunch of attributes to God. There is only God! There is only Reality. There is only Perfection. There is not Perfection and non-perfection. There is not degrees of Perfection. There is not degrees of non-perfection. There is only One Thing, Singular. Period!

So, talk about a Trinity, OK? Only to those that believe in separation. They are the only ones it'll make sense to. Because Everything in Oneness doesn't see a difference, doesn't experience it. It's just in The Knowing of the Oneness. So, it's only important to those that want to dissect things. It's like you guys talk about a mind and a heart. I have no idea what you are talking about, a mind and a heart! There is only Oneness. Oneness is not made up of a bunch of things. It's Oneness! It's One! And you have a hard time comprehending what that means, because to you Oneness is when everybody comes together. If you can get all the parts, then you think you've got Oneness. It's nuts, it's nuts! There is no such thing as parts in Oneness!

Isn't that amazing? It's good news, isn't it? This is all just about good news, that all the things you have been looking at and trying to sort out through what you know, through the utilization of perception, are only ever going to lead you to one conclusion, perception is never going to reveal The

Truth to me! And, all your questions involve perception. So, somewhere you are going to have to recognize you're running the same loop, the same pattern. Over and over and over again! And what you really want is something that is outside of that patterning. The patterning itself is made by you. But, you didn't make Reality! So, what you are looking for is not made by you. It doesn't even require your comments because your comments are about something that you insist is not you and therefore is as useless as all your perception.

Q: How does Reality relate to The Light?

R: Yes, well, see, is The Light you?

Q: Yes.

R: Then why do you call it The Light? Why don't you just say It's Me? Because, you like to use me for the ego that perceives, and you don't know the difference yet.

Q: No, but I feel like a victim of The Light.

R: Let It get you then! Let It get you wholly and totally then! Then It'll show you that The Light is You! And, the you that you think you are will disappear in The Light. What does darkness do when The Light shows up, anyway?

Q: Disappears.

R: Has anybody ever found It? It's just all there in your mind.

Q: Isn't there the fear to melt into The Light? To disappear, I mean.

R: What?

Q: When The Light becomes very strong inside of you.

R: It already is. It doesn't get weaker and stronger. It is what It is.

Q: Yes, sometimes.

R: No, no, no, no, It is what It is! You either pay attention to It or you don't!

Q: But It kills me!

R: Yes!!! Yes!!! Isn't that great?

Q: My bank account.

R: Yes, your bank account too. You don't need it anymore. You've got the bank account of Perfection. It gives you Everything. It gives you stuff more valuable than money. Isn't that good news?

Q: You tell me about good news all the time.

R: There is no such thing as bad news.

Q: Yes, there is!

R: No, there is no such thing as bad news!

Q: There wouldn't be good news if there weren't bad news.

R: See, that's what perception tells you. Perfection does not tell you that. And I am representing Perfection here tonight and every night and every moment that you'll ever run into me. I'm here to represent Perfection. You can choose what you are here to represent. And you will get the result of what you want to represent. And I get the results of what I want to represent. You can join me if you want. There is plenty of space available. There is a specific space reserved just for you in Perfection. Isn't that great?

Q: Really?

R: Yes, I am sure of it. I don't even have a doubt about that at all. It wouldn't make sense to have a doubt about Perfection.

Q: This Oneness is always new.

R: Well, because in Oneness there is nothing new and nothing old. It just is. It's Isness. It's Being, it's Eternal. There are no days, there are no hours in The Eternal. Eternal is not a lot of time! It has no time in It. Eternal has no time in It! None!

Q: Because It's one, It cannot change. So, there is no time.

R: OK.

Q: It is confusing if you say there is a place just for you in Perfection. I feel like, OK, so there is a single me, but you say we are all One...

R: But, if there is only One and It is just for You, guess what? You're the only One! I'm trying to give you your True Identity. And your True Identity is confusing to you. It will be until you accept it.

Q: In complete Oneness can you still play cards?

R: If you want to. If you wanted to, you could. Do you want to? Would you want to in Perfection? You could play with your Self then, couldn't you? Since It's Oneness. And you'd be the cards too. And you'd be the winner and the loser! Just kind of like the way it is here if You're Everything. If It's all in your mind. It's kind of like this in a sense, isn't it?

Q: I heard somebody say in church that we're all one God that's looking through millions of eyes and speaking through millions of mouths. Is that something to experience?

R: Yes, you can experience that. But you'll never know that because that's not a part of Knowing. But you can experience that if you want.

Q: How do we get there?

R: Where?

Q: In the knowing and in the Oneness!

R: You're already there! My hope for you is to help you see what you're doing to not know you're already there. Is that clear? Does anybody have a question about that?

Q: Yes, what am I doing?

R: Why are you asking me that question? Where is the answer to that question? Where is the answer to that question?

Q: Well, in my mind.

R: OK, in your mind. Now that's where you're going to find it. You just look in your mind for the answer.

5

FEELINGS HAVE NOTHING TO DO

WITH LOVE

Analyzing / Limitation / Enlightenment /
You Get the Result of Your Thoughts

Q: Is there no sex in Oneness?

R: Yes, eternally. But it's not sex, it's Love! Sex is just a... I don't know if you would understand if I put it that way or not... it's like a poor man's substitute for an eternal orgasm, which is what Love is. Creating is orgasmic, it's passionate, it's Life. Sex is associated with an activity that is derived from an idea in man's mind to make more bodies, which is a substitute idea of creating. You think when you have children you've created them. Do you understand what I'm saying?[11]

Q: Yes, I understand.

R: It's a substitute for the idea of creating. But in Reality You are creating, and so the orgasmic experience, the energy some people tend to call bliss or whatever label you want to put on it, is the constant climate of Reality. You're constantly passionate and constantly creating. You don't have to huff and puff and then have a, you know, a climax, after which you smoke a cigarette...

[Audience laughing.]

---

[11] *Like in 'A Course In Miracles' Rananda distinguishes between creating and making. Creating is what is going on in Heaven/Eternity. It is the extension of God, i.e. Love extending as Love. Making is what is going on in an illusion; it has no real cause and therefore no real existence.*

R: ... and then ask if it was good for them, too...

[Audience laughing.]

R: ... because, if it wasn't, then you're guilty. None of that kind of stuff is going on in Reality. It's just a constant orgasmic, passionate activity of creating. Q: Some use sexuality to be in Oneness.

R: Man has a lot of very strange thoughts! I will make a claim to you that most of you will not like. And, that is that there is no part of the illusion that can cause the ending of the illusion! So you can employ whatever techniques you want, they will not end your illusion. The only thing that can end an illusion is Reality!

Q: That is what an Indian Master said...

R: [With an Indian accent.] Oh, that is very good. It was probably me, then, in disguise...

[Audience laughing.]

Q: He said that many years ago, that an illusion cannot be analyzed, because it has no substance...

R: No, it's just the opposite. Illusions are analyzations; they can never be Reality. But, that's exactly what you do, you analyze your illusion. Constantly you analyze it. Should I do this, should I do that, what is the right thing to do, how can I keep money in my bank account, oh my God, what am I going to do if my bank account doesn't have enough money? That's all you do, analyze all day long. You analyze the illusion. It's exactly what you do. And that's why you don't know Reality, because you cannot analyze Reality. That's what you cannot analyze. You can *know* It, but you cannot analyze It. Because It doesn't have parts to analyze. Isn't that really good news?

Q: Are there still preferences in Reality?

R: No, there's only what occurs to you.

Q: What about eating...

R: Not in Reality. Only in an illusion. And you do that because you think your body will die and then you won't be alive anymore. So you believe in death, too.

Q: So, why do you choose to stay in the illusion?

R: For You!

Q: For me?

R: Yes!

Q: You do it only for me?

R: Yes!

Q,: You don't do it for yourself?

R: You are Me!

Q: We eat together.

[Audience laughing.]

Q: You are Me, I am You. There is only Reality; there is only Oneness. Yet you are here and I am here.

R: It looks like that.

Q: It looks like that.

R: I'm telling you, that's not The Truth. But, because you believe it's The Truth, I have decided to be here to help You. When I went through my Awakening, I did not have to be here any longer. So there are certain things I have taken on.

Q: And is that not a preference?

R: Well, from the perspective of Perfection you should be glad that it was a choice for me to do that and to be here for you. I would be really grateful if I were you. And since I am You, I am.

[Audience laughing.]

R: It would be nice if you would share that with Me.

Q: Yes, we are very grateful that you made that choice for us. That's how I experience it. It is a great gift from you to us, to have chosen at a certain moment to continue to eat...

[Audience laughing.]

Q: ...so that we may learn, so that we may learn from you Oneness.

[Audience laughing.]

R: This really is a funny place, isn't it? We don't have conversations like this in Reality. This is the only place you can have them.

Q: But, honestly, I'm very grateful.

R: You're a wise man. If you want to be wiser...

[Audience laughing.]

R: ... give up your analyzing, and the wisdom that is inherently Yours, that You share with Oneness, will be all that You're left with. Which is what you really want.

Q: Yes, that's Pure Love, that's Pure Love.

R: Whatever It is, you don't have to label It, you don't have to analyze It, you just be It. Just stop analyzing and let It reveal Itself to You. And if you come up with fears, which you tend to do from time to time, recognize that fear is not a part of Perfection, and therefore it cannot be anything more than like a cloud. It can't stop you.

Q: You talked about perception, the senses, that they are always part of the illusion and only Knowing is part of Reality.

R: No, it's not part of It, It is what Reality is.

Q: It is Reality?

R: Yes. Isn't that good news?

Q: Yes.

R: See, I can't help it. These are really very important things that you keep rejecting. And when I hear it, I consider it to be incredibly beautiful good news that that is true! Because, look at what you're doing when you don't accept that as Truth, look at what you're stuck with, look at the pain and suffering that you keep on drawing to yourself. See, to me good news is a thing that brings me to a realisation that I don't have to be a part of suffering any longer, I don't have to be a part of pain any longer, causing it. Things can change, I can remember What is Real. Because, it's all in my mind.

Q: So, bringing our kids to school is a waste of time?

R: No, well, I don't know about your schools. It could be, but...

Q: Now that I realize they already know, why would I do it?

R: See, they already know, just like you already know, and they're rejecting the Knowing, just like you're rejecting the Knowing. So, what would really be nice is if the teachers knew and could help the children remember. What you guys do as parents, is you do everything you can to get your children to stop remembering what it was like before they came here into the illusion. If they have unseen friends, you say they're going nuts, they'll get over it. And you try to make sure that they don't talk to anybody who's next to them that they know is actually there. Because it is there. It's in their mind.

Do you understand what I'm saying? So, you have this program set up to stop everybody from remembering. Now, if your schools were set up to help people actually learn...

Like if you as a teacher would know, that would really, really be helpful; you could help the children recognize how they're getting the results of their thoughts. That would be one of the greatest things a teacher could do. Because then a child would understand why he's learning, how he's learning, and that he's making choices to learn. Or not to. And he will get the result of that. And then they won't blame the teacher, they won't blame the parents, they won't blame the children they're playing with. Everybody will take the responsibility for getting the results of their thoughts.

And, then you can ask, "Well, where does that stop?" And, then you come to this incredible conclusion, "It doesn't stop here in the world. Everything in the world I know, is in my mind. So, if I don't want this world, I should have other thoughts." And then some of the wise ones will go, "Is that possible?" And then you say, "Yes, it's possible." And then they're going to really open up to... "Wow, what would that be like?" In that moment a quantum jump is possible from being bound by their own thoughts to this world, to the Realization of their True Nature. It doesn't matter what age they are, they'll jump and they will remember and they'll start to tell you the things you always wanted to know and that you wouldn't let yourself make that jump. Because, they don't have so much of a barrier yet, you know, they have not taken so much for granted as you have.

Teacher, teach children and adults that they get the results of their thinking. It's more important than telling them the idea of right and wrong, because they will understand when I put my hand in the fire, it's not the thing I really want to do. And, I'm not saying don't advise them that that's what will happen, but did you ever burn your hand? Did you? Ever? On something hot?

Q: Yes.

R: Yes, see, you know then. And in that moment you went, "Oh, that's why mom and dad...," or "Oh, that's why..." See, you have to have that thing, that really lets you know. So, certainly your children will have a certain trust in you, but what they really need is to know. You need to help them find it in their own mind. You need to help them see they're getting the result of their thoughts. And, you'll find people that are addicted to drugs, alcohol, sex, whatever the addiction is, they will begin to lose it, because they will be aware that it's just a choice. And, you know, this is true, because like in Alcoholics Anonymous one of the things they'll tell you is, "Do you know how not to get drunk?" Do you know how simple it is not to get drunk? If you don't pick up a drink, you won't get drunk. That's how easy it is. If you want to stop drugs, don't pick up the drug and you won't be addicted. OK? Are you following what I'm trying to say? It's actually really easy. The question is, are you willing? But the activity is actually with great ease. For the willingness on the other hand, you might need to really dig around in there to find where the willingness is. And, this is why people don't come into their Awakening. Because they like to talk about how they like it. They like to talk about how nice it would be. They like to talk about somebody they've met who has undergone their Awakening and how incredible it was to be around that kind of individual. But when you ask them why aren't you like that, then they come up with their incredible, long list – shall I start at the top or at the bottom? – as to why they don't let It happen, as to what parts of consciousness of perception they don't want to let go of.

And, I tell you, trying to go in opposite directions at the same time never succeeds. And, this is like that quote from the Bible which says you can't serve two Masters. That's what it's saying. You can't serve this world and serve your Awakening. You're dedicated to one or the other.

Q: Have you ever been in love?

R: Right now.

Q: Yes?

R: Of course.

Q: OK. Another question.

[Audience laughing.]

Q: Well, Love is about feelings. True?

R: No.

Q: OK.

R: Love is about Love. Feelings have nothing to do with Love.

Q: It's not something solid?

R: Love is, It's the only Thing that's solid, It's the only Thing that's Real. Love has nothing to do with a body and that's where you have feelings. Love is Perfect and Pure and Whole. It never changes. Love never becomes something other than Love.

Q: Bhagavan, India, he uses one percent to give deekshas. Why is that?

R. : I think you should ask him, if that's what he's doing.

Q: Yes, but you went there...

R: Yes. You think I only got one percent? You think I only get one percent of anything?

Q: No, there must be levels of something...

R: That's the illusion, there is levels.

Q: How helpful can blessings be, then?

R: They can be very helpful, if you give them the purpose of being helpful. So, let me ask you a question, OK? Can I ask you a question? How much Light is Perfection?

Q: Well there is no answer to that.

R: Yes, there is. That's why I asked the question.

Q: Three cubic meters.

[Audience laughing.]

R: [Laughs.] That's a really small Heaven. I would say we really would be crammed in there, if that's all there is.

Q: Well, Eternal...

R: Yes, all of It. All The Light there is, is what Reality is. However much that is, that's all of It, that's all we know. OK? And who is all that Light for?

Q: Everything, Everything we...

R: Everything there is? Are You part of That?

Q: Yes.

R: Then, who would limit You to one percent? Are you going to let somebody do that? Are you going to let somebody limit You to one percent of Heaven?

Q: No, I just heard it.

R: No, I'm just asking you a question. You don't have to defend yourself. I just want to look in your mind with you. I really want to know, is that really what you want to do?

Q: No.

R: OK, then don't do that. And begin to think that Everything in Your Mind is available to You, because You deserve It, because You're a part of That. OK? And, if anybody ever tells you that anything should be limited for you, tell them, "Thank you very much, but I want the whole deal. I'm not depending upon you to give it to me, but I am depending upon You to share It with Me. Because it's not mine alone, because You're with Me in this. And if you want the whole enchilada, it's yours." But remember what you're asking for, because you're going to get It." OK?

If you agree to be limited, you will be limited, that's all I am telling you. If you don't want to be limited, The Eternal is available to You, and that's what I'm encouraging. I'm encouraging you to get so passionate for God, so passionate for Reality, that all the things that you hold onto you let go of and you let Reality reveal Itself to You as You. It reveals Itself to be You. But all that you have thought will disappear. And, All That is, is All That will be left. But, you know what, that will be enough. Because it's a little bit more than three cubic meters… That's really good news, isn't it?

Q: Yes.

R: Yes, that you're not limited, that you don't have to be limited and no one can do that to you, unless you say in your mind that that's OK. You deserve Reality, Heaven, Light, Love as much as anybody does, regardless of who anybody tells you those other beings are. You deserve it just as much. It's yours just as much. That doesn't mean you don't accept their help and their wisdom, but that you know the Whole Thing is for You. And that's what you want, you want the Whole Thing. OK? Let that guide you, so that you don't limit your Self. When I went to India, I didn't let myself be limited by anything. By anything or anyone. And those that understood joined me in Everything.

Q: But, you said two percent; it would be too much for us to handle it, the deekshas. What is that then?

R: Well, I can get a ton of weight and put it on your head and that's too much for you to handle. I mean, what's the big deal? Why is anything too much for you to handle? Or anybody else? Why did people, when they received the Golden Energy, when It was being offered the way It was at that time, why did they have a problem with it? What was the problem? What is the problem? Well, were they afraid they were going to lose this world? Or were you afraid you were going to lose them? You just can't be sitting around, being in The Light all day long. You've got to be a productive member of society. You don't expect me to take care of you when you're like that. You're supposed to take care of yourself. You know, your thoughts are the ones that limit you and your brothers to what's going on in this world. Why weren't people ecstatic that somebody couldn't do anything and they were just in The Light and radiating that Energy for everybody to benefit from instead of freaking out? That's just a question that I would have.

See, I could give you so much Light, you wouldn't be able to get out of that chair, unless somebody grabbed a hold of you and carried you away. But why would I want to do that to you?

[Audience laughing.]

Q: Well, maybe to make the process faster or something, remove the blockades and...

R: If I were to do something like that, it would be so you would remember what Perfection is like. No, the question is for you. Are you ready to take the responsibility if all of that was revealed to you? Are you willing to take the responsibility of holding all of that Light?

Q: Not yet.

R: Well, see, so then you won't get it. And, what happened in the early days with Bhagavan is that lots and lots of Light came and it was given to people who were not willing, but said that they wanted It. And then they had certain, what you call practical, problems and there was either no one there to take care of them or those that should have been taking care of them didn't want to take care of them, so they became a problem. Then Bhagavan has to deal with that, doesn't he? He says, "OK, if that's the way it's going to be and everybody is having a problem with what I'm doing, I just have to give them a little bit less." And then, you know what they do when you give less? Then they complain that they're not enlightened.

[Audience laughing.]

Q: Yes, true.

R: Yes, so that's just the way it is with humans, that's just the way it is. Something else and somebody else is always the problem. OK?

Q: Is that good news?

[Audience laughing.]

R: Yes. It's good news that the illusion will always be the illusion, yes, and it won't change. It will always just be that and you can always see right through it. When you have eyes to see, you will always just see that the illusion is the illusion. You will realize how you've tried to make it real You'll realize how you tried to squeeze out of it something that's not really there, and finally where you found the frustration is where you'll find your joy. In the same exact stuff that made you frustrated at one point you now will find joy, because the joy is coming from within you and you're recognizing it can't come from there any longer. And, you're just happy that it's true, that you can't find it there any longer. If you want to know whether or not you're on your spiritual journey, if you've "made progress", which is also an illusion, that's one of the ways that you can tell. Where something used to upset you or caused frustration or anger, you're actually happy now. The same exact thing is happening, but now you're happy, because you see it's an illusion rather than Reality. Right? And then, because it's not, you know – You being Love – You bring Love to that moment, because it's obvious that Love is missing in that moment, in that situation, however you want to look at it. And you know Who You are and It's flowing, because Love moves, It's a movement, It's passionate, and so It comes forth from You to where It's needed. And, this is Love's attraction to Love. And it will work that way. You will get everything that you can handle. But, we don't give you more than that, because then you're not helpful at all. Unless your job is to just sit there in that Light. And if that's your job, you'll get it tonight. If it's not, you'll get whatever it is that will help you, whatever you're willing. And that is usually an indication of what help you need, your willingness.

Q: But, there is no me that can be enlightened.

R: That depends on what you consider Enlightenment to be.

Q: Well, I don't think there is a meaning in Enlightenment, because it's the dissolving of the me.

R: That's what Enlightenment is.

Q: So, so...

R: And, what is left when the illusionary you dissolves, what is left?

Q: The We, the Oneness.

R: Yes, so that's what Enlightenment is.

Q: Yes. So, that's why It's also a kind of a group thing.

R: No, It's Oneness, It's always just One. Actually, one of the biggest problems with people who are on a spiritual path is, that they want to be around to know they woke up. And you're not, it's not going to work that way. Your Awakening is your disappearance, the you that you think you know.

And, What takes its place is the You that has always known Everything.

Q: It takes over.

R: It doesn't take over anything. It's just always been exactly What It is. It doesn't battle with anything, It's not in competition with anything. It's what Everything is, there is only One Thing! But that's all that's left, because you're finally not trying to make something other than What Is. It's very simple, actually, it's so simple! And all you have to come up with is some willingness. But, if willingness is required of you, don't you think it's already there? If it's a requirement, don't you think it's already there? Where would it be? Ah, so you know where to look for your willingness.

Boy, this is getting so clear. Is this helpful?

[Audience laughing.]

I have noticed that some people don't consider good news helpful. In fact, they get angry at me.

[Audience laughing.]

* * *

Q: Can I ask you something totally different? There are people in certain parts of the world that practise black magic.

R: Ooohh.

Q: They have an influence on other people and stuff happens. But what is happening? Can somebody do that to me or is it my illusion or my creation? What is it?

R: It has nothing to do with Creation; it has everything to do with an illusion and if it's happening to you or in your world, then it's yours. That's taking responsibility, isn't it? Let me ask you a question. Is there anything in this world that you know of, that's not in your mind? Hello?

Q: No.

R: No. So everything is your thoughts?

Q: Yes.

R: OK, and the idea of black magic, those are your thoughts.

Q: Yes.

R: Oh, OK. Let me ask you another question. Everything about this world is in your mind?

Q: Yes.

R: And some guy called Jesus Resurrected and Ascended?

Q: That's the story, yes.

R: Well, yes, it's the same story as black magic, isn't it? It's a story.

Q: Yes.

R: Oh, OK.

Q: I'm choosing the thoughts...

R: You do get the results of your thoughts! We established that very early, didn't we? We get the result of our thinking. Yes. So, if you believe people can die, they die.

Q: In my mind they do die.

R: Yes, and if you believe they can't, then they don't?

Q: That's right.

R: So, if in your mind there's an illusion of separation from Perfection, then people will die.

Q: I'm trying to get what you're saying, but...

R: Well, I'm saying if you have ideas of death in your mind, people will die.

Q: Yes.

R: Yes. But if you allow that idea to be removed from your mind, can they die?

Q: No. But other people still die.

R: What other people?

Q: This confuses me.

R: In the beginning you don't quite know which is which, because you've always just known your idea of yourself. You've always just thought you were one. And you don't understand, you know, until you get it, you don't understand that you've been split and there's literally two different things coming into your mind. And then, when you begin to see it, it's a little confusing, because how are you going to deal with it? And this is where the strength of getting together with your brothers and looking at these ideas and staying true to what you want, is really, really helpful. You talk to one another about what you want. Because, if you don't, you'll talk to one another about the illusion and you convince one another that this really is real and you really are bound by it and you really are limited by it. So, it's really helpful when you can get together with those that want to tell the same story. And, then you can begin to break the patterns in your own mind and set yourself free and begin to have different experiences. Those that indicate to you that there is Perfection. And, then you have the inspiration and the encouragement to keep moving towards The Light. And then you begin to recognize. Within your own mind the remembering that everything that I've been saying is actually true, will be unfolding. You come into the remembering of it. You'll have moments of faith, that go beyond faith. It is the faith that there is something that you haven't yet remembered. But in that moment of faith the remembering will be fulfilled. Then you have the certainty. From that place of certainty you can begin to work with a greater self-confidence that this is, in fact, an illusion. You already know it's not Eternal. There's a good clue right there. The fact that things die is a real good indication that this is an illusion.

Q: But, it is real if the body dies, isn't it?

R: It's a part of the illusion, it's real to the illusion.

Q: But, there is stuff getting buried.

R: In the illusion, yes, not in Reality. It's not about denying that things look that way in an illusion. I'm trying to get you to admit it.

Q: It looks like that in an illusion.

R: Yes, it doesn't look like that in Reality; it looks like that in an illusion. Because, Reality is Perfection and it could never look like that in Perfection. Just admit that it's an illusion instead of trying to make it real. That's, that's, that's… [Rananda laughs.]

[Audience laughing.]

Q: Finally, starting to live.

R: No! Dying has nothing to do with Life, nothing. They are a denial of one another. Life denies death and death denies Life.

Q: But when you're dead, you cannot…

R: Who?

Q: When you're dead, you can no longer have the illusion that you die; so you have to live.

R: No, no, no, no. See, you… [Sighs.] Look, thoughts cannot leave their source. They're just thoughts. A thought cannot leave its source, can you understand that? Thoughts are in your mind. They don't leave your mind. You're a Thought in the Mind of Perfection, of God. You're not going to leave there.

Now, here is the key that you keep missing. There is no source to an ego, because the idea of an ego is an illusion. It's not a Thought in the Mind of God. And only Reality is in God's Mind. Can you hear what it is that I'm saying? Illusion is not in the Mind of God. The only Thing in the Mind of God is Reality. So, the thoughts of an illusion will be removed from your mind for you, not by you. And, that's easy to do, because it's nothing. And, if you don't give it value and hold on to it, it will just disappear. And, you know that it's true, because there are thoughts that you have had, that you value, that at one point you saw, ah, I don't have to give that any value, or, gee, that's not true, and it was gone. And it was gone! Everyone has had these experiences, you know that this is what happens in the mind. What you don't like to admit is the ones that you're holding on to.

Q: Is it an intramental affair? If I hold on to an illusion, if illusion exists in my mind, the thought of holding on to that illusion also exists in my mind. So, this illusion is just an intramental affair.

R: Yes, that's what I am saying, you get the results of your thoughts. And you say, "This is my thought, that's my thought." You don't say, "Oh, those are the thoughts of an ego, they're not even mine." You don't do that. But you could, if you wanted to. And then, when the Thoughts that can be shared with God come into your mind, you can go, "Wow, that's My thinking, that's what I feel true to, that's what makes me feel really, really good." You could do that; You might find it helpful.

Q: The Thought of God is total...

R: It has no opposite.

Q: And therefore, even if you say it's certain, it's a shortcoming, it's more than that, it's total, it's eh...

R: It has no opposite.

Q: Yes.

R: It's not something you can analyze. It has no opposite. Analyzing means you have to have more than one. It has no opposite. There only is What Is. Isn't that good news?

Q: When you talk about these things, something in me gets so elevated...

R: Yes, It should, because I'm talking about You, the Real You, the Truth of You.

Q: I notice that the words you're using lead more to division than to Oneness in my mind. I hear elevated, I hear Light, Love, these are all words, which immediately in my mind separate Love from what It is not...

R: Yes, that's what you're doing in your mind.

Q: Yes.

R: Yes. Don't do that! There's another thing you can be doing when those words come in. You can apply that to how your illusion ended. It's really easy. Elevated takes you out of the illusion, lets it disappear. It doesn't elevate you to a point where there's somebody below you and somebody above you. It not only takes you out of the illusion, but it dispels the idea that illusion is still in your mind. There's lots of ways where you can find a way into Singularity, if you want to look. I can take any thought in the entirety of this world, any thought, and I can go to Perfection with it. By the way that I think. And, this is what I'm saying to you. You can take all of those words and not let any of them bind You. They can help you to find the relationship to Singularity, through those words. Which is what I'm doing, I'm trying to lead you from where you believe you're stuck to a point where you can be grabbed and pulled out, pulled out of time and space.

Q: And could that be for me in my case by not using words like Love?

R: It's not important what words you use, what's important is how you think.

Q: Is it how we think or how we know?

R: You start with thinking, because you already think that you're in the illusion, and when your thinking is transformed to not wanting or not having any ideas that are perceptual, then you will know. So, coming from a point of saying, "Hey, I'm dealing with all this and I want to awaken," you're saying, "I want to awaken!" You're making a declaration that you're not awake. From a point of making a declaration I'm not awake, you do need to awaken. However, when you awaken, you will then know and realize you've always been awake. So I can teach you've always been awake, but only so that you know there is something other than you think everybody has to put up with until they die. There's even ideas that, when you awaken, you still have to die. And I'm bringing the idea that you don't even have to do that. You don't have to die. It's an idea that is useless now. Its time has passed. Its value is no longer valuable.

Q: What will happen instead?

R: You'll be a Master of Infinite Creating instead of a master of limitation.

Q: They call it the dying of the illusion.

R: Yes, I know. It's pretty humorous, isn't it? Something that isn't can die. See, that's the ego's way of teaching. It wants you to think that you have succeeded and then you can overcome it. My teaching is, you never succeeded and that's the only way it can be overcome, easily, because it never succeeded. But if you succeeded and you are separate, then you have defiled Perfection and there is no way that you could return to Perfection then. Because there is no Perfection to return to. Because you succeeded.

R: That's what I teach. In Indian terminology they use the idea of non-duality and Pure Non-Duality, where their idea of non-duality is what you said, "You can die to that and then...," but Pure Non-Duality says, you can't die to something that never was. And that's what I teach.

Q: And what about the other one you mentioned. The first one of what the Indians teach?

R: No, they teach both of them, and you can accept whichever one you want. But I'm telling you, one of them is instantaneous and the other one is actually impossible and you will come to a point where you let it go and you'll accept the instantaneous. So, why wait? Right, why wait, why not just give up that idea of non-duality and pick up the Pure Non-Duality?

Q: It's also what is said, that we as human beings have fallen from Oneness into multiplicity.

R: That's the idea.

Q: And you have to come back to Oneness.

R: That's an idea. And, it's valuable to you while you believe that you have done that. That's what I'm telling you. You can't take that away from somebody. You just have to help them come to the point where they can see more than that, where you can remember that that never happened. From here it's important that you see it that way, so that you'll be willing to do what's required to remember. But you have to be careful what you believe, because you get the result of it.

See, there's a point where you have to come to, where you have to admit you already believe it. So, you have to be healed from your own belief, which means you have to begin to recognize that those thoughts are not actually yours. Because what belongs to You is what belongs to Perfection.

Q: Thinking is never Knowing, because Knowing is immediate; knowledge, thinking is in time.

R: Well, if you're analyzing, it is. But if the thoughts are just coming to your mind and they *are* just coming to your mind, that's all that it is.

Q: They expand?

R: Kind of like that, but they do have spam filters now. My program has a thing on there that says, "Empty."

Q: I want that too!

R: So, I just go on there and I go click, and it's all gone. It's called Yahoo. Yahoo!!!

[Audience laughing.]

Q: What I'm trying to refer to is that knowing is immediate, there's nothing...

R: There's no time in Knowing.

Q: There's nothing between That What is Known and the Knower.

R: There is no Knower and Known, they are the same.

Q: They're One, that's right.

R: Yes.

Q: With thinking there's always the distinction between the One Who Knows and What is Known.

R: You only think that way because you think you're separate. I guarantee you that God thought You into existence. And it didn't take time. And You're not separate from God. And I know that you don't understand that, but that's OK.

Q: I think it is not a matter of understanding.

R: Well, from here you better have an understanding of it or you'll never get to The Knowing.

Q: The Knowing is immediate, It's not understanding.

R: Yes. I'm not here to argue with you, I'm not going to do it.

6

WHY DOES HAPPINESS COME AND GO?

Happiness / Illusion / Our Last Choice

R: Is it fair to say that people of this world want to be happy? Is it fair to say that people of this world are pursuing happiness? Is it fair to say that they are not doing a very good job at being happy? What's the problem? Why are people not happy? If everybody is pursuing it, you would think somebody would find it, wouldn't you? And when somebody finds it, don't you think that everybody else would want to know about it? Has anybody found it?

Q: It is found sometimes.

R: Well, does it like disappear then? I mean, what happens to it? Or, why does it disappear? I mean, why is it sometimes? If it is sometimes, then you would still be seeking, wouldn't you? Because you lost it, you're going to find it again. And then in between you wonder, did I really have it? Was that really happiness? So that you are not even sure what you called happiness is actually happiness, are you? You called it happiness, but where did it go? If it was happiness, where did it go? What kind of happiness are you seeking for? Some people get really happy when the sun rises in the morning. When it disappears at nighttime they go, "Oh, nooo! I hope it comes back." That is what you used to do about ninety-eight lifetimes ago. You got really excited when the sun rose and you went, "Oh, thank you, thank you, thank you." And then, when it left, you were worried whether it was going to come back or not. And now you are really smart, right? Now you have something that goes tick, tick, tick, tick, tick, like that, that keeps track of it for you.

Right? So, you have really made a lot of progress in your pursuit of happiness, haven't you? But see, no one has actually answered my question. Where did it go? Why does your happiness come and go?

Q: Everything comes and goes.

R: Everything comes and goes? That means you haven't found something that doesn't come and go yet. That is what you are actually telling me, right? That is why you call it everything? Now what? Now I feel important. And this now, and this now, and every now that you'll ever come upon. But, don't slide away from my question. Because, there might be something here that is really helpful to you.

Q: I think it also is a matter of whether I am aware of it or not.

R: So, you are telling me the way that you utilize awareness is that there are times that you choose not to be aware of happiness. You choose not to be aware of happiness.

Q: Is it a choice?

R: I am asking you! Oh, so there is somebody else in control then. So, there is somebody else doing that inside of you? Is it like more than one of you in there? Are you telling me there's more than one of you in there?

Q: I think one hundred thousand or so.

R: Oh, that really must be crowded in there! Who gets to read the newspaper in the morning first?

Q: I don't know.

R: And, when you go to bed at nighttime, who says their prayers first? See, the attempts to avoid my question are very interesting — to watch you guys do that. You can't simply just face that, can you? That is difficult, isn't it? But, the path of Enlightenment or the path of Awakening requires that you look right at what is happening in your mind and be with that and let things be revealed, so that the changes that you long for can be fulfilled. So, somewhere you know it is nice to be Enlightened and happy and everything, and so it should really be nice to be sincere about those opportunities that you have for a change from the temporal to The Eternal. And that is what I'm helping you with right now. I'm asking you to look why in your mind your happiness comes and goes.

Q: I'm not really happy. I have joy sometimes. I feel very much like it doesn't matter what happens and that's another kind of happiness that makes you feel... you understand what I mean...? But my English is not so good.

R: It is not about English, it is about how you use your mind. I understand your English very well. My question would be, "Why would you do that?"

Q: I don't know.

R: See, this is what I don't understand. It is your mind. It is you, you are in charge of it, and you do things with it. And I say, "Why do you do that?" and you say, "I don't know." So, somewhere you are doing something with your mind to not know. And then you say, "I don't know that I'm doing that." But my question is, "Why would you want to do that and on the other hand say, 'I am very much interested in Enlightenment or Communication with God or only Love.'" I mean, you say these really beautiful things and then you do these strange things with your mind. And all I can help you do is first of all declare to you your own Perfection. And then, as you tell me, things come and go, the only thing I can do for you is help you see what you are doing or why you are doing it, so that you might not want to do that anymore. Because, when you don't do that anymore, then your Perfection is all that you would be left with.

See, You s   don't have to become Perfect, you already are Perfect. I don't mean perfect as a human. I mean Perfect as You were created. And you are confused about Who You are, because you are not telling me about Perfection. You are not telling me about Eternal Happiness. You are telling me it comes and goes and things happen and I don't even know why they happen. You are describing a self that is not The Truth of You. But, perhaps it is the way that you experience you. OK? And I am trying to get through to you that you experience the way that you choose to experience.

Nothing is making you experience what you experience. Those are your choices. OK? Some of them you are not aware of and some of them you are. Half an hour ago you said, "OK, I'm going to go to that place." And, then you did what you did and you came here. So, right now you are sitting in recognition within your own mind of, I made that choice and I'm getting the result of it, here I am. But there are other choices that you are making without you being aware of them. And that was a choice. To not be aware. Alright? So, somewhere I'm saying to you, you have a purpose in making choices so that you don't know that you made that choice. And until you uncover that, you continue to make choices, say you don't know about it and profess that you are not Perfect, Enlightened or whatever words that you want to use. If a teacher is going to help you at all, that's what a teacher is going to do. So, they'll help you look at what you are doing in your mind and help you get in touch with that sincerity that allows you to make a different choice until there is only One Choice being made by you.

The best choice that you can possibly make, according to me, is to make no more choices and just accept what is. But What Is, is not what you have been telling me is. That is an illusion. And illusions do not exist. That is why we call it an illusion. So, I am not saying choose what is going on in an illusion. I am saying What Is, meaning What is Real, What is Eternal. Let that be What It Is. Choose for That to be what It is and stop trying to make something up to replace It in an effort to find happiness, to give yourself an identity. You have already been given an Identity by your Creator.

Q: So, on the one hand you say you should be conscious, be aware... And on the other hand you are saying many choices seem very natural. But if you do this, is there something happening then? Because, in my opinion you do nothing anymore.

R: My question to you would be, "Why are you trying not to be What You are when anything is happening?" My question to you would be, "Why are you trying not to be What Your Creator created You to be? Is anything happening?"

Q: A good question!

R: Yes. I've got lots of good questions! You understand what it is that I'm showing you? If you want to align yourself with Perfection, you have to hold Perfection as your model. And then you have to see if anything supports that or not. And if it doesn't, you have to say, "That must be the nature of the illusion then." And, if it does, then you know that it has something to do with What is Eternal.

See, what you don't trust is that Spirit can lead you through this, without you having to tell Spirit the incredible things why you are in an illusion. Which is nothing. It is a lot about the illusion. But the illusion is nothing, so it is nothing. All you are learning is literally nothing. And that is all that you learn, that this is nothing and you can let go of it and let Everything that has been given to You when You were created, replace it. But, everybody is so fascinated trying to find happiness where they cannot find it. And then feel disappointed when they don't find it. When you get a little juice of something, you know, you go, "Ooohh, it is not so bad here after all." And then, all of a sudden it disappears and you go back to, "Hey, why would I want to be here if I can't get any happiness here?"

But you missed the point. First of all the point is, You are not here. The second part is, that pursuing it is what the problem is. Everyone is pursuing happiness here, didn't we talk about that in the very beginning? Everybody is seeking happiness. Didn't everybody agree with that in the beginning? I could swear I asked that question in the beginning. Didn't I ask a question in the beginning? I did, and you all said, "Yes, we are all pursuing, we are all seeking happiness, we all want to be happy." Is that not what you said? OK, got you!

So, reclaiming The Truth of You means that you have to stand up for That, rather than standing up for the illusion and saying, "Prove it to me, Perfection; prove it to me Perfection." Instead you stand up for Perfection and say, "OK illusion, let's see you deal with that. Show me The All-Powerful here. If this has something to do with The All-Powerful, show me The All-Powerful here." If this has anything to do with the Source of Love, show me all the Love. Hold up your illusion to Perfection and see how it stands, instead of saying, "Well, this is the way it is; we all know it is this way," you say, "Come on God, prove it to us. Come on Spirit, do your thing; show us that we should be worthy of You." And who do you represent? Who do you want to represent? The master of illusions or the Master of Perfection? And you do choose in every moment. Therefore, if you can come to the awareness of, I can make one last choice, I won't choose this anymore, I will let that be, then it would be. Unless you take your choices back again. OK? And if you do, you would then have to finally admit you don't actually want That. You only want It sometimes.

And, that is why you always get the sometimes experience; sometimes happy, sometimes not, sometimes dealing with the world, sometimes trying to deal with God, sometimes meditating, sometimes not meditating. Sometimes you are awake, sometimes you want to be asleep. You basically like sometimes. It is almost like a mantra. It is the biggest mantra I discovered since I have been in The Netherlands. I really like to pick on you. And the reason I do that is because you come. So, you are the ones I can pick on, Yes. It is a Love affair.

Q: You use a mantra?

R: Yes, I did, as a TM-student. Once I forgot my mantra. I went to my teacher and I asked, "Can I say it out loud, is it OK to say?" They sound very much alike, you know. There are only like seven of them and I expected her to remember, since she was the teacher. But she was new, I guess. Do you remember when you first started to meditate and you really were intent on doing it right? Do you remember that feeling? Like you really were sincere. You were given something and you wanted to do it right, something you really wanted to work with. And didn't you want to do it right? You were really concerned that you were not doing it right. It is funny now, isn't it? Isn't it? Do they still sell mantras? They do? Well I give you mine for free.

I mean, what is the right way to be Perfect? Do you see the humor in that? Is there a wrong way of being Perfect? There is either being Perfect or being Perfect. You won't have an option. Perfection doesn't give you an option. Now, how can Perfection know about non-perfection? How is that possible? It would be impossible, wouldn't it? Yes. So, is there a right way and a wrong way of being Perfect? That wouldn't make sense, wouldn't it? Hello? Yes! And then, at one time I was looking and I thought by myself, let me see, if I was born deaf and a mantra was required for me to remember my Perfection, my Creator would be extremely cruel, wouldn't He? Right, if that were required for me to know God and I could not hear, I would really be in trouble, wouldn't I? And that would make for a very cruel God, wouldn't it? Wouldn't that, guys, wouldn't that? Don't you think that would be a cruel God to do that to you? It would, right? So, I knew there was something about a mantra that couldn't be God's way, because God wouldn't give you a way that was impossible for you and then have you be born without being able to hear. Now, I'm not saying a mantra can't help you, am I? I didn't say that. I'm just saying, what comes from God must be for everyone. Right? So, if you have to hold your hands like this [Rananda forms circles with thumbs and forefingers.], and you were born without hands…

My point is, let us look at some of the things that people insist you have to do in order to know God. I am saying, those cannot be from God; those could not be God revealing. They could be man trying to figure it out, but they wouldn't be God revealing. Are you with me? Can you hear what it is I am saying? Because God is not cruel to you. OK? So, it can't be that you have to have hands because some people were born without hands, right? It can't be that your legs have to be crossed, because some people have been born with legs that can't do that and it can't be a mantra, because there are people that can't hear. So, what are you left with that everyone must be able to connect with? Well, now you are on the spot, aren't you? So, what is It? What is It that could come from God to us that everyone would be able to recognize?

Q: Joy in the heart.

R: If you recognized the Joy in your heart was self-effulgent, that would be true. But if you are pursuing the happiness in the world, then you could be confused about what it is that brought the joy. So, that's possible, but you know, once again I'm looking at what everyone is doing with their mind What's going on with humanity? Has God touched us in a way that everyone could be touched in that way, because it's really important that whatever it is, is universal. Our Communication with God must be universal if it's from or with God.

Q: Is it about the one universal thing that you make contact with and that everybody can feel?

R: I understand the words you are using, but probably it's not a doing and probably feeling has nothing to do with it. But, I understand what you're trying to say. There is something that is recognizable by everyone. And it is universal. Let's try awareness. Everyone is aware of what is universal. And now we don't have to feel anything. And, if you don't speak English, and you do a translation to German of French or Dutch or whatever, and you would use the word feeling, you're going to find a word that is comparable in that language. And feeling is not a word that you should use when you're talking about a universal experience. OK?

Q: Awareness is better?

R: Yes, OK. So it's nice, we agree. I'm just trying to help you express, so that there is no confusion, OK? Because words can do that, can't they?

Q: Is Awareness the same thing as Knowing?

R: That's the way that I use it. I do not use the word consciousness for Knowing or Awareness. I use consciousness for perception and illusion. And if you try to use them for more than one thing, you open up your whole mind for confusion.[12]

But I know that for those of us that came from the "New Age" maybe it's still new. We tend to talk about feeling things. I felt that energy, you know. We tend to use that word.

Q: Is this not playing with words?

R: No, we're not going to play with words. We're going to find out what's really going on in our mind and be true to it for a change.

Q: The closest then would be direct perception, without words, without explanation, perception without description.

R: And that's wrong too, because God doesn't have anything to do with perception. God has to do with Knowing and Being. Perception has to do with consciousness and what people do in an illusion. OK? And what we're talking about is that which comes from God. Right? That must be universal. It cannot be perceived. It can only be Known. That's what your point was. Yes. That's why it's not a word game, but it's about a clarity game. I'm not interested in playing with words. But I'm very interested in making sure that your mind gets very clear. Otherwise there is no communication.

I'll show you exactly what I'm talking about. I have an image in my mind and I'll use a word, OK? And I'm going to say that word and then you tell me what image is in your mind.

---

[12] *Rananda always makes a very clear distinction between consciousness and Awareness. Consciousness is of the illusion. We are always conscious of something – which implies duality. He uses Awareness to indicate the experience of Truth or Reality, which can never involve an ego or personality. Knowing is not the gathering of information or concepts, but the experience of Truth.*

Alright? And we will see if that's the same. Have you ever done this before? OK, here we go. Are you ready? **Boat**. Does everyone know the word boat? See what image comes up in your mind in association with the word boat. Do you have it? OK, what did you see? Can you describe it a little bit?

Q: Yes, it's a ship, I think.

R: Aha, and then, does it have a sail or not? It does, it has a sail? OK, cool. And what did *your* boat look like?

Q: A rowboat.

R: A rowboat. With oars, we call them oars? Yes, but no sail. See, they didn't look alike. And the same word. What did *your* boat look like?

Q: A sailing boat.

R: A sailing boat. Kind of like a modern day sailing boat? With sails, aha. Do you see what I'm talking about? We can use a word. Now are we playing a mind game about words? Or, are we understanding that some would use words and we don't actually have the same imaging with one another? So, this is my point. If I'm working with you in the realm of Spirit, you'll do the same thing with these words. So, I do take the time to try to communicate with you. Certain words really do represent God's World, if I can put it that way, and there are other words that use the changing of consciousness in an illusion. Some belong to perception, your senses. Some belong outside of your senses. And, to use the same words like consciousness for both of those, can be very confusing. And, there are other words that are very similar to that, like forgiveness. So, I'm not interested in playing word games, but I'm interested in finding a way for clarity and communication with one another. So, that when you walk out of here, you don't say, "Jesus, I'm not sure exactly what he was saying." It's very clear to you.

* * *

Q: What from God is available to everyone?

R: Oh yes, I asked that one, that was my question.

Q: Yes, I want to return to it.

R: Does that mean you have the answer?

Q: I don't know what to say. I don't know anymore. I think it's The Eternal, I don't know.

R: Well, that's true. Whatever That is would be Eternal. That's true. OK, let's look at that this way. What we are looking for comes to us from God, because that's Who knows, and you can use any other word you want. You don't have to use God, if you don't want to. You can use Perfection or Wholeness or Singularity, I'm not concerned about the words that you choose to use to represent Perfection, because everybody here is confused, right? Even your gurus, who say they woke up. So, everybody is confused and something happens and they're either less confused or more confused or whatever. But all I'm saying is, it's not a technique from here. It must come from outside of that, because every technique from here is not universal. Right? Do we not discover that?

I feel like I'm losing you, guys. Are you with me? I'm saying that man has employed techniques in order to know their Creator. From mantras to who knows what. And I'm saying, each and everyone has been of the nature of this world. They have some limit to it that someone cannot be involved in. And if somebody cannot be evolved in it, it cannot come from Perfection. Because, Perfection is universal and therefore, whatever would literally lead you there, would have to be available to everyone. If anybody was excluded, you can be sure it's not from God. Because God is inclusive, not exclusive. Even some of the churches and people would like to tell you otherwise. Right? That's what I'm talking about.

Q: Some people have used, for instance, some meditation technique and reached Self-Realization.

R: Perhaps. How do you know? How do you know what they reached? What I'm not going to do is assume anything other than if something comes to me that is universal, everybody will know about it. And everybody can share in it. And it will not be in a way in which someone cannot share in it. If it excludes anybody it's not That. That's what I'm saying.

Q: So, a teacher like Nisargadatta Maharaj in your opinion didn't realize The Absolute?

R: I have no idea. I have never sat with him and joined in an experience where God was the result of that joining. I'm not here to judge him. All I'm trying to say is, if you come into Perfection, it has to be through something that is of Perfection. It cannot be of something that someone is excluded from. That's all that I'm saying. OK?

Q: That's why you can't reach everyone.

R: Who can't? God can't reach everyone? Anybody that He wants?

Q: OK, you can't change everyone.

R: Well, I can if I let God do the reaching.

Q: God created us different so, maybe...

R: Who told you that? Who told you God created differences?

Q: Because you see all the nations or people...

R: Oh, see? Now you're using perception in order to know about God. And you can't do that, that was my whole point. You see, if you use perception, there would be lots of differences and then you go, "Yes, this is different and this is different and this is different. So, if they are all different, they must have a different way?" Yes, but that's the illusion.

Q: That's where I started.

R: Yes, you start with the illusion, but you have to let go of it if you want something that is not an illusion.

Q: Oh, if I understand correctly, all the people talking here are all talking about reaching somewhere now. And the picture is completely different, it's like we already are, all of us.

R: That's what I have said.

Q: All of us together... not all of us but everything around us, we are God, we are that.

R: No, everything around you is not God. You've got that part wrong. An illusion is not of God and all around you, and even your idea of you is an illusion.

Q: Yes, I'm not talking about ideas. I'm talking about the energy.

R: Yes, I'm talking about the energy too. The energy is all an illusion, too.

Q: So, it already is, and all the experiences that I'm having in my life and everything that...

R: All an illusion.

Q: Yes, all illusion that I have, I have it like...

R: What had all those experiences as an illusion?

Q: It's like a sort of veil and when you clear it up, you are already there. You don't have to come anywhere. You're already there. All you have to do is clear your view.

R: No, you don't even have to do that. You're already there. Period. End of story.

Q: Or let's say, "stop bothering about it, all this talking."

R: Yes, but you can't stop bothering about it and continue to do the bullshit.

Q: Then you'll have to change.

R: You'll have to change thinking that You're not already Awake, and then stop acting like You are not already Awake, too. That's what I mean. But, you have to stop the bullshit, too. You just can't play the game, "Oh, here is the theory, honey, hey, we're all Home, we're all Perfect, nothing is really going on." And then you go and kill one another. You want to fight with one another and you're arguing with one another. You know there are concepts and there is What Is.

Q: The moment that you see what you are doing...

R: Or not. It has nothing to do with acting. It's about being. And, you see, as a person who believes in the reality of an illusion or an illusion as Reality, you think you are actually in charge of what you are doing from moment to moment. Not only do you think they're in charge, you want to be in charge of what's going on from moment to moment to moment. But The Truth of You is that you're never in charge, and Creation or Creator or Perfection is All there is. And You are not allowed outside of that. You can think that you are but You are not allowed outside of that. So, coming to accept what already is, is the requirement. But accepting it means you no longer think that you are a doer. Instead you are a Be-er. You Be. And you're not concerned about doing. Because in doing you then will become a perceiver and an actor rather than a Be-er. I don't know if that makes any sense to you or not. But you've got the part right where You are already there and there is no way that You can become That because You are already That. But you have to understand, it's an understanding. And your understanding and the way that you present yourself to your own mind from moment to moment do not match. There is a gap in there between what you say and what it is that you are demonstrating. So, something does have to happen. OK? So that that mind can let go of that activity and Be. And this is what we are talking about. People try to put techniques in there in order to get to that Perfection. And I'm saying, if you're using a technique that was put together by man, it's going to be imperfect and you're trying to use part of the illusion to awaken from the illusion. I'm telling you what has to be used must come from Perfection. It's the only thing that would work. And that has to be something that's for everyone. That has to be universal. Because, if there are some that cannot, then it could not have come from Heaven or whatever you want to call It. Perfection. It could not because Perfection encloses everyone. It wouldn't do that. It just would not do that.'

Q: If you re-employ your own energy...

R: Re-employ? I don't understand it. I don't understand re-employ.

Q: Well, you just said that it can only work when everybody is included in it.

R: Yes, because of where it comes from.

Q: Exactly. All your Being is That.

R: Yes, your Being is That. And all that's happening is, The Truth of You is being revealed to you by The Truth of You.

Q: I find it hard to describe in my mind how it works.

R: OK, that means you haven't come into the Wholeness yet; there is two of you. But the you that you think you are that is an illusion literally disappears. There is no re-employing in that. There is just a disappearing act. Act three. You came here, you thought you were here, you disappear. Act three.

* * *

Q: You still function in the relative light?

R: If you need to you will. But if you need to – and you will – you will not maintain the Totality, because in order to stay here you cannot stay here with The Awareness of The Totality. You will lose some of It in order to stay here and fulfill helping the rest of You, helping the rest of You, not someone else. Helping the rest of You. Accept what it is that you are experiencing.

Q: But then, once you accept it you disappear, because You can't live on the earth.

R: Well, not only that, there will be no earth to be on.

Q: Are you to be on it?

R: Are you to be on it? Yes, that's the program. Otherwise, why would you want to stay in an illusion when You're awake to Everything? And when you're awake to Everything, doesn't that deny that an illusion is anything?

Q: But you're staying on it to help us?

R: No, it looks like I'm here. What I'm doing is actually the same thing you're doing. I'm just projecting an image here where you have projected an image. And I'm trying to get through it to you to stop doing that. Because, you're fascinated with trying to find happiness here instead of finding happiness within yourself, in your communication and relationship with your Creator. That's where the Source of Joy is, in that relationship with the Source of Love. Now we're back to what it is that I really want to get to. OK? That what is really helpful to all of us must come from outside of the illusion. No part of an illusion can end the illusion! That's what I'm saying. Does that make any sense? OK? OK! It's important to look at that and understand that, because if you don't, you will employ parts of the illusion with the intent of having an eternal experience and you're doomed to fail. It could take you thirteen, fourteen, fifteen years or lifetimes of pursuing that before you're willing to say, "Ohhhhh! Enough of hope, enough of hope. Let's get on with the Real Deal now."

Q: So, the Thing outside the illusion is what God created?

R: You can call It that. Yes, you know, in my words and in the words that I'm comfortable using, there is nothing but God's Grace that affects the disappearance of an illusion. God's Grace is the only thing that does it.

Q: So, we're not awake because we're still waiting for it?

R: I wouldn't wait on God. The idea of God is like Eternal and Infinite and All-Powerful. What would you wait on something like that for? I mean, when is It not there for you if It's Infinite and Eternal? In what moment would It not be there for you? So, for me there is no need to wait. It's about accepting What Is. Which is where we were when we were talking about making your last choice, which is no more choices to accept What Is. OK, now you're not waiting for anything, you're accepting What Is, and you're saying, "Oh, my perception, right, what I'm seeing for instance, is not What Is. That is an illusion." And, if I keep accepting that, then what I'm saying about The Eternal doesn't become my Knowing. Because I'm holding It off by preferring my perception. But, you can't do it, because grace does it. So, what are you left with that you can do? This is really important, because now you're getting down to, what can I do with my mind? If I'm pursuing all kinds of things that aren't working and that are actually keeping me away from receiving the grace or recognizing the grace, then I want to know. And this is what I said. I'm trying to help you see what you're doing in your mind and you're kind of fighting with me.

You have noticed how you're kind of fighting with me about your willingness and unwillingness to see what you're doing in your mind. And every time that you do that, haven't you noticed that you have always chosen something with perception as to who you're representing? Have you noticed that that's what happened tonight?

Q: I surely have to choose awareness, that's the only choice I have.

R: Yes, but once again, you cannot make it happen. If you're doing that with the idea you're going to make it happen, you're connecting two ideas. One is, I have a choice and one is, I can make it happen. It's wanting. See, you won't be able to do that either. That's what the grace does. But, and this is what I was saying last night, what it is that's required is not denying perception. OK? Not trying to make perception not happen, but let it happen and then recognize you don't want it. Rather than using it, recognize you don't want it, because What you want is Eternal. Alright?

Now you're turning your mind to The Eternal. You have to remember that you're the one that made perception. So, fighting against it is fighting against yourself. And it would never work that way. You would just be in the struggle. And you would never rise above the struggle that way. Right, trying to make it happen, nee, nee, nee! [Dutch for *no.*] Oh man, I did it again and you know how it seems like sincerity, but actually it's just a trick. And so you're fighting with yourself. You never get beyond it when you're fighting with yourself. There has to be an acceptance that it is happening, but that it can never be what Reality is. In fact, I don't want it to be what Reality is.

Now you're open for That that is outside of time and space, That that is Perfect and Pure and Whole, to be able to communicate with you. Why? Because you're not holding It off any longer by preferring your perception. Or insisting that you have to deal with it. Who is that you that says it has to deal with perception? Well, it's happening in the mind, that's true. And if you're talking about the eastern way of talking, they do say the word mind for the ego. I never use the mind as a problem, because for me Mind is What God is. God created My Mind. And He only had Himself to use to create Us; so God is My Mind.

I see there is this thing ego that people seem to call mind, but that's different. That's just a thought system that is employed in the mind. [13]

And the mind is that that has the choice and makes choices. Until it makes one final choice. OK? Then there is the heart or what you all call heart. You know how you guys love to talk about heart? Heart is actually the part of the mind that is in direct communication with The Divine. It's not a separate thing. You're not made up of many things. You're One Thing. You're not a mind and a heart. Alright? So, if you have a problem with mind, then let heart be Everything. And

---

[13] *Like in 'A Course In Miracles' Rananda employs the term 'mind' as the instrument which receives messages (thoughts/ideas) from two sources, ego and Spirit. And the mind gets to choose which thoughts it is going to value, those from Spirit or those from ego. And we will always get the result of our choices. We will always get the result of our thoughts. If we don't like these results, we only need to change our mind, which – fortunately – is easy, although ego likes to tell us it is very hard to do!*

if you have a problem with being heart, then let mind be Everything. But don't battle with mind and heart. Because what separation is, that's what multiplicity is. And if you get caught in that you will be caught in perception. Thinking that it's good to push one away and embrace another, you still have the two. And you want to bring them together. You want to see how there is only One. That's what you're after. You reclaiming your Oneness by allowing Oneness to reclaim You.

Q: How about involvement?

R: The closest you get to involvement is what you tend to call surrender. It's releasing your willingness to make choices. That's what surrender is. You're not just surrendering to anything. "Oh, I'm so open!" No, no, it's not about being so open, it's about being open to Perfection. And not anything else! Hello! Enough of that sixties stuff where you're open, oh, and grounded too! That's another one that always really gets me going. Open and grounded. "Oh, honey, I'm open to everything. I've been around the block. I'm really grounded now. I used to think about God all the time but I'm grounded now. So, I'm doing good!

7

GOD HAS NOTHING TO DO WITH MAN

Relationship with God / Healing / Separation / Undoing / Morality / Longing for God

Q: I was thinking about the concept of remembering. Is it God Who remembers us or we who remember God?

R: God doesn't have to remember anything, He hasn't forgotten anything.

Q: And, secondly, if you remember God. How is this possible? How can Infinity infuse a finite structure and still stay finite, or do we become Infinite?

R: You already are Infinite and just lost The Awareness of what you call Infinite.

Q: He says we live in Him, in Him we live, are and move. So, it's hard not to remember God. How come we do not remember Him, then?

R: I don't know, what are you doing not to know? See, you would have to actively be doing something not to know, wouldn't you? And, if you knew what you are doing to actively not know and didn't do that any longer, then you would be left with your Knowing. Does that make sense?

Q: Yes, but the question is then, how do we know when we remember God?

R: There's nothing else like It. You won't miss It. It is self-evident.

Q: OK, thank you.

Well, one more question. Is remembering the essential relation to God? What is it that binds or connects us, or is the same in human beings and in God? Does it require an initiative of man to remember God, or is It God who inspires the Holy Spirit to remind man of God?

R: Yes.

Q: So, God drawing Himself to Himself – us – to Himself.

R: It will look that way from those who are asleep.

Q: And what does it look like from Those Who are Awake?

R: It has always been.

Q: One of the relation aspects between men and God is that God is Creator and we are created. Is that right?

R: No. God has nothing to do with men; What God created is Spirit.

Q: God has nothing to do with men?

R: No, thank God. But He has everything to do with Spirit.

Q: Spirit is also called His Gift, isn't it?

R: Spirit is an extension of God. God extends Himself as Spirit.

Q: And Spirit works through men? Or in men, or...

R: Men is the attempt to not be Spirit.

Q: So, as long as we are here, think we are here...

R: While you think you're here, you will get the result of that thinking, won't you?

Q: So, God is not Spirit?

R: That's kind of a tricky question. God, your idea of Spirit, is certainly more than that. But Spirit is What God has extended as The Truth of You. So, in that sense God is Spirit. But God doesn't go around, you know, everywhere saying, "I'm Spirit."

Q: In the song that was playing on the tape-recorder, it said, "Please, Holy Spirit come."

R: Mm, mm.

Q: So, from there I took it that there is something men can do to enhance the influx of Spirit.

R: That's true. You can stop doing what you're doing not to know that You're Spirit, and that would really help. That's true. You can find a place of gentle tenderness within yourself that reaches to your Creator.

Q: So, the remembering is stopping anything that blocks Spirit.

R: Actually, the remembering occurs when you stop doing what you're doing not to remember. Then the remembering occurs. And when it's complete, then there's no remembering.

Q: And if I in my boldness say that I think that sometimes I have remembered God and I lost it again...

R: When God reveals Himself to You, You're not going to forget it.

Q: Yes.

R: It's an Eternal Knowing!

Q: But can you be 24 hours in the Presence of God?

R: Not as a man. There aren't 24 hours in Heaven. Can you still be you and have God revealed to you?

Q: Yeah.

R: No, not completely, no. Because what God reveals You to be is not a man.

Q: Isn't it somewhere in the Bible that nobody can see God and live, I mean continue to live as...

R: That's really good news, isn't it?

Q: Yeah.

R: Yeah. Who would want to be here after being with God? Who would want to remain in an illusion of pain and suffering and death, when you can be with Eternal Life? The only reason someone would truly want to do that is to help those who are still asleep, so that they can stop their willingness to experience pain and suffering and their idea that you are something that has to die.

Q: One final – for the time being – question is that the previous time I was here, you gave me some kind of energy after the talk. I don't like to define it, but I felt that if more had been given, it would not have been good for me.

R: That's the ego.

Q: Mmm. Because I had the idea – but that's probably the ego – that if too much was given, I would not...

R: You'd die.

Q: Yes.

R: And that's not an idea of Spirit!

Q: So, it can never be too much?

R: It is possible that the energy has effects upon the physical body that you would find discomfort with.

Q: OK, thank you for your answers.

* * *

Q: I'd like to ask a question that has to do with healing. Are you aware of Arten and Pursah, the two characters in Gary Renard's book *The Disappearance of the Universe*? I think it was Pursah that when she, in one of her past lives, became aware or woke up, she died in that life from some illness. I often hear that people who are Enlightened are aware that they have some illness or physical ailment, which causes them to die or to have to live with a very impaired body. What is the relationship; why does that happen? In my mind I think, well, if you're that awake or that aware, you'd have a very healthy physical body. Apparently that's not the case.

R: I do understand that many people have those ideas, but I don't see the correlation myself. However, there is one demonstration in your world where even the illnesses all the way to death were overcome. That's the one that I would look for; that's the one that I encourage people to use as their model. There is so much going on within the mind that is asleep, that is not in full awareness of Reality, that it's extremely difficult to know in any particular individual expression through the body as to why certain things are the way that they are. You have ideas and you have laws of your world, and you expect everybody and every expression to follow those laws, and if they don't, you have a lack of understanding. That's very common here. Go to your doctors and ask them what happened when a miracle took place and somebody got off the operation table. It happens quite often and all they know is that they cannot explain it. So, your laws are constantly being violated and whether it's a spiritual law, the idea of a spiritual law or a physical law, there's just way more going on than can be expressed in a philosophy or a concept that everything must demonstrate. Because Reality is not like an illusion in any way whatsoever. And, those who are still utilizing a physical body and yet dedicating that physical body to helping your brothers, you might say, understand the True Nature of Self as Spirit and still have some bondage to the world. And, when that bondage is complete, then the body is recognized for exactly what it is. So, whether you lay it down or whether you send it into a Light factoring is a choice. Now, those who do not know what that choice is, see it from their own awareness, and from that awareness you would never know why it looked the way that it did, other than what you tell yourself you are capable of knowing. So, it is extremely difficult to know why someone like Jesus came down from the cross and experienced what he did and then went through an Ascension, and somebody else, like Buddha, was poisoned and yes, his body went through the death process and he took another lifetime to complete what he needed to complete. But does that mean that somebody else might not have the body go through that death process, and be completed? There's no law that you can go by to say, because they laid the body down they were not enlightened.

And, then you have the question, what is Enlightenment? What are you enlightened to? Are you enlightened to the Reality of God and the denial of the material world? Or are you enlightened to that it's an illusion, but you still are not enlightened to the full Truth of You; you have the concepts, but you're not in the Knowing of That? So, there's many ideas, and there are many ranges – because that's what the illusion is – many ranges of light experiences. In fact, there is a whole range of illusionary light experiences that many spiritual people are very familiar with. They make up wonderful light experiences for themselves, that have nothing to do with Reality. But, they satisfy some longing that is happening within the individuals who partake in that activity. And, many of them do not allow themselves to be aware of what it is that they're doing, because of that deep need to be spiritually recognized. The idea of not being loved is very deep in humans. It needs to be satisfied. However, there's only one way that that's going to be satisfied and no substitutes will ever work. And that's when Love Itself reveals Itself to You, not when there is an experience of your own making. I hope that was helpful.

Q: Thank you. Is it possible to ask another question? You said a moment ago that there are many more things going on than what we normally are aware of. And you also said that there are many ranges of light experiences. Must I understand that there are levels of experience in levels of light?

R: That's what the illusion is, yes.

Q: So, I was wondering, in remembering God there are stages in which there is more nearness.

R: That's an illusion.

Q: So, nearer to God is an illusion? It's All or nothing?

R: It might be what you experience, but the experience is an illusion.

Q: So, it's either All or nothing?

R: That's right.

Q: So, you cannot come nearer to God, you can only come to God.

R: From the perspective of an illusion you will think you're coming nearer. In fact, you'll even have the idea of evolution. And in that sense evolution is so. But, it's part of the illusion; it has nothing to do with Reality. Reality is the only Thing that has to do with Reality. Levels, degrees, all of that is an illusion. It satisfies you in your mind, because of the fear that arises and you only will allow so much at a time. Well, then that's the way that you're choosing, but that's not God's Choice. Reality is what It is and It has no degrees involved in It.

Q: A person is not very holy or less holy. He's either attuned fully to God or not at all.

R: Well, what I'm saying is, you can be awake to levels if you want to, because you have levels in your mind. But those are not levels of God; those are levels of your own making. When you're done with levels, then You'll know God. What do you want, levels or God?

Q: I want God!

R: OK. Keep your eye on that then.

Q: Sorry that I insist, but when I experience more nearness it is so beautiful...

R: I won't take that away from you.

Q: But from God's perspective...

R: God doesn't see levels.

Q: Right.

R: God doesn't have a perspective. God knows!

Q: So, when there's no more nearness, you realize there's never been a nearness.

R: Once You know, You know You've always known!

Q: Yeah.

R: As a mathematician you must know that you cannot have half something all the way to zero. That isn't possible.

Q: It isn't. [Laughs.]

R: Alright? So, my point is, you'll never get there that way. It's impossible. Salvation is immediate. Your Awakening is your Resurrection. Is that helpful?

Q: Yes, it's great news, great knowledge! But I think the transition from...

R: Is an illusion.

Q: Right.

R: But enjoy it, because it's the best part of the illusion. But don't get attached to it, because it's an illusion. What do you want? Do you want the higher ranges of giggling, joyful, bubbly, blasting with light, or do you want God?

Q: I think in reality, that when I go home tonight and somebody is sitting on my couch and says, "Hello, I'm God..."

R: That's not Reality.

Q: Well...

R: That's a fantasy.

Q: Can one survive the immediate experience of God?

R: No, the ego will not survive It. That's your problem. People don't want to admit that they don't actually exist. They're more fascinated with their ego and their sense of self than with the fact that They are What God has created. And so there are all kinds of philosophies in your world. The Truth is not in your world, however, It's outside of your world.

Q: In order to get a very clear understanding of that, can I ask a small question related to that? Suppose I'm a very rich man and I have millions of euros in the bank, but I've forgotten it. And I come here and they say I have millions of euros and I say that's a lot. So, suddenly I realize that I'm a rich man. My relative world completely changes. Is it like that, to remember God?

R: No.

Q: So, it's not something that you have forgotten.

R: What? What is that something that you have forgotten?

Q: Well, if it is said that one can remember God, this to me implies that we can also forget about God.

R: You can think that you can, yes. And you will get the result of what you think. And if you choose to be something that has feelings, then you will be a man; you'll be part of mankind. Because, there's nothing in Reality that feels. Reality knows Everything what there is to be known. Feelings have nothing to do with it at all; feelings have to do with bodies. Until you believed you're separate and not in the experience of Reality, you never had anything called a feeling. No intuition, none of the strange things that you like to teach one another here.

Q: So, the Love of God is not a feeling?

R: No, it's not a feeling.

Q: It's a Knowing?

R: Yes, it's a Knowing! And nothing in this illusion remotely resembles the Love of God! You don't have anything going on here that resembles the Love of God. It's so Pure! It has nothing to do with situations; It has nothing to do with people. What you have here is a reflection, that's the most that you can get. So, you have kindness and you have compassion, which are worthy of mankind. But, it also is part of the illusion and must be let go to know the Purity that is outside of all of that.

Q: Is our human love a kind of – what you say – reflection, a kind of...?

R: That's what I just said; it's a reflection, yes. The Divine is active; there's nothing just sitting, being nothing, trying to remember What It is. God does not forget What God is. Reality does not forget What It is. It's actively creating, constantly, without time, without end, without beginning. It has nothing to do with the concepts that are representative of the world as you know it. That's one of the greatest pitfalls for those that are attempting to awaken or remember. So, this is what I was saying a moment ago, you tend to use your reference point and project it on to What Perfection might be like or What you would like It to be like or whatever, and as soon as you do that, you've reduced It to what you are capable of imagining. And you'll never be able to reduce Reality. That's what the illusion is; it's an attempt to reduce Reality. It will never work.

Q: I still find it difficult to understand how God's Love can be Knowledge, is Knowing.

R: You won't understand it; you will have to experience it!

Q: So, if Love is knowing, is knowing also Love?

R: Yes, of course. If there is only Reality, then any words that you use are just talking about One Thing. The question is, why do you want to keep picking It apart? Why won't you let It just be One Thing? Why won't you let Reality be what Love is, instead of trying to make It fit into this world? Why don't you let the world disappear and you fit in to What Love really is? Mankind has everything upside down!

Q: Can I ask a question? I'm pretty new to all of this, so eh ….

R: Me too.

Q: [Laughs.] I'm at page 100 of *A Course In Miracles*, so I'm really a beginner. Why did we break off? I know we haven't broken off, but why do we think that we've broken off? Why have we fallen asleep? Why has it happened?

R: You really have to ask yourself that question. In books like *A Course In Miracles*, *the Bhagavad Gita* and many others, there are answers. And you can choose which one you like, if you want, or you can let all the answers go and demand the direct revealing, which is what I recommend. Because, the answer is never going to be good enough. You're still going to say, "But I don't know that. I read it, but is it true or is it not true? So and so says it this way and so and so says it this way. Are you an authority that I can ask which one is true?" No, I'm not going to be an authority that you can ask which one is true. I'm going to encourage you to enter into the experience itself and let it reveal itself to you, so that you will know. See, because Knowing is what Reality is, not hoping, wishing, not learning the concepts out of some book. It's Knowing Itself, It's Being the Love Itself. That's what you want.

Q: So, really I'm enlightened, but I just don't know it.

R: Exactly. And the coming to know it is what some people call Enlightenment.

Q: So, I could really make this all very easy and just go home tonight and say, "OK..."

R: You wouldn't even have to go home tonight, you could just go Home tonight.

Q: [Laughs.]

R: Like right now.

Q: Yeah.

R: The Real Home, your Real Home, where You already are. If I so choose, I can depart this world, and it's not death that makes that possible. [14]

Then, what makes that possible? That's a question. I'm looking for an answer from you.

Q: That's a good question.

R: It's a very good question.

Q: [Laughs.] I'll think about it. I'll get back to you.

---

[14] *From 'A Course In Miracles', The Workbook, lesson 226.*

R: OK. And salvation is immediate!

* * *

Q: I understand that we can't do anything to get to know that we are God...

R: That's good news, isn't it?

Q: Yes, but I still ask myself or you, "Is there something we can do?"

R: This is an age-old question. It's a matter of fact. It's a question that has been with humanity since humanity thought it was something. What can I do? And the answer is: you need do nothing! Because, everything you do gets in the way.

Q: So, even being here tonight gets in the way?

R: Well, it could. Some people can use this talk, this opportunity to share Love, as getting in the way. You are in control of what you want to think, and therefore you can decide what is being said and what it means to you. There's lots of things that can happen in your mind. My point is simply this, Reality is not an option, because It's Perfection and It's Eternal; It's All-Powerful and It's Infinite. Now, you hear those words and they have either some meaning to you or you only hear them as words. And then, beyond that is the Knowing of what those words represent because words are just symbols. Are you with me so far?

Q: Eh, more or less.

R: Well, I want you more and not less.

Q: [Laughs.] Yes, but we are all, I mean the people I know, we are all seeking; we all want to get that realization of God.

R: That's right, it usually starts that way for humans.

Q: And my question is, what can I do in my daily life, so I get this realization?

R: OK. Now, let me ask you a question then. You won't let me do it the way I want to do it, so I'll do it this way. What do you do in what you call your daily life not to know that You are only what Love is? Why do you not let yourself be aware that you are what Love is in what you call your daily life?

Q: Because I don't experience it all the time.

R: Yes, but what do you do not to experience it all the time?

Q: It's a good question.

R: I've got very good questions.

And, I've got the answers. But, they are answers that came to me when I asked the questions and allowed my mind and my heart to be opened so that revealing could take place. And I don't want to take that away from you, because I wouldn't be a friend or a lover with you if I were to do that. I'd be fulfilling some need in me to be a teacher or something like that and what I'd really like to be is just a person who is Home in Heaven with You. So, if you'll look at what it is that you do not to know, and then you don't do those things, the Knowing will replace what you're doing not to know. So, you don't need to do anything, you can stop doing what you've been doing and the beauty and the Perfection that You already are will shine through.

Q: Thank you.

R: OK.

Q: Connected to her question, semantically speaking I could say then yes, you do have to do something, you have to be aware or you have to allow yourself to be aware of what you're doing not to be The Love and The Light that You are.

R: This is the teaching that ego wants you to hear, because the awareness that you were created to be is already aware. And when you stop what you've been doing, that awareness is there with what is Real. Ego is the one that says, "Yes, but you've got to do that." And I'm saying, "No, you're just not going to give up, are you? You don't have to do it, You already are that. If you stop doing what you've been doing, You'll be what You already are, which is not a doing." See, the ego insists that there's something that you have to do, because as long as you're doing something, you are in alignment with the ego, you're in alignment with perception, you're in alignment with the illusion, you're buying into the program. Believe me, Awareness is not a doing, it's a Being. Do you understand what I'm saying? Your Awareness is not a doing. You say you have to do that to be aware. No, you're already aware. What you're doing is keeping you from Awareness. So, when you don't do that, Awareness will just be there, being what it is.

Q: That's a nice idea.

R: OK. That's a start. That's the way communication begins. You begin to look at ideas; you begin to share those ideas. The ideas begin to have more value to you and in that value – because they are reflections of What is Real – you begin to recognize What is Real. Why? Because you're letting go of the value of what you were doing. And then, when you're not doing that, you're not putting any value on the doing and what is valuable then comes into your Awareness, which is Awareness itself. Isn't that nice? Isn't it nice that it is that way?

Spirit is always encouraging you to look at Thoughts that you would be able to share with Perfection. That's what Spirit always does; always encouraging you to look at Thoughts that you can share with your Creator. It doesn't care about doing at all, because it knows doing something in an illusion has no meaning whatsoever other than what you choose to give it. And if you choose to give it some meaning other than this, it ends the illusion through the activity of Love. Then all you're doing is finding a finer realm of confusion in your own mind. Like morality. Be a good person rather than not being a person at all. See, what you fail to realize is, if your goal is not to be a person at all, goodness will flow through You constantly, Love will flow through You constantly. But, when you want to be a good person, it will be defined by whatever you and your world that you populate think is good. Which can change from time to time, can't it? Some people say it's good if you were to pick up a gun and go to war and defend your country, for instance. And another person would say you should never do that, that there are other ways of solving problems. There's lots of things that happen in this world that are in certain "situations" considered to be OK. Like if you had a sister and somebody wanted to kill her, some people in this world would say to you that it's completely OK to kill the person that wanted to kill your sister. And some other people will say that under no conditions should you take another person's life. This is morality. I'm offering you something that's beyond morality and will guide you to share What It is that God wants to share with You, what your Creator wants to share with You, which is not circumstances where you have to figure out what is the moral thing to do. There's none of that going on in Reality. That only goes on in illusions. That doesn't necessarily help you, if that's the situation you're in though, does it? Unless you can rise above it. That would be a different option, wouldn't it? One that's not provided in morality.

Isn't that good news?

* * *

Q: I've got a personal question. The last couple of days I was painting and my thoughts were very negative and, eh, it's...

R: ... want to repaint?

Q: [Laughs.] ... and it seemed, it seemed like that it was shattering me...

R: No, I meant that.

Q: Pardon?

R: I meant that.

Q: Repaint it?

R: I said you might want to repaint.

Q: Repaint. I do not understand.

R: Well, you painted and had all kinds of negative energy...

Q: Yes.

R: You might want to repaint that and this time do it with Love.

Q: Yes. Yes.

R: Or, that's what you will keep.

Q: OK.

R: Now, what was your question?

Q: I was reaching out to God and to Jesus, but one way or the other I was staying in the negativity and I couldn't ehm...

R: You couldn't make it happen.

Q: Make it happen, right.

R: Thank God.

Q: [Laughs.]

R: It's not your job to make it happen. It's your job to have an open heart and an open mind and let Them come to you.

You're a female, you receive. Let Them be male energies and let Them come to You. Men need to do that, too, by the way. You need to let your Creator come to You.

Q: OK.

R: But, your longing can reach out and let Them know that you're longing. But when it reaches the point where there's some frustration involved, and the feeling of doing something wrong or I'm not lovable, because something that I hoped or wanted to happen didn't happen, then you're letting the ego get involved in what came from a very pure place. That doesn't mean that your longing can't get deeper and stronger and deeper and stronger and deeper and stronger, because it certainly can.

Q: Because I know I want that Love.

R: Yes, there's nothing wrong with that. You deserve it!

Q: Mmm, mmm.

R: Aha, now there's something to look at. And deserve it.

Q: Yeah.

R: But, as long as you have that question whether you're worthy in there, it won't happen and then you'll do one of two things. You heal, or you say, "See, I knew I wasn't worthy; I knew those thoughts I had about myself were real, and now I'm getting the proof." Don't tempt your Creator. That's not the way. But being true to the longing and letting it do whatever it does by just being with it, that's really beautiful.

Q: Thank you.

R: Frustration is always a clue where it went off. So, you're going to be painting again tomorrow, is that it?

It is so amazing that our Creator loves Us so dearly. We've convinced ourselves that we don't know that and that we have no idea what that would be like. We're absolutely convinced that the Creator's Love is not Something that we are worthy of. We say that we want It and so on and so forth, but when the Purity of It is actually available, we turn to fear. And then the different thoughts come up in association with that fear, like unworthiness or whatever else shows up; guilt, shame, all those different things, even anger sometimes will come up. But none of that can withstand the purity of God's Love. Nothing can, because that's all there is. That is what Reality is, God's Love, God is What Love is. That's all there is then, It's Love. People in this world have a word that they like to use, it's called energy. They don't really know what energy is, but when they talk about God, then they say It's One Energy. Whatever God is, It's that One Energy. But the energy that mankind is aware of is part of the illusion. And to think of God as one energy is basically just an attack upon Purity. Just like when people talk about having light experiences.

Q: I have a question about that. Because, you also said that a lot of people make their own light experiences...

R: Yes, that happens.

Q: ... and I still sort of wonder whether they made them themselves or not.

R: Everyone knows. Everyone knows when they're making the light experiences that are happening. They might choose to deny that, because they find value in being one that had light experiences, because that's what you call Awakening. And so it's very easy to make experiences for yourself and then call that God or Jesus or whatever. But there's another one that happens and that is not of your own making and you know you didn't make it. And believe me, you do know the difference between the two.

Now, what you might not know, is when you meet someone else that says, "I've had an experience of light," you might not know whether that was of their own making or whether it was a gift. However, it usually shows up sooner or later. The other part of it is, rather than trying to judge them, see The Light that they are anyway, regardless of what they say they have experienced. "I want to see you as the Purity that You are." And you can tell me I'm aware that that Purity has been revealed to me, and to me it would be, well, that's good and that means that's what you want to share with me. OK? And that's all that I want to see from you. That's all that I need to know and vice versa. If they want to see something other than your Purity, regardless of what they're saying, then there's more healing that's required. In my years of wanting and practising and devoting I had different insertions of Light. Not just one, had more than one, that I did not make happen. And there were years when I was meditating and so on and so forth that I made up some very nice things that I felt very good about. Guilty too, but I kept that very, very hidden, because I wanted to feel good about spending all those hours and years doing meditation practices, not wanting to admit that what was happening was not what I had actually wanted to have happening. So, you're in an illusion and all the imaging is not so easy to walk through with great clarity, because of the nature of it, and so the pathway is to remember what you want, and as you get thrown off from time to time, you come back. But remember what it is you want, because it's in that remembering what you want that eventually you get caught unaware. You're in the longing, but you're unaware. You know what I'm saying? It's in there and it's alive, but you're unaware in that moment of that Reality, and then it dawns on You. It doesn't dawn because you're begging and pleading and crying and doing all those different things and your meditation techniques and so on and so forth. That's not what makes it happen. No, what makes it happen in that sense is just the willingness and the presence, being present in your willingness. Because The Eternal is already Eternal, it's already everywhere, it's already Everything that It is, and You're already Everything you're ever going to be. There's just something that's still happening with your mind, that keeps the awareness from being there. Do you know what I'm saying? And that's how you get caught unaware.

I hope this is helpful.

Q: A moment ago you said that possibly you could expand a bit on what you mean by, "Be with the longing". So something could be desired there, and there's a certain attitude that we have to...

R: No, I didn't say anything about desiring that.

Q: But then with the longing...

R: The longing is a call that was put in you by Perfection Itself. It's a point of Light and It's in the deepest part of your mind that you call the heart. It gets activated when touched by The Divine, and as that touch occurs for you, the longing comes into your awareness. And if you let it grow, if you let it blossom, then it will take the place of your thoughts of limitation, littleness, and you find yourself thinking and longing and acting in ways that represent thoughts that You can share with your Creator. You become compassionate, you become kind, perhaps even a bit gentle, but not necessarily, but gentle with yourself, and that gets extended to your brother. But you might be very strong – you know what I'm saying? Like gentleness does not necessarily mean a lack of strength and it also does not necessarily mean not firm. But gentle in the sense of not attacking, not judging.

Q: So the longing means, as I understand it, that the heart is the finest faculty of the mind.

R: No, it's not a faculty.

Q: The most refined.

R: Ehm, I'm only going to say it the way that I say it, because I don't know how else to say it. It's the deepest part of your mind that receives direct Divine impulses.

Q: Aha.

R: Divine is what Love is. So, when you say your heart is aware of Love, that's what you're actually saying. But it's a part of the mind, it's not separate. You're not made of separate things, You're One Thing.

Q: No, I just said that the heart seems to be the most refined faculty, refined part of the mind. It's the interface to God.

R: The Heart is not a thought. Don't reduce it. The mind is What God is. The heart, being a part of that mind and unable to separate from it, is also what God is. Just like in Christianity they say the Father, the Son and the Holy Ghost. There's not three things. Jesus told you, "if you knew me you would know the Father; if you would know the Father you would know me. The Father and I are One."

Q: It's a Trinity.

R: Yes, but it's not really a Trinity, it's only 'perceived' that way because of the way that you choose to think in separation of all of that. But when you're talking about that, if you want to break it up, you'll never know the Singularity of it. All you'll know are the pieces that you keep breaking it up into. Hence, my talking the way that I am what I say, the deepest part of the mind where divine impulses are received, is what you call the heart.

Q: Mm, mm.

R: If you want to experience it and different words occur to you, maybe you can express that in a way that's very particular to the way that you are. And then those that can hear that and experience it that way through you, will be there for you to express that. I'm expressing it this way, because this is the way that I experience it. And that's not explainable. God is not explainable, Perfection is not explainable, it just is what it is. It is You. It's just what it is, you are just What It Is. You are What has been created by extending Perfection as You. Now, that's one thing. See, here you cannot understand how something can expand and then have a name for that and not have two things. See, to your mind that's the way It has to be. And I'm telling you that the mind that you're using, the way you're using it, is not the way it is in Reality. And so, if you want to know what Reality is, you're going to have to let your mind be used the way It is in Reality. If you keep trying to make it fit here, if you keep trying to reduce it here so that you can understand It, you'll never succeed. You've got to let go of here and be there, in the sense of a here and there, which is also an illusion.

8

THE AWARENESS OF TRUTH IS A CHOICE

Being Love / Split Mind / Truth / Christ Mind-Buddha Mind/ Advaita Vedanta / Creation-Extension

Q: I have these repeated experiences that what I am is Love. But then I lose that again. Apparently I am blocking being what I am. My question is, what should be changed?

R: I already answered this, haven't I? Whatever you find yourself doing to not let Everything be What it is, stop doing that. You know that analyzing has nothing to do with Reality?

Q: Yes, but in the dream...

R: No but! Analyzing has nothing to do with Reality!

Q: Reality...

R: Yes, that's right.

Q: Because Reality is Pure Love?

R: It's Knowing.

Q: Knowing?

R: You do not have to analyze anything when you know it. You analyze it, because you tell yourself you don't know it, but that's a lie. So, if you intend to analyze to know what after buying into the lie that you don't know, how could you possibly know? You are in an activity of not knowing. You have to let go of that. Analyzing has nothing to do with Reality and it will not lead you to Reality either.

Q: Can I, once more, ask you about this love? If a human being speaks of love it's always in terms of relationships. But that love which I have, which I have experienced is not related to anything or to everything. Is that the criterion for love?

R: If you are talking about it as a human...

Q: I don't know. There is a kind of love which is intrinsic and that's...

R: Love Itself, in Reality, is an activity of creating. It creates constantly by extending Itself. It does not see other things that It is not. So, there is only Love! Period. End of story! Not a love in Relation to anything. There is only Love! There is only Oneness!

Q: Yes, the movement is that it loves in itself...

R: Any movement that you don't perceive through eyes or anything else is the activity of creating, which is an expression of Love. Not observable. It's You being What It is that You are. I keep telling you, you keep on looking at everything through the eyes of something that is separate. And you keep on trying to grasp what Perfection is through the eyes of something that can never experience That. And I keep on saying, the only way this is ever going to work is when you stop doing what you're doing, all the analyzing, all the perceiving. Then, What is not That, will be What You're left with and that's why many people use the analogy of a sculptor. Right? He's got a big block and he takes away what doesn't belong there and then what's left is what everyone likes. It's the same thing with you, when you let everything go away, what's left is You. You have tried to add on to You. You keep trying to add on pieces of information hoping that somehow these things sticking on to you answer your questions, as if they are going to give you something, some insight or some something and I am telling you, those are the things that keep you from being You.

* * *

Q: When I communicate with you, something starts to flow, which is special.

R: Yes, that's right.

Q: Rananda, when I hear you I get so excited.

R: Why is that?

Q: Yes, and at the same time...

R: No, why is that?

Q: I don't know what to...

R: You have no idea ?

Q: No, yes.

R: Oh, you do have ideas.

Q: There is always this excitement when I hear you and at the same time I am afraid of you.

R: Of me?

Q: Yes, of you. And at the same time I could burst and scream and say I love you, I love you.

R: Really?

Q: Yes.

R: What keeps you from doing that?

Q: Hahaha, I don't know.

R: Don't you?

Q: Yes. Chose the wrong answer, huh? That's the double thing, the fear.

R: Yes, it's called the split mind. You have two sources of thought, you see. This is something I have found extremely difficult to help people with. Because, when they talk to me, they talk to me with the idea in their mind that they're one thing. But they're not.

Q: No?

R: No, they're split. In their mind they have two different sources of thought. So, sometimes you are listening to one source and sometimes you are listening to another Source. But you, who are listening, you think you are one. You don't understand that you have two different guides in that sense, two different teachers. One of them can tell you, "Oh, this is really scary." And you know which you can make judgments, right?

Q: Yes.

R: Criticize someone. Or you can love them. And those two do not come from the same source and that's what needs to be healed. So, instead of having your mind split, It's Whole. That's what this is all about.

Q: Yes.

R: You get excited because you can feel the healing happening. And it is also why you get afraid, because the thought system that is bringing you the fear knows that it's losing control. So, its range goes from suspicious to vicious. Suspicious of what he is saying and suspicious of what his intent is and suspicious when he talks about love, whether he is really loving or not. Suspicious. And then it goes to vicious. "You can tell me that he is loving. I see things he does that are not loving…" So it goes from suspicious to vicious. That's the full range of one of the thought systems. And the other one talks about Love and It has no degrees in there. It's just either recognized It's Love or not.

Q: Yes, I only love you when I see you.

R: Well, if it's Love, then that's what I am saying is there. You won't see degrees in that. When you begin to see degrees of more or less, then you're talking about what the ego is bringing to you and that's what analyzing is. That's what analyzing brings you.

Q: I don't want that anymore.

R: Then you won't.

Q: So many years...

R: If you don't want that anymore, then you won't. See, when you're split, there is one of you saying, "I don't that want that anymore," And the other one is saying, "Wait till I get her home."

Q: Yes. [Laughs.]

R: Until that is healed! The only way it becomes healed is when you begin to see what is truly valuable. And what is truly valuable is only what your Creator would share with You. Choose the only thing that really has value. And if your Creator is loving and creates by extending Love, then what do you think the Creator does with You?

Q: Yes, oof.

R: So, when you have experiences that are not loving, guess what? Those are the things you are putting in the way of knowing What You are. Who You are. Who your brother is. The Nature of God. Just stop doing what you're doing. Then that Love will just be there. The You, the Love that You are. Then the communication with Everything else that is Love is natural. It's not something you do, it's natural. See, you don't know what's natural, because you have been teaching yourself that you're separate from What It is that You really are; that you don't even know What It is You really are. Love is natural. It's all that there is! God is Love! There is nothing but Love. In this world you have ideas you love and ideas you hate, feelings and emotions, and love is one of them.

Q: Yes.

R: In Reality there is only Love! Here you will be able to experience other than Love. Because, that's what here is all about. That's also why this is not Reality. It is what you choose to experience, OK? So choose wisely. Especially when you say you'd like to have experiences of Love and Light.

Q: Yes.

R: Well, then you have to choose differently.

Q: Truth is not a choice, is it?

R: The Awareness of Truth is a choice. Truth is not a choice. And it's not an experience. It's Knowing, because It is What You are. And to not know What You are doesn't make sense to anybody.

Q: I don't have to think about It?

R: Don't think about It, I agree. Now what? Don't think about It. Be It and know What You are. That's absolutely true. But there is a difference between Truth and true. There are many things that are true in this world. But there is no Truth in this world. Truth is what Perfection is. That's What You are. And Perfection knows What It is. Doesn't doubt, doesn't think about It. It's too busy being It. I consider that really good news. But, you know, the thinking about It, that's the analyzing. And that's what tends to happen in the mind when you think about It. The ego doesn't make sense at all. Who, what would want to do that? Doesn't make sense. To see how the mind works, on the other hand, is very valuable. Because it is your tool. The mind is your tool. And, if you let that mind work with the guide who wants to bring thoughts into that mind that do not represent Thoughts that would be shared by Perfection, then you will get the result of doing that. In fact, you would have to want to do that for it to occur. And that's what we are talking about here. Seeing what you have been wanting to allow in there. Seeing the result you get from it and then choosing differently. See, stop doing what you do. When you describe a self that's involved in an illusion, when you're involved in analyzing an illusion, you will not know that You're creating. It's impossible.

R: Was that OK? Was that helpful? You can just shout out if you want to. I LOVE YOU. It's OK.

Q: Hahahaha.

R: I don't hear that very often but...

Q: Hahahaha.

R. It would be OK.

* * *

Q: I would like to ask what's the difference between Christ Mind and Buddha Mind?

R: Well, they spoke a different language. [Rananda Laughs.] That was a joke, right?

If you look at it in the sense of Buddha Mind being the Awareness that Buddha allowed himself to access and The Christ Mind being the range of Light or awareness that Jesus allowed himself to experience, the difference would be that Jesus realized he is the Christ. Which is the only One that there is! Buddha came to a point where he heard a voice that encouraged him to come back and share what he learned, which means he didn't learn that there was only him. The Christ learned that the Only Thing there is, is The Christ. Christ is a word or a label that you would put on all of Creation. That's what The Christ is.

Q: It is also said that The Christ Mind was a portal of Love. Is Buddha's Mind a different portal?

R: Well, once again, if you limit yourself in time, then you have like a chunk of what it is that you associate as Buddha and a different segment of time chunk you say is associated with The Christ. But, you see, there is only One Mind that Jesus and Buddha both came forth from. And even since that time frame where Buddha went through the death process, the Mind that he eventually recognized as Self, is The Christ. So, even now The Buddha Mind is The Christ Mind and there is no difference. That's why I made it very specific if you're talking about time frames. I can show you whether there is a difference but that really doesn't have any meaning any longer, because not only were they always the same, but since then they have become the same exact thing.

Q: So, they're the same.

R: Yes. Unless you look at the time frame. Because the only place you could find differences is in a time frame. Right? Like, if I were to talk to you, how old are you now? Just make it up. It doesn't make any difference what you say.

Q: Forty.

R: Forty. OK. So, there is an image of you as ten years old. And if you look at that image, it doesn't look the same. But you're still you. You were you at ten and you are you now. So, it's just the time frame that has a different image, that gives a mind the opportunity to say there is a difference. But if it doesn't see that, if it only sees what You really are, then the time frame has no meaning whatsoever. And you saying I am forty and I was ten has no meaning whatsoever. Unless you wanted to give it meaning. But if you do, you do it because you don´t want the Single Thing.

Q: I asked it, because I thought The Buddha Mind was different from The Christ Mind and that Christ was Love.

R: That's true, but that's what the illusion is. I mean, Buddha, it is said, represents compassion and Jesus, it is said, represents Love. OK, when they taught, they had different programs that they taught. Like Jesus taught the path of forgiveness. And that's not the path Buddha taught. But when you talk about the mind, they are the same thing now, whether you want to follow the precepts of the Buddhists or the precepts of the Christians. The thing to recognize is that Jesus taught Resurrection and Ascension and Buddha did not. But, both of their intent was to know Reality completely. So, to me the differences are only significant in time reference. For instance, Buddha taught, because I did you can. But Jesus teaches, when I did You did. And there is a difference, you see. One is teaching Oneness and one is teaching we are not the same, but we have all the same capabilities and we have the same Source. So, one was looking more at time and the other one was looking at how time has no meaning here whatsoever other than to love one another. And help one another so that you can come to know that we all have the same Source and therefore we are all Children of that same Source, we are all expressions of that same Source. And then, once he went through the Resurrection and the Ascension, he had a whole offering and that's what people call *A Course In Miracles*.

Q: Thank you.

Q: And from the point of Advaita Vedanta?

R: That's the closest I can find to what my experience is. Like, for instance, when I listen to... Well, this is a little tricky because I can say things and you hear what I am saying and then you do with it whatever it is you do with that. Now, this is all being recorded and somebody can listen to that and can decide to interpret that whatever way they want. And, if it is written out and then put into Dutch, you could have who knows how many different translations of what I said. So, my point is that for instance with Ramana Maharshi – who to me was probably one of the best expressions of that teaching – when I get an English translation of what it is that he said, it is a different interpretation or different choice of words from the person who knew the language and translated it, right? So, when I first started listening to that, I went, "Man, this is so, this isn't so, this isn't so." And then I came upon the book that was published by the person that was considered his librarian, the one he chose himself to take notes and keep records and so on and so forth. When I read his book, I went, "Oooh, of course, oooh, yes of course, ooh, of course." When I look at that representation I see that it matches what happened with me. And I also recognize when he taught Hindus, they were trying to get him to express through their tradition or platform of religion. He tried not to do that and then, when they insisted, he said, "Well, OK, that's the way that would look." He tried to get them to give up their effort to put his teaching into their thought system.

Q: Is Creation going on now?

R: Yes, It's Eternal. It's just, you know, how are you going to talk to people that don't understand? You have to use a language in terms that they do have some understanding of…

Q: But my question is, if there is Extension and Creation going on, how does that fit in with Pure Non-Duality, which is what you teach? Because an Extension and a Creation seem to imply some difference, which is not the case with Pure Non-Duality.

R: Alright. OK, try this out, let everything you know disappear.

Q: I'll try?

R: No, don't try, do it. Empty your mind of everything you think you've learned, right or wrong.

Q: I experienced that once.

R: No, now! Do you want it now? [Laughs.] Do you want The Presence of your Creator now?

Q: Yes, yes, yes, yes.

R: OK, then let go of everything you ever thought that you have learned. Whether you think it's right or wrong. Just let go of everything that you think you've learned. Let it go. Come unto your Creator with empty hands. Mmmm…

Q: That's the Extension?

R: Reality is What Creation is. Creation has occurred by God extending Himself as Reality. Call It The Christ, call It whatever you want. I don't care what anybody calls It. Allow It to be What It is, regardless of what you call It.

Q: Yes, but I was trying to convey what I experience. I'm trying to do what you say and how I experience that.

R: No, Extension is creating! There is no creating going on in an illusion.

Q: Then, what is It that gets created?

R: The Extension of Yourself. More Love.

Q: So there is eternal Extension going on?

R: Yes, Creation is eternally created. No beginning and no ending. There is nothing going on but Creation. And that's not what's happening here. As fascinated as everybody might be with what they call their life and what they are doing and thinking and experiencing, it is still not creating.

No matter what role you think you're playing. From the greatest teacher to the one who hasn't begun to teach yet, it's all an illusion. The only Reality is creating. And That's not here. This is an illusion; this is a dream. Isn't that good news?

But when you let go of all that you've taught yourself, Reality can reveal Itself to You as It is. Not as you prefer it. Not as you like it to be. Not within the Christian story or the Hindu story or the Buddha story or the Celtic or whatever. You know what I am saying? It's just, those all have flavors and I am not saying there is anything wrong with that other than the fact that your relationship with Reality has nothing to do with a religion. It's about what was there before religion showed up.

Q: So, could you say anything that has to do with matter would be a part of illusion?

R: You can look at it that way. It's really necessary to recognize that all thought manifests in some way. OK? When it's thought in association with an illusion or fantasy, then you make up all kinds of things and that's what matter is. Matter is something that is made up that would contain images, fantasy. All of Creation is of Light! But, you have to be so careful when you say that, because people think they actually know what you are talking about. But they don't remember The Light that I am talking about. It doesn't have any color to It or anything like that. But there is no other word in your language that you can use to convey It. So, we use imaging like light and darkness, right? Asleep and awake, you know? Because it's what your mind is familiar with. But Reality is not like what your mind is familiar with. So, it's just as easy for me to say there is nothing that you can go by. That apparently is frustrating, but it's meant to be encouragement to let go of what it is that you think you've learned and the words that you used to try to describe it. Now, that can either disappoint you or get you really excited, because if It's not like this in any way, It means no pain, suffering and death. It doesn't have bodies and people that you like or dislike. You know what I am saying? And clothing that you like or dislike and the things that you like to do. Those are not happening there either. So, that might disappoint you a little bit and give you a little fear. Then, as you describe yourself as someone who has choices, you make a choice. Whether the idea I am presenting to you seems really exciting to you, or whether it seems fearful, because you still value what you think you are going to lose. It's not like this in any way. I have to help you see that what you have been valuing has no value to begin with. And then, when you begin to see that, you'll be willing to experience something not like this, because you don't feel there is loss involved.

Q: So, in Reality you are One with Everything, but you still have some kind of personal identity?

R: It is not separate.

Q: Some kind of personal flavor of something that you still are you?

R: Yes, but let me put it this way. I don't know if this will work for you or not, but this is the only way I can look at it. When you see a cloud in the sky, part of it is dense and part of it you might be able to see through. OK? But, it's a cloud. The cloud knows itself as a cloud. It doesn't know itself as dense or not dense. It only knows itself as a cloud. You're the one that makes a distinction. OK. So, if you were one of the particles in the cloud, you wouldn't make any distinction. You would just be that particle and your awareness of the cloud. Everything. That's all you are aware of, you're a cloud. Now, I know that's not a complete analogy for what I am talking about, but it's kind of a close imaging that might be helpful. If anything happens at one end of the cloud, the back end of it knows exactly what's going on. Everything experiences everything that any part of the cloud is experiencing. Here you all think you are part of Oneness, but you don't know what Oneness is experiencing. See, that is what you've lost. That's what you are willing to give up.

Q: I think that that's a very important point, because I think that a deeper sphere here in the illusion is that you would lose yourself. What you think that you are.

R: Yes and that's true, you will. So, it's a true thing. But the question is, is it worthy of fear? Or, is it worthy of joy? I mean, take a look at that thing that you think you are. What is so great about it?

Q: Thank you.

R: Love does not inspire fear!

9

GOD'S LOGIC IS NOT MAN'S LOGIC

Awaken from the Dream / Perfection / Learning from Love

R: There is nothing easier than being what You already are. The only question there would be, is that what you want? Do you want to be Who You are? Or, do you want to be something that changes with the day, with the seasons, with whom you are talking to? One ends in pain, suffering and death and the other one sets You free. It's up to you and there is nothing making you make the choice that you make. There is no magical force somewhere, no Heavenly Father zapping you if you make a moral decision that is not to His liking. It is just not like that. It is just you and your thoughts and the results of your thoughts. That would be enough, wouldn't it? I mean, what if it were true that you got the results of your thinking? What kind of thoughts are you having?

Q: Many today.

R: Yes, but what kind?

Q: Loving thoughts.

R: Ah, so you have lots of Love today.

Q: Yes.

R: Just like every day.

Q: Yes, just like every day.

R: So, when you are dreaming, you usually don't know you are dreaming, you are just dreaming. And, then you say some things happen after that. The dream ended, and then something happened, and then you were aware that you were dreaming. And that's what you call waking up? I woke up and that's how I knew I was dreaming? Is that the way it happens for most people? Yes. And then sometimes you are dreaming and you are aware you are dreaming. You are awake in the dream. And what you are awake to is that you are dreaming. Right? You are not awake to its reality, you are awake to that which is dreaming. Like, sometimes when you are dreaming and you make your dream do all kinds of things, change the colors, and do all kind of things, you play around with your dream. It is fun to play around with your dream, isn't it? And the only reason it is fun to play around with your dream is because you know that you can wake up. Otherwise you would be stuck in the playing around, wouldn't you? Then you call it a nightmare. So, there is waking up in the dream and there is waking up from the dream. Which one do you want? And then there is getting drunk in the dream and getting drunk on the dream. Buddha calls that pursuing the pleasures of the world, which is the cause of all your pain and suffering. You desire that that cannot relieve you from the pain and suffering; so it brings more of it. Wouldn't you first have to wake up in the dream, before you can wake up from the dream? That sounds logical doesn't it?

Q: Yes.

R: God's logic is not man's logic! That's why I was just checking. I had a sneaky suspicion, but it can happen that way. You can find yourself awake to the fact that this is a dream.

Q: But are you saying it is not necessary, that God's laws are not sequential?

R: That's right. Time, the ideas of time and sequential, is the illusion. It is like back to the idea of instantaneous. Most of the individuals that I have had an opportunity to talk with, that have gone through what is considered by them to be Enlightenment or Awakening, have had more than one insertion of Light or Light factoring that altered them in such a way that it allowed them to become aware of what they were not aware of before that factoring happened. I haven't met anybody that had like one zap and everything was completely wide open.

Q: But you teach the instantaneous because otherwise you are not upholding the Integrity of God.

R: That's right. And The Truth is, there is only one Awakening. The idea that there is more than One is a part of the illusion. But, that's what this is, so that is the way that it shows up. Until you have the last disappearance. And in the disappearance there was only one disappearance, the world of perception disappears once. Everything else is temporary.

How many times would an illusion have to end? And see, when it ends you say, "How can something that didn't have a beginning, have an ending?" But knowing that and having concepts about it, are two different things. When you speak of Reality from the perspective of Reality or from the knowing of Reality, you say things like, "There is no world." But from being part of the dream, you say, "It might be true that there is no world, but I need to come to know that. And therefore I need to be involved in the coming to know." But once you know, you know that you have always known that there is no world, that there is only Reality. Illusions have done nothing, have had no impact whatsoever upon Reality. How could they? They are nothing. So, you have a dream and in the dream your house burned down and you went to the bank and they decided to give you a billion dollars to build a mansion instead. You don't have to make monthly payments or anything and you only wait five minutes for the builder to be done with your billion dollar house. And then you woke up and there you are in your apartment. What do you do, you close your eyes and try to get back into your dream again?

Q: Sometimes.

R: Or would you go, "Oh, boy, I was just saved from having a billion dollar house, I am so grateful, thank you, thank you, thank you!" Because, it depends on what you value, on what you are pursuing. The wealthy man thinks the poor man has got it made, because he hasn't got all that money to worry about and the poor man thinks the wealthy man has it made, because he has got so much money he can have anything he wants. So everybody thinks someone else has really made it. Everybody always thinks that somebody else's situation is a lot better than theirs. To be grateful just for what it is that it is with you is really helpful; just being grateful for what is happening. And recognize from whatever it is that is happening with you, there is a doorway into the Remembering of The Truth of You. The differences of an illusion are the differences of the situations that you find yourself in and literally have nothing to do with your instantaneous or immediate access into Reality. They have nothing to do with it; there is no situation that is easier or harder than another. An illusion is an illusion; it's an illusion of differences. So, you can look at anybody that you want, make any kind of comment about them that you want, but they are not better off than you. They might be willing, be more loving than you are and therefore there is somewhat of a difference in what you would call the quality of their life. But that's a choice and that can change in any given moment that you decide that Love is more important to you than what you have been pursuing. And instantly it can change, or you can practise and let it make time. It is your choice, until you run out of time. So, I wouldn't take too long if I were you, since you don't know how much time you have left. Do you know how many breaths you have left, before you don't have any more breaths? Then don't waste them. When you don't know, don't waste them; use them wisely. Gratitude is really good, isn't it? It's a good idea, gratitude is a good idea. Until you wake up and you don't need it anymore. Isn't that good news?

Q: Yes.

R: Your Awakening cannot be far behind a grateful heart and an open mind. Anybody here grateful?

Q: Yes.

R: Does anybody here have an open mind? Be careful, here comes your Awakening. And if your Awakening didn't just happen, guess what? Somebody is a liar. Honesty is important too, isn't it? Is it fair to say that as long as you believe you are something or someone that is an experience in an illusion, that there is still something that has not occurred for you yet?

Q: Yes.

R: So, then it doesn't do a lot of good to play the innocent role, does it?

Q: No.

R: It makes sense to play the role of one who is in some range of transformation. You are in your Awakening, this is what your Awakening looks like. It looks like this; this is part of it. You are not waiting for it to happen, this is its happening. How long does it take?

Q: I would say it takes as long as it takes until it disappears.

R: Yes, until you accept it. It takes as long as it takes for you to accept it! This is your Awakening. Otherwise you are thinking other thoughts, aren't you? Right? You are not accepting this as your Awakening; you have other thoughts, so you get the results of those thoughts. You see how simple this is? I mean, what I am teaching is not really sophisticated. In fact, it is really simple, but the rejection of it is relentless. And it is the rejection of it that keeps you in the need for complexity, because the simplicity of it is — were you to accept it — that you already find yourself Home in Heaven. It is not faster, it is not difficult, you don't have to do anything. In fact, all that is being asked of you is to stop doing what you are doing, so that The Truth of what it is that is being said, will dawn in your mind. Call It Enlightenment, Awakening, Resurrection, I mean... see? You just throw words at it instead of being It. And the simplicity of It is that what you talk about is What It is What You are, already. There You are already, You are all ready, ready!

Q: Can I ask a question?

R: Ja, ja. [Dutch for *Yes, yes*.]

Q: I have a question about being awake in the dream and being asleep in the dream. You are talking about rejection. At least when I am awake I can be more aware of the thoughts that are coming into my mind and I can choose them or not. When I sleep I think I am like dead, but I assume that at that time I am also either accepting it or rejecting it, but I am not aware of it.

R: You are choosing not to be aware of it, that's right. Your Awareness is Eternal. You are always aware of something. In a dream, and this is a dream, you can choose to not be aware. So, that is a choice too. But, you will be aware of something. Because all you are saying is, "I choose to not be aware of this dream." And that's what you call sleep, because you cannot obliterate your awareness. So, you go into what you call sleep and your awareness is just focused somewhere else, in another thought patterning. And if you are really fascinated with this one, then your dream sequencing will also be much like this one. But, let me put it to you this way. There is a Master who once said to you, "I am with you always." So, whether you think you are awake here or sleeping, and aware of something else or even not aware, that Master is still with you, that Christ, that Buddha, that whatever words you want to throw at it, Reality, You as Creation, You and Perfection, that is always available for you, no matter what thought patterning you find value in. And to me that's one of the most beautiful things to begin to prefer, because apparently, in your dream, you think you have a choice. So, while you have a choice, it would be nice if you preferred to be aware of Perfection. And as you did, then everything would begin to change, because it is the way that it is, because you are preferring the dream to Perfection. Do you follow what I am saying? So, waking up is a preference in that sense, besides the fact that you don't really have an option eternally. It is nice that somewhere along the line you say, "Hey, I have had enough of this." I mean, why would you... You know, like if you listen to a lot of the teachers that come out of the eastern tradition, most of them will tell you that you have been doing this for lots and lots and lots of lifetimes. Hello?

Q: Yes.

R: Aren't you tired?

Q: Yes.

R: I mean, aren't you tired of doing it over and over and over and over and over and over and over and over and over and over and over and over and over again? I mean, how many mornings you want to sit with your legs crossed and how many evenings you want to fall asleep? Sometimes it feels like you are going to break your neck.

How many lifetimes before you finally say, "Hey, something is not working." Has anybody ever pleaded with their idea of God or whatever, to stop this nonsense? Have you ever felt that way? "Please God, please, so and so, mama, papa," whatever. You know? Have you ever done that; have you done that quite a lot? Yes, and here you are. Has anybody ever yelled at God? Do you ever like scream and get really angry?

Q: Yes.

R: "This is unreasonable," and maybe you even stamped your feet. Did you ever do that? Have you ever done that? Did that work?

Q: No.

R: Did you ever like meditate just right on through the night and then into the morning? And there you were and it was time to go to work and you didn't sleep and you meditated all night long. Have you ever done that?

Q: Yes.

R: Did that work?

Q: No.

R: Let's see... What else have you tried? How about not eating food? Have you ever tried not eating food?

Q: Yes.

R: Did that work?

Q: No.

R: Let's see... have you ever tried eating a lot of food?

Q: Yes.

R: Did that work?

Q: No.

R: So, can you grasp what it is that I am trying to say? It is just like practising things that you make up in order to try to adjust to the illusion or the world that you are aware of. It hasn't worked. It hasn't worked. And you have been pretty sincere about it, haven't you? As far as you are concerned you have been pretty sincere, right? Obviously everybody was going to say, "Yes, as much as I could be," and then you can always judge yourself, "Oh, I wasn't good enough." Right? And that's what your teachers will often tell you, "Well, if you were better at it, no wonder it is taking you all those lifetimes." Right? So what does it take? What does it take for you to let go of focusing on an illusion and let What Is, be What Is?

Q: You have to be willing.

R: Yes. But if I ask you, "Are you willing?" what would you tell me?

Q: Sometimes.

R: Oh, that famous Dutch word, *soms*. [Dutch for *sometimes*.] But how about if I told you, you only have to be willing once? That would be a tough teaching, wouldn't it? Because you are already absolutely convinced that you are willing, aren't you?

Q: Yes.

R: You have had moments where you are absolutely convinced that whatever was happening in that moment you were being willing, right? And yet, your Master tells you that all that is required for your Awakening is a little willingness. So, now you are mad at your Master? Or do you look at your own idea of willingness? So, that you can begin to sort out your own lies and begin to recognize that of many of these words that are used, you don't actually know the experience that is associated with them when they are said by a Master.

You have an idea of what those words mean, based on one who is not awake. So, when you hear the Master say that, you think he is saying what you think, rather than you wanting to know what he means by that, because you need to join with him in order to know, because he has got the Awakened Mind. This is the problem when you listen to someone like Jesus. You interpret what you think that statement means. And you forget that one of the things he is asking of you is to not put new wine in old skins. Don't take these precious ideas and put them into your old ideas and think you know what's going on. It takes a certain humbleness, a certain sincerity that is truly willing for a revealing to take place that does not fit within what your experiences have been up to that moment. That is why you are beginning to hear the word quantum used more and more in association with spiritual teachings. The way that I always taught this is, what you are looking for is an experience that is not of your own making. Because, if it is of your own making, then it is not Perfection. But, you are looking for an experience that is Perfection that is going to reveal Itself to You, so that You can know What Perfection, Wholeness, Oneness is. It is not what your idea of It is. When you describe yourself as something that is separate, your idea of wholeness is taking the things that are separate and putting them together and now it is whole. That is not what Wholeness is. Wholeness is That that cannot be separate. One more time. You cannot look at all the parts, like all the people or all of your ideas, and think that if you bring them all together that that is what Oneness is. And that is what you try to do, because you think you are a part of Everything. Which is true, but when you think of that, you are thinking of everything that is in the illusion.

Q: So, I can like what you are saying, but is it better that I don't understand? I mean, at least the me that I think that I am? I don't know. What you are saying sounds really good to me, but I don't think I get it.

R: You will.

Q: OK.

R: Look, if somebody uses the word Perfection, it is a symbol, isn't it? It is not what Perfection is Itself, it is just a symbol that represents It. OK? If you are aware of symbols, you are not aware of Perfection. If you are aware of the symbol and someone talks about Perfection and you think you understand Perfection, you are just kidding yourself, because Perfection is not the symbol. What you understand is something about That. You understand the concepts that words represent, which can be translated into Perfection. With the advent or the will of Perfection, these concepts can be converted into the experience of Perfection. There are these events, some people call them what, event horizons? Some people call them holy instances, some people call them a moment of blazing Light where you become Awakened. See, there are lots of ways for people to talk about these things, but something can happen when you get that concept clear in your mind, realizing however that it is only a symbol. And that you won't be satisfied until the symbol is replaced by the Beingness in that Perfection. So that what it is that you think you are that is not Perfection, is literally removed from your mind for you. So that there is not something that is in the awareness of differences and separation, that is then only aware of the Perfection. It disappears and What is True and What has always been, is all that you are left with. Got it? That is what I am talking about. But, if what I am saying is satisfying to you, then you think the symbols are enough, and that's what I am saying. How can they be enough? They are not Reality, they are symbols that represent It, or point to It. And many people are just, you know, they are happy being able to say the words and they are still very much afraid of being That.

Q: What is left then?

R: Everything.

Q: You stop thinking?

R: No, I have never said that. I don't know where you got that idea from. I never said you would ever stop thinking.

Q: What about the symbol?

R: Yes, well, you won't have symbols any longer. You will be Everything; you will just be creating, having fun. That would be nice.

Q: OK, but what about my feelings?

R: Feelings only have to do with illusions.

Q: So, you have good illusions and bad illusions?

R: Yes, in illusions that's true, but not in Reality. There is not good Reality and bad Reality.

Q: Can I say then that I have good feelings?

R: Yes, you can have good feelings or bad feelings, but they have nothing to do with Reality. They have to do with the illusion.

Q: So, when I am in Reality, what is That?

R: That is what I am trying to say. The symbols are not It, that's my whole point. And unless you let go of your fear of being directly in the experience, you won't know. And then you will say, "Keep telling me, keep telling me, tell me more, tell me more, give me more symbols, give me more definitions, give me more descriptions, give me more of the images." And I keep saying, "No, I don't want to do that, I want you to come into and have the direct experience. Don't waste my time and yours in images." I only give you as much as you can pull out of me, which I hope is really little. Because I want you to be so frustrated that the symbols are not enough. You know what I am saying? Because, it is the passion of That that turns away from what you call your ego and turns into spiritual grace.

Q: I'd like to experience That.

R: Well, of course. It is your Divine Right. But guess what? In order to experience that, you have to stop doing what you like to do.

Q: Then I don't do much.

R: Well, I don't care how much you think it is. It is enough to keep you from experiencing Perfection.

Q: OK.

R: See? So, whatever it is you do, some people think they do a lot, some people think they do a little, some people do as little as they can, some people do a lot of littleness.

Q: So, I stop experiencing Perfection, what then?

R: No, that is what this is. When you stop experiencing Perfection, that is what this is. When you stop this, then you get to experience Perfection.

Q: So, the fact is that even though I think that I am willing, I haven't gone beyond the symbols. This means that I actually haven't even had enough willingness to go beyond the symbols.

R: And that's the only thing that you are asked the willingness for, that you go beyond the symbols. Now, see what I am trying to show you; this is what Buddha taught, what is so beautiful, right? That you keep pursuing things in this world rather than allowing the world to disappear, because what you want is not in this world. Now, when that happens, when you stop pursuing what you want in this world, all of a sudden you are going to find it a happier world. Why? Because you are just letting it be what it is, and you are not trying to make it what it is not. Because, you are trying to make it a place where you can find Perfection. Did you ever notice how, when things don't work out, you get really sad? Or disappointed? Well, why? You had expectations that you would find Perfection there, or something would go right, or somebody would respond in a way that you had hoped they would. You see, you have expectations that somewhere something within you is going to be satisfied, that is what this expectation is. And sooner or later it falls apart, because you have tried to get something that is not actually there. So, sooner or later, at some point in time it has to fall apart. Now, every time that that happens, there is an opportunity to recognize the nature of what you are doing with your mind, and if you don't, you really have not taken advantage of all the pain and suffering you have been willing to go through. You wasted it, you waste pain and suffering. You might as well use it, if you choose that path. You understand what I am saying? Let your pain and suffering help you see that that is not what you want. Don't go after it and after it and after it. Now, that is one way of pursuing knowledge. However, that is not what I am teaching. I am just teaching, if you are going to do that, don't waste it. What I am teaching is, let Love show you the way, let Love guide you. Don't waste those miracle impulses, don't waste those Love impulses. Can you hear the difference of what I am talking about?

Q: No, because I don't think I really know what Love is.

R: Yes, but you have impulses within you, that Divine Spark that is sparking. It is sparking and everyone is being sparked by The Divine. And you do something with it. Some people have lots of sex, some people eat lots of food, some people read lots of books, some people meditate it away. I mean, they do all kinds of things, they go fast in planes or boats or cars. These impulses are happening to connect with The Divine, and you put them into whatever it is that fascinates you. OK? When God fascinates you, when Perfection fascinates you, when that spark happens, you turn in that direction. Now, that is following the path of Love. If you don't, you are taking that spark and you are putting it into the world, and then you get the pain and the suffering and you just think, well, I messed up this time, I keep trying, maybe there is another guy, maybe there is another girl, maybe there is another town, maybe there is another language, maybe there is another guru. That is always a good one. People love teachers, they collect them like credit cards. I talk to people and they will say, "Oh yes, I went to see this teacher and that teacher, and this teacher and that teacher, and this one over here and that one over there." And I say, "Well, why didn't you just learn from the first one?" "That wasn't a nice thing to say to me." "Well, I am sorry, I am trying to be helpful. If I knew you didn't want help I would not have said anything." A spiritual credit card is no good in Heaven. All it indicates is your unwillingness. Sooner or later, what will they tell you to do? They tell you to get scissors and cut it up. Right? You're going to cash it one day and they stick it in the machine and they go, "Huh?" And they have that look. You know that look? The one who is about to cut it up, looks at you with that kind of look, "Oh, I am sorry, this card is not really, you know," and starts to get the scissors and you say, "Give it back to me!" And they go, "No", and then they cut your card up. There goes your spiritual credit card, just cut in two. And you thought it was going to get you into Heaven. Boy, talk about disappointment.

So, you know, really, what we have been looking at here is that when someone is a teacher and is teaching from their Awakening, you have to understand that what is being asked of you is not for your teacher to join you in your unawakened state, but you are being given an opportunity to join in the Mind that they are representing. You join in that Mind. Not by taking what they are teaching and stick it into what you know, but realize if you are not awake, it is what you don't know that you want to join with. And you can call that humbleness for a moment if you want, you can call it whatever you want, but if you don't come to a teacher with that kind of an understanding, you will think that what you came for is pieces of information that you are going to add to your credit card, your spiritual credit card, so that now you have lots more of information that is of a spiritual nature and that, somehow, is going to have value for you. And I know you have been doing it for lifetimes, and I am telling you, something with you in your willingness to do that has to change. You have to see what you are doing, what I am talking about. You have to see that you are actually doing that and say, "Oh, something else... I'm... uh..." And we call that joining. That something that you are not doing is actually joining, which is what you say you want. You want to know Oneness. Oneness is the idea of being joined. Hello? But you don't want to do that, because that would take away everything that you already value. Which is your sense of self, and you don't want to lose that. And while you are in the fear of losing that self, there is no Awakening. Impossible!

Q: Rananda, after an evening like this and after an evening in Utrecht [Another place in Holland where Rananda teaches.] and all this, then I change my idea of willingness and it is a better idea. I replace my idea of willingness for a better idea of willingness, but I will always have then my idea of willingness. And it will never be...

R: No, some day you are going to have what willingness is.

Q: Yes... But I will always have an idea, "Oh, now I should..."

R: Until you let it go. See, at some point you are going to say, "Oh, I am starting to get this, I don't get it, help." And then the help reveals. Then, what you have is a revealing, not a getting, because what you think you need to get is already there and the revealing just shows you where it is. You just keep not looking at it. You keep looking at what you choose to look at, because of the fear that you have placed between your idea of you and what You really are. And, see, I happen to know some of your stories – actually I know everybody's story. I happen to know your story and I know that it is true for you that there have been moments where, when The Light is really bright and you begin to have access into brighter reflections of Who You are, it generates fear in you. You need to find out why you do that. You need to find out why fear is still valuable to you when you talk about being in the Presence of Love Itself. See? And I know, if I say those words, everybody will say, "It doesn't make sense. Love? Why would I be afraid of Love? Love is Love, there is no fear in Love." Yes, that's true, there is no fear in Love, but there is fear in you, according to you. When Love is revealing Itself to you, you choose fear. See? And it doesn't make sense. I grasp it doesn't make sense, but you do it anyway. So, you need to know why you do that, so that when Love is revealing, you don't choose the fear.

Q: How do I do that?

R: OK, I just told you. You have to see what you do to choose fear instead of Love. When Love is here, you have to see It. Or, don't see fear and choose Love. I don't really care which way, which is the preferred way, right? The preferred way is that you see what is going on and you choose Love. And eventually that is the way it will be. But, perhaps, to move from where you are to where eventually you will be, you need to see that you are actually choosing fear. Some people don't even realize they are choosing fear, they are saying, "Ah! It just happened to me, I didn't know... I don't know how that happened! Boy, that pissed me off when that happened too. I am going to tell you. Boy, I was right there and there was Love and ooh, it was all coming and then just all of a sudden it was gone! Freaked me out, I am going to tell you!" Right? You are not honest, you don't go, "Man, there was so much Love I was afraid I was going to die." What? "There was so much Love I thought I was going to die!" What? "OK, there was so much Love, I thought that I was going to die." Well, that is the way it was, I don't know why you cannot understand my simple language, right? Because, you are still going to try to convince me that what you are saying is the way it is. Can you hear what I am saying? And Love is constantly just here revealing Itself to you, It is Eternal. There is never a moment when Love isn't revealing itself. But listening to people is like, "Well, boy, I missed that chance with Love." Well, which one? Which one are you talking about, of all the billions of moments that you have decided? See, so somewhere you have to pin this illusive self down, so that you can see, first of all, how you have been valuing this pitiful, little thing. And when you see that that is what it is, then you don't want to choose it any longer, because you see what it is.

Then, when you see what it is and you are not choosing it, then you stop seeing what it is, because you are so attracted to Love, because Love is attracted to Love, Light is attracted to Light. You learn through Love rather than through pain and suffering. And that is what I am trying to say. You guys are fascinated by learning through your pain and suffering. Some people love to tell their stories about how much pain and suffering they went through, until finally they had this incredible recognition. They wear it like a badge of honor. See, I don't have any, see? No badges, no honor. But eventually you will let Love teach you that fear is nothing, because that is the only time it shows up. You don't pull it out of your bag of tricks until you are threatened, and the only thing that can threaten you, according to the bag of tricks, is Love. Because Love says, "There is no such thing as death." So, you are afraid you are going to die. Love says, "You are Eternal", but your fear says, "No, I am not. Everything here dies. There will be a day when I do too. I'd better really get meditating, because... I don't know."

Let's see, the Christians say, "All I have to do is believe in Jesus." The Krishna devotees say, "All you have to do is be saying the word Krishna when you die." See, everybody has this thing, if you just do some perceptual thing, somehow that is going to transport you. Well, listen, if you could do it, why don't do it right now while you are dying? "Krishna, Krishna, Jesus, Jesus, Christ, Christ, Christians, Christians, Hindus, Hindus." How come I just didn't spring out of here? You know what I'm saying? Oh, you have to wait until you are dying and then do it? Well, this is what dying is. This is a rejection of The Eternal. This is what death is. I am not very reverent, am I? But do you understand what I am trying to say? It is just like you have been sold a really damaged bill of goods. You have paid a high price for something that is not going to give you what you have been told you were going to get. But, God is offering you something that costs you nothing, no sacrifice, no loss, just Love.

But from the point of view of the ego you do have to let go of your image of your body and of who you are. That means death for the ego. So? The ego is nothing, what do we care what the ego thinks? Why are you so concerned about what the ego thinks? "Well, that is a good question." Why are you so concerned with the ego? Why don't you say, "This is what Spirit thinks and I am really grateful for all the help that Spirit is giving me and indicating to me that I am Eternal and that the ego does not exist, unless I give it the energy for its existence."

I understand while you are in the identity of, I am the ego, you are going to say all those kinds of things and all kinds of thoughts are coming into the mind. OK, I understand that. When are you going to see that they don't have any value? When will you choose when those thoughts come into your mind, "Oh, there they are again, those worthless thoughts, want me to be something that can die, want me to be something that can be hurt, want me to believe that I am, you know, so little, want me to think I am not Home in Heaven. OK, the thoughts are there, I don't want them to be in control." Now you are looking to what is actual help in your mind. In fact, you are turning away from the teacher of pain and suffering to the teacher of Love. And then you will be led, believe me, you will be led.

See, this is something that people... that you don't trust. Literally, so far, but you are going to, because it is inevitable. You don't trust that you can be led in every moment of every day through Love. Because, there is a Voice that speaks for Love, that is within you, that you can hear when you want to hear only that Voice. It can lead you, it will reveal wisdom to you in every moment. And when I am using the word Wisdom, I am talking about the Thoughts that you can share with your Creator, not the wisdom about this world. And that Wisdom will allow you to be in such a freedom, in such a power of Love within this world, that whatever comes through you, will be, what you would call, Light activity. You don't have to be concerned to do the right thing, your concern is to be connected with that Love. And as you stay connected with that Love, that Love is what guides you. It is not about morality, it is not about doing the right thing, it is about staying in contact with the Love. Then You are the Love. What do you think Love does?

Q: Love.

R: Well, then what are you concerned about what you would do? You will just be The Love. Ego is the one that goes, "Oh, man, you really get hurt then, you would be so exposed; everybody will take advantage of you." See? You have always got this other system that keeps wanting to talk to you that you are so small and that you can be hurt and that you can be abused, and all these ideas about you. And it is not helpful, except unless you want to be that. Then it is really helpful to you, but not forever. Eventually you get so fed up, you will stop. Because that is the path that you are following, the path of pain and suffering. You want to learn through pain and suffering. I am here to tell you, "You don't have to do that anymore. You can begin to trust me and walk the path of Love." But it will be a change from what you have been doing. You cannot take what I am saying and stick it into your way of doing things. You have to understand that the path of Love, the way of Love, learning through Love, will be different than learning through pain and suffering, much different.

Q: So, then there is an admission that you actually don't know the way.

R: That is what I said. I said that a while ago, right? That you don't know. That is exactly what I said when she asked the question. I gave her my Zen response. Right? And then, you know, true to form I had to explain it all.

Q: I have a question about practising. You are saying, "Just follow the path of Love." What comes up in my mind is, when I keep practising always choosing the path of Love, God, Universe, whatever, isn't that also an illusion?

R: Yes, but it is better than the other one you have been practising.

Q: Yes, true.

R: It has a different result.

Q: I know, but last time I was in Utrecht you were reading a section from *A Course in Miracles* and it was about freedom, which is here immediately.

R: Yes!

Q: You know? You remember of course. You repeated that lots of times and it was all in my mind. Over the past weeks it has been in my mind, but now I am also confused...

R: Oh, how did that happen?

Q: If I choose the path of Love and keep practising that all day, and try to do it as much as I can and as much as I remember, then I am still in the illusion that there is a path of Love, so that there is a choice and when you say, "Here, it can be here, right now, immediately," then I am confused. What am I doing? I can choose the path of Love, but freedom is here already.

R: Exactly, what are you doing?

Q: Yes, what am I doing?

R: Exactly, what are you doing?

Q: Meeting my blockages?

[Giggles.]

10

GET OVER THE FACT THAT

YOU HAVE FAILED!

Practice / Willingness / Joining / Quantum / Hope / Love

R: You see, you have an illusion that is set up, so that the activities of that illusion – because they are activities of the illusion – are activities that support and represent the illusion. Except for what you give the purpose to end the illusion. When you give it the purpose to end the illusion and you are not giving it the purpose to continue the illusion, there will finally be a difference.

Q: I don't understand.

R: Oh, yes, you do; yes, you do. You looked right at it and you went, "Hmm..."

Q: Yes? Oh.

R: Yes. Activities of the illusion are activities of the illusion. However, you give them a purpose, you give everything a purpose. OK, now, until you heard this message, you gave things of the illusion the purpose to believe in the reality of the illusion. Until you heard this message that said, if you do this the illusion can end. That's when they become something different. Because you gave them a different purpose. OK, now, are they still a part of the illusion? Yes, but with a different purpose. So, it will work because of the purpose that you have given it. OK? But remember, it has to be an undoing, not a doing. Because when it is a doing, you have bought into the ego's program that says, if you do this, you can overcome what has already happened.

But if you are hearing what I am saying, the overcoming will happen because it never happened! The overcoming will happen because it never happened! Not because it did and if you do this you can overcome it. That is never what I said. I said, "You have the ideas in your mind and the way the ideas are removed from your mind, is when you don't do what you were doing to value those ideas. Without the value they disappear." It is an undoing in that sense, OK? Now, what happens is that many people hear this teaching, or they don't hear it, but they hear it, and then they think they have to do lots of things, rather than hear the message. No, it is an undoing; you have to stop what you have been doing to make this world. That has to be your purpose. In that sense your purpose in life, you know, what they call life here, has to be the undoing. And when that is your purpose, it will be undone.

OK, now, how long does it take for it to be undone? It will take as long as it takes for you to accept it never happened! However long you take, that is what you call practising. So, practise, because somewhere in that practice you are going to say, "man, I have had enough of this practice shit too." Now that usually comes from the ego, but you are going to hear the message of that and you are going to go, "Oh, I can be somebody that practises all the way to his death." Or, "I can accept what I am practising, rather than practising like a mantra. I can accept what it is that I am practising. What am I practising? There is no reality to this and I am Home in Heaven." Well, somewhere you will be sincere. And because it is true it will dawn upon your mind. And this is what I am trying to help you with. So, yes, you are free in this instant. Why? Because you are already Home in Heaven. It would have to be instantaneous and time cannot be what it is about. Your rejection of instantaneousness is what time is. The result of rejection is what time is. So, when you stop rejecting, time will disappear and you will be in the fulfillment of no longer doing that. Because, when you don't do that, The Eternal is there. Most people go, "Oh, yeah, but..." And they tell me their stories. And I go, "Well, OK, then you didn't have the willingness." "Oh no, I was really willing; that is because I wanted to..." You see? And there is not an acceptance of that activity that needs to be accepted so it can be healed. Instead of trying to play the innocent role and hide what is really going on there, which is some range of fear that you are going to disappear. Well, you are going to disappear, that is the fun part! "Ooohh! I didn't recognize it as fun. How do I recognize it as fun!?"

Q: So, how is it for you sitting here while we are all looking at you and hearing what you say?

R: Do you want me to tell you The Truth?

Q: Yes.

R: OK, I am not here!

Q: So, where are You?

R: Where You are! All I am doing is projecting this body so I can bring this message. All you are doing is projecting a body so you can hear it. Once it is heard and joined in, there will be no here necessary any longer and Your Awareness, Which, as I said, is Eternal and You always have Awareness, will be where We are doing what We actually do, which is creating.

Q: I am just so curious... I don't know what to call you. God, Jesus...

R: The only way you are going to find out is to join. Otherwise we are back at what I was saying earlier. All you have are these symbols and definitions and descriptions, which are never going to satisfy you.

Q: No.

R: The ego will say, "I like these and I don't like those." And somebody else is going to say, "Well, I have heard it said this way and I heard it said that way, and guru so and so says this." And you know what? I am not really interested. I am not going into descriptions. All I can tell you is that I am aware that I am not here and that I am using this to communicate with you and that You are not here. But there is a belief in that and that will be healed. And that is what I am about. That is what I am doing and You are too. And how aware you are of that activity is what it is all about. It is about returning to the Awareness that allows you not to be limited in Awareness, OK? It is like, you were created as – I will say it this way because it is a good way of saying it but don't get too bound by it or anything – it is like, you were created as a Master of Limitlessness and you have been trying to be a master of limitedness and you have done a really good job. However, it has no value. And that is where the rub is; you have been pursuing something that has no value and you don't want to quit because you have to admit it has no value. But you have been at it, and at it, and at it, and yet I am coming to tell you, no, you have to understand, please hear me, You are a Master of Limitlessness and that is where the fun and the joy is. Get over the fact that you have failed.

Q: Because that is the ego?

R: Yes, that is what we call the ego. Is that helpful?

Q: Yes, it is. I find the ego a fearful idea.

R: You can apply fear to anything you want. The question is, why would you do that? What do you get out of applying fear to whatever it is that you choose to apply it to? Why do you do that? We are not going to debate any longer with you guys that you do that. Hopefully you recognize you do that and so you are not fighting that battle any longer. New guys usually do that. They come in and hear me and they want to slit my throat, spiritually of course. I will be a sacrifice for them or something like that, you know? And they just think it; they don't say it out loud usually. Until I get like three quarters through the evening and I am relentless, and I am relentless and finally they go, "Grrrrr!!!" you know, because their ego has been really nice in there, kind of being a gentleman. They have been storing up all this anger and all this frustration and eventually it cannot be contained anymore, "Grrrrr!!!" It just wants to roar and tell me how much of an asshole I am, you know. And then, eventually, you really do begin to hear what is being said and you look at what you are doing and what is happening in what you call your life, and all of the sudden you go, "That crazy guy. There is more going on there than I thought was going on there." And that is even worse, because now you are beginning to accept it, which means you are beginning to accept you are as crazy as that guy. And then you really get confused, because now you have got two sets of thoughts going on in there, where before you always thought you were just you. Now you are beginning to recognize there is a split and that is what you call crazy; here in this world you call that crazy. Me, I just call that normal, I am a Gemini. You have to have a sense of humor!

Is this helpful?

Q: Yes.

* * *

Q: Love is very important for me to reach. Every now and then I reach a state I think is Love. It comes again and again. It started five to six years ago. It became more frequent and stayed longer. It was combined with a feeling of compassion for everything.

R: Yes, those are the early stages, compassion.

Q: I would like to be that very much.

R: I would like you to go past that.

Q: Yes, me too; takes time.

R: No, it doesn't take time, it takes willingness.

Q: Well, I am open then.

R: If you are open to going beyond it, you will, that is a fact! And, if you are not, guess what? It will just take longer. You want more pain and suffering before you are going to be willing, that is all. It is inevitable! We are not giving you a choice. God said, "There is my Son in Whom I am well pleased." Well, let me see, Who is that again?

Q: To reach that state, you know, you must be open.

R: Yes.

Q: You must be willing.

R: Willingness, that is all that is what being open really is.

Q: OK, I sit somewhere in a chair and be open in willingness.

R: You can walk down the street and be open and willing. You don't have to sit in the chair. But you can sit in the chair and do it too, yes.

Q: That is how it started with me, with mantras, meditation.

R: Yes, that is what you wanted.

Q: Well, that is what they taught me.

R: You wanted a teacher, you went out and found one and that is what they taught you.

Q: And I wanted to break out.

R: Yes, well...

Q: Now I have this Moola mantra; feels good to repeat it now. It blisses me up.

R: Yes, that is nice, there is nothing wrong with it.

Q: But now in half an hour I think, well, that is enough, let's forget the moola mantra, and then it goes on.

R: That is the worst, isn't it, though? When you think you have had enough.

Q: But then I am in a state that I think is Love.

R: Who is thinking all that? Who is thinking they have had enough and who is thinking they are in a state of Love? Who is doing all that?

Q: I don't know who thinks that.

R: Is it the same one that thinks he needs to wake up?

Q: I'm sometimes bored and I want something.

R: Who wants something, who is bored?

Q: Someone I think is me or something.

R: Oh, you think it is you? OK, see? That is my whole point, right there. Spirit is not thinking like that; Spirit is having a blast, you know. It is dancing and radiating Light and Love and it is whispering sweet nothings in your ear about how much you are loved and everything, you know. And ego is there, going, "I don't know, man, this is way too much Love, I have had it, I have had enough." And, because we are so identified with It, we go, "Yeah, that is the way I feel." And we think that it is us, because we are identifying with it. But Spirit, which is the True Us, is going, "No, don't give up, honey, don't give up! Don't give up!" Kind of like that, you know, but ego is just like, "Oh, boring man, can't you learn a new dance or something? Do something to get my attention here, just don't shine. I have had enough of that mantra; you have got another mantra I can repeat?" And then you go to a different teacher because they might give you a different mantra.

Q: Now I experience that I don't need the mantra.

R: Of course you don't, you never did. Unless you thought you did and then you did. You see, it is always what you are thinking and you always get the result of your thinking. I am presenting to you ideas that are coming to you from your Creator. Your Creator is telling You – you want me to try it? – OK, here it goes, "I created You Perfect already without the ability to be anything but The Perfection I created. So, give up your story and accept mine, because I am All-Powerful." Got it?

Q: You've got power, yes.

R: No, no, I don't have any other power than you have. I was just representing God there for a moment.

Q: You can express it.

R: Yes, so can you.

Q: Well, I...

R: No, you can, I just shared it with you and I bet you can say the same thing.

Q: Yes, I think so.

R: And you can probably feel it the way I feel it, if you wanted to. But you have to want to. You have to be like over the top. You have to be willing to look like you are crazy in front of other people instead of a good meditator who is nice and stable. You know, I used to be like that, I did. Before I woke up I was more meditative-like, because I had an image that someone who is enlightened or awakened would be this kind of cool person, you know, like really in control.

You listen to gurus. I have listened to a lot of gurus, by the way, and they all talk pretty much the same. They have this cadence and this way of talking.

Q: Why is that?

R: It is a learned thing. You learn it from your Master. You sat at the feet of another Master who was like that and that is just passed down and somewhere what is really being passed down is this, be You! You are enough, don't try to copy your teacher. If you are going to copy anything about your teacher, copy the part that lets everybody be what They are. And demand it of them! Because what They are is The Christ, is this incredible Thing. Demand that your brothers be that, see only that, and let them be an expression of whatever... The beauty of your expression is how it is that God created You. Don't be trying to imitate some teachers, believe me, it is a waste of time. Eventually you are going to get fed up. Not only that, you know what you will do in a short period of time? You will start attacking them for being that way. You make them an idol and you have to cut them down. "Who does he think he is? Look at this and look at this and look at that." And what are you doing? You think you are setting yourself free, but all you are doing is binding yourself to these other ideas that you employed in that relationship with that one trying to help you and you just found a way around it.

Do you follow what I am saying? You've got really slippery in not letting go. You just justified your way of attacking That that is truly there to help you. I used to meditate sixteen hours a day. Yes, seven days a week and it didn't help. No, it did help. What it did help is, it helped me be able to concentrate. But there was no spiritual thing that came out of it. But my mind was able to focus. Now I can focus my mind very easily for long periods of time, because I trained it. You follow what I am saying? But it wasn't trained in focusing on God. I was focusing on the mantra and other things that I was told to focus on. And I know there was an intent to go beyond the focus somewhere. Oh, fine, but what? What is beyond the focus? God is going to be happy us focusing on a mantra? While I am already in Heaven in God's Mind? Come on, give me a break, will you? Look at what you are thinking and telling one another and encouraging one another to do and be involved with. All I want to do is encourage you to love God, that is my whole thing, in case you haven't gotten it. That is my whole thing!

You have a relationship with That that created You, OK? I don't care what you call You. I don't care what you call the Creator. I don't care what you think that story is. I don't care how you think it happened. I don't care if you think it had an ending. I don't care if you think it's eternal. All I am telling you is, whatever It is that You are, Something created You. And, because Something created You, You have a relationship with It. And if you don't know what that relationship is, you are missing the most important thing about You. That is what I want to teach. That ís what I am teaching, OK?

Now, the reason I am teaching that is because I had a revealing happening to me in that relationship. And in that relationship the revealing was Love, so I can talk about It as what has been revealed to me. But I know when I use the words, you think you know what Love is, and so it is a little difficult, but it is what I've got to work with. I've only got to work with what you think; I cannot work with what you don't think, because you will say, "Say... what?" Right? For instance quantum. "Well, what do you mean? What do you mean quantum, quantoem; what do you mean quantum? What is quantum? That is what scientists talk about, this is spiritual. Why do you use the word quantum?" And then I, what? I try to explain to you the value of the concept of quantum, because it is a reflection of how You create, hello? And, how the world disappears from your mind is quantum. In other words, quantum is... I will reduce it, OK? You start here, you have a quantum moment and you wind up there; and there has nothing to do with here, OK? It is like, you are in an illusion, you have this awakening experience and you find your Self in Heaven. Heaven has nothing to do with here; here has nothing to do with Heaven. Here has nothing to do with how you wind up knowing that You are there. Being there and aware of the fact that there has nothing to do with the idea that you are here. It is quantum, OK?

And that is what I am teaching, I am teaching an experience that is not of your own making! You cannot make yourself have a quantum experience, but you can allow it to happen. And the way you allow it to happen is to stop doing what you are doing to limit yourself in timefulness, because limited in timefulness is the denial of the ability to experience quantum, which is the natural movement of your Mind as You were created in Perfection. That is how You create in Perfection, You have a thought, "Oh, I like to create that", boing! "Oh, I like to... how about...?" Boing! It is instant, it is just instant, because there is no time in Perfection, there is no time in Reality. There is only You and there is only the extension of You that happens through your thought. So, every time a thought comes, it manifests something. Do you understand? That is how You are. That is what You are like. And here you have it really slowed down. So, sometimes you don't see how your thoughts are actually manifesting. You say, "I don't remember thinking that thought, I don't know. Hey, I didn't want that to happen to me!"

Here you are very much like molasses. You know molasses? Have you ever poured molasses? That is what it is like here, molasses. But in Reality it is instant, instant. Everything is instant. Americans would really love Reality. Everything has to be instant, you know? McDonald's, you probably have them here now, don't you? Yes, so the Dutch are becoming Americanized too, aren't you? But if you can get what is really behind it, there is an attempt to get into your dream, the idea of instantaneousness, because that is what you are like in Reality. And you do everything to try to slow everything down. "Don't talk so fast, take it easy, let me meditate on that for a while." Everything is just kind of like, you know, slow things down. No! Speed it up, so you can get into a quantum experience! It is passion; it is speed up! You will get so fast, You wind up before you began, which is what you want. You think you had a beginning here; you want to speed up so fast, that you get to where this did not begin, before it began. That is What Perfection is, that is What Reality is, before this began. Why? Because this never happened, it is just an idea! You will speed up so fast that that idea is not in your mind any longer! It is not sitting and being really, really slow; that is nuts! I don't know who would teach you that, slow down, slow down, so you can find the now. No, speed up and you will find now. Slow down and you will hang out in your past. Speed up and you will not have a future! Vroemmmm... right past your future!

I am a little nuts. I know, but you know what? I don't have a problem with it. I don't have a problem with being nuts and I am not going to be here for very long. So, if you are going to crucify me, do it fast. Otherwise I will be gone and you'll go, "Oh man, we should have gotten him when we had that chance." Talk about a useless journey, huh? Do you know when Jesus actually brought that message in he didn't say useless, he said foolish. It is a foolish journey.[15]

So it is a useless journey, no doubt about that, but you are awfully foolish in thinking that it is OK to prolong this journey.

* * *

There is no value in hoping. Boy, you guys love to teach each other that, don't you? "Don't give up hope!" Don't you? Don't you love to teach one another that? "Don't give up hope!" You think hope is really valuable, don't you? Hello? It is really valued in your world here, isn't it? Hope. Right. And then someone crazy like me comes along and says, "Give up hope, give it up. There is no hope for you here." And it goes completely against everything you are teaching one another. It is like your ace, right? You are playing cards and you have this ace hidden. Hope, and you are just waiting for that moment where you have to play it. "If you think I am going to give up that ace, you are nuts!" Right? And there is that other guy that is playing with you, you know, and he is all kind of listening and listening to music and you are trying to find out what you will do with your cards. And he couldn't care less what you are doing with your cards, because he knows you don't have any hope. He knows you don't have any hope, and you go like, "Oh, man, shall I play it now, shall I play my ace now. Oh... man, he looks awfully confident over there. I don't know, maybe I should just... no I got that ace there, maybe I should..., maybe I should raise the bet. No, I don't know, he looks awfully confident, maybe..." You

---

[15] *In the original edition of 'A Course In Miracles' [ISBN 978-09764200-5-7, pocket edition, 2010^2] Jesus says, "The journey to the cross should be the last 'foolish journey'." In the second edition of 'A Course In Miracles' this has been changed into the last 'useless' journey.*

know? And you are just in the confusion of your mind, right? Trying to figure out what to do, based on what? All the input that you can get through your body, right? Thinking somehow you are going to be able to figure it out. "What is the right thing to do?" But the guy you are playing cards with, he couldn't care less what you are doing because he is just trusting there is no way you can lose.

So, I guess what I am telling you is, there is another way. There is the way you have been pursuing and hoping in association with the world and in association with the you that thinks it can wake up. And then, there is another way that you give up hope and you expect What already Is, and then it sorts out. It sorts out by What you are true to, because you can say one thing and be true to something else. So, what you are true to is how it sorts out for you. If you let go of the pursuit of this world, you will be pursuing something else that is not of this world and you will get the result of that. If you pursue this world, then you will have lots of this world to bury yourself in, or burn your body and toss it wherever you guys like to get it tossed. Right? In the wind, on the water, on the mountains, somewhere where you can be free! And part of mother earth, instead of with your Creator, you know. I mean, give me a break! You have such a thing to get through, don't you? You have been teaching yourself so much crap that you have to sort your way through, you know? I will tell you, you know the best way to sort through all the crap? Heavy stuff falls to the bottom.

Q: What do you mean?

R: Figure it out. If you want to be heavy, fall to the bottom with all the other heavy things, if you want to be Light, then rise up. And whatever you choose is what you will experience. OK?

Q: I want fun.

R: Yes, fun. Me too. But the thing I have been revealed is, the only fun is in Heaven; it is not here.

Q: I think that too, now.

R: Yes. Go Home!

Q: I believe I have.

R: Yes, go Home!

Q: OK. I see that, I see that.

R: Take everyone with you, though. Don't think you can go there all by yourself. That was a clue. I forgot to tell you about that. That is the next time I teach.

Q: The company in Heaven.

R: Is this OK?

* * *

R: Look, I have been saying this a lot lately, and I want to say it here too, OK? Because, some of you haven't been around me too much, but you have been on what you call a spiritual path for many lifetimes. So I want to say this again. And I hope you feel the intensity with which I mean it, because I am really intense about it. OK? Now, I can't do it without being really intense, right? I want you to know, this is a very intense thing what I am going to say, because you guys have been on a spiritual path for lots of lifetimes, but you are not living Love. You have been hanging out with concepts long enough. You have been pretending long enough. What you want is the fulfillment of being Love, and you are not being happy until you let the shift take place. And, the shift that I am talking about is away from hanging out with your concepts about how spiritual you are and pretending with everybody else how spiritual you are.

What is required, is literally loving one another; not talking about it, not hoping, not saying that you get there someday; not talking about how you are not good enough, but really practising what this talk is about. Really being there for one another, really helping one another to enjoy The Light, rather than doing things to pull them out of The Light, calling it friendship. Really, actively being present for one another, really practising this. It is OK to say the words that need to be said. It is OK, but it is not as important as being The Love Itself. Being What this is, is much more important than being able to tell somebody the words.

That this is all about, OK? I am asking you, please, step forward with your Love, put yourself on the line. Or, you can see that being loving is a challenge to your fear, so you can see that your fear is nothing. And that The Love will mean so much to you, that you will go there and you will go there and you will go there, until at some point there is no going there any more, you just are That. And it could, believe this or not, it could just take once. It could be. The next time you are willing to do that is the only time that is required of you. You don't know, because time is not what brings you into that Awakening.

But I am telling you, because I have seen it. I have traveled your planet, I have seen it. I know what is going on. I see how people are talking and not being. They talk about things, but they are not there for one another. When somebody really needs help, everybody has something to do. When somebody needs help, there should be more than enough people saying, "I will help, I will help, I will help!" That is the way it ought to be. Why? Because you are all talking about how you want The Enlightenment, how you want to know God, how you want to be Who You really are, how The Christ is important to you to be revealed within you.

And yet you are given these opportunities, every day, to step forward with this incredible Love that is already there within You, but you are just so afraid to let It out. You have got to face this, this fear, you have got to face this fear that you have been valuing and let the change take place. Challenge yourself to live This, to be This, because It is The Truth of You. It is already The Truth of You. You have got to let It out, you have got to set your Self free, because that is what it is all about. And when that begins to happen, You will represent such a force field of Light that what you see is going on on your planet will not be able to maintain that kind of activity because of your Presence.

Don't be afraid! That journey has been completed, that foolish journey has been completed. Your Awakening is assured, because one of us has already completed it. Actually more than one of us has completed it in The Oneness. But when one did, the certainty got in. Can you hear me? When one of us completed it, the certainty got in, because one of us got it completed. Since then others have completed it. And the more you join in that, the easier and the stronger that Light factoring will be for everyone who comes in time behind you. In fact, you cannot go Home without taking them with You. And that is how it becomes stronger and stronger and stronger.

Jesus is not willing in his mind that You are not Home in Heaven with him. In fact, he is so unwilling, he is telling you there is only One Mind. So he is telling you You are already there, but it doesn't do any good if you don't know it. It is good for God, it is good for Jesus, it is good for those who have allowed that Oneness to be completed in the Awareness, OK? And it is a nice message to bring to you, but it doesn't do you a lot of good until you accept it. Accept it! Accept it! Do you understand? The acceptance is the demonstration of the willingness to be It. And that is what is being brought to you.

You can delay it if you want to, but you can't do that forever. And why not do it now, when you have got people who are willing to support you? Why not step up now and say, "Man, I don't know if I can do this alone," and then we all say, "No one is asking you to do it alone; we know you cannot do it alone. Why do you keep running away from us? Why do you keep saying the nasty things that you say? We are the ones that you need to forgive, so that you can know what it is like to forgive. And as you know what it is like to forgive, you will see that you are only forgiving yourself when you think you are forgiving us." This is the way it works. Somewhere you are going to have to forgive The Perfection that You are that you think did this. And I know, see, I know that doesn't make sense. "Hey, It is Perfection, why should I forgive Perfection? Come on Rananda, you are not even consistent."

You understand what I am saying? This is what I have been trying to say. You cannot hear it from here, you cannot hear it from here; it doesn't make sense. What I am teaching doesn't make sense if you want to be here. It only makes sense if you look at here and you go, "Man, this is an illusion, there is something strange going on here." Instead you go, "Well, I don't know if I can really get that. I don't know if I even believe that or not." But you know what? It would be an explanation as to why things don't seem to be quite right here. And then everything just starts to fall apart. Because, until it falls apart you will not know What is Eternal, because Eternal cannot fall apart. But here it starts to fall apart, and then you try to hold it together. Why? See? That is where you see what you are doing, that is where you become honest. "Oh man, I don't want Perfection." See? "I don't. Yes, I do. No, I don't. Yes, I do. I know it is a terrible world, but it is all I know." Yes, you want to leave it. "No, I just..." See? You have got a split mind. And the reason it is split is because you have let it be that way. You have not held onto The Light as if your Life depended upon It. And It does. Your Life does depend on you holding onto The Light. Because The Light is your Life. And this is nothing!

Q: Don't you need another light to be able to trust this is nothing?

R: No, you only need willingness, sweety. Then all The Light and Everything else that is there will be revealed to You. It is there already. Everything you need is there already. You need to focus where in you is willingness. That is what is required, OK? And you have lots of help to do that. I will help you, Jesus will help you, and I am sure there are other brothers in this room that will be really grateful, happy, more than willing to help you. And there are other Masters that have gone on before that are willing to help. All the help you could possibly need, you have. What you need to focus on, is your willingness. Not how big the problem seems to be.

Q: Or how big the ego is.

R: Or how big you think the ego is. But, remember, that you are dealing with The All-Powerful, All-Knowing, Everywhere, Who created You. Keep the picture clear, or you will buy into the littleness, which then makes it very, very difficult to get past the fear. And it is the same with your brother. Don't treat your brother little. Treat your brother like he deserves to be treated, the way God, the way Jesus would treat your brother. Treat your brother with the same Love that Jesus treats your brother with. Because you deserve to be that way, and so does your brother. And, if you don't treat your brother that way, you won't be that way. You cannot be anything that your brother is not. So, if he is a pig, you are a pig. If He is the Son of God, then You are the Son of God. If It is a beautiful Spirit, then You are a beautiful Spirit. If he is an asshole, then you are an asshole. What you make him for you, is what you are, OK? It cannot be any other way, because that is the way it works.

So, remember what you want. Stop your spiritual stuff and let yourself be What You are. You don't need any more concepts about your Self in a spiritual nature. You just need to find where the willingness to be loving is within you, and then let that challenge everything. People will come with their incredible spiritual stuff about guru this and guru that and so and so this, and so and so that, but if there is no Love there, what is it? What is it? It is like a little cub, trying to roar like a lion, "ggrrr..." and it hears its dad go, "GGGGGRRRR!!!" Did you ever hear a little cub go, "grr, grr...?" They try to roar like their parents, you know. They are really cute, aren't they? And then, when they get a little more of their voice they go, "ggrr." They open their mouth like that and sometimes all of a sudden "gggrr..." comes out. Then they close it. You know what I mean? They are really cute, they are trying to be like the grown-ups, you know. Kind of like what you guys do. You try to copy your parents, the older people, because you think that is what you are going to be. And parents love to teach you to be just like them. Most parents have children, because they want them to be just like them. Hello? That is how you got here. Somebody wanted you to be just like them. And you got here and you said, "Say what? I've got my own ideas." And immediately you had a battle. All you are doing is playing it out, over and over. Groundhog Day.[16]

Just stuck playing it and going around, and around, and around. You wake up every morning and it is the same old story, same old story. That is the world; that is what happens in the world, yep. "What am I going to do today? I am so excited." But how about you give the world a different purpose? Then you would go, "Yes, there it is, a place without Love, YOO-HOO!!! This place is mine! I can give Love everywhere here. I don't even have to try to figure it out. There is Love nowhere! I can go anywhere here! How exciting! Where should I go today...?" And you just begin your journey.

Q: But they will think you are crazy.

R: I don't care what anybody thinks. I am crazy! I don't care if they think I am crazy, I *am* crazy! I am not well in this world! Neither are you, that is why you are sitting here, listening to all this. Are you guys OK? Did I sufficiently disturb you tonight? The thing I really want you to hear is the thing I said at the end. I really want you to grasp that there is something expected of you. And, what is expected of you is that you begin to live the path of Love, that you begin to be more loving than you were this morning. Now, I don't care what your image of yourself is. I want you to look

---

[16] *Groundhog Day (1993) is a movie from director Harold Ramis. A bad tempered weatherman, a female producer and a cameraman cover a yearly event in a small town around a groundhog whose behavior is supposed to predict the coming of spring. The weatherman rushes through the item with a lot of reluctance, to discover the next morning that the same day repeats itself. This goes on until eventually he begins to make other choices during this repeating day. His total resistance to his job, the small town, his colleagues eventually gives way to love (also for the producer) and thus the loop in time is broken and he can 'move on'. He wakes up in a new day, finally new himself.*

in your mind and find the place where you are willing to be more loving than wherever you think you are now, OK? And it doesn't matter how that shows up for you. Just find that place of willingness within you that says, "I am willing to be more loving than I am right now." And if that shows up with a person, that is OK. "You know, that person I haven't been so loving with? I am really going to make a great effort to be more loving with him." I don't care how it shows up, to me that is not important. It is just the beginning. It is just the beginning of you finding the dedication and the willingness and the determination to allow Love to be there more and more and more and more for you. And not just some spiritual idea that somewhere in your Awakening that happens. You know what I am saying? It is not like that. It is right now it happens, because you value it, and you are with it. That is how it happens. It is not something five years from now, ten years from now, whatever. It happens because you are willing and you are active with it. And you let go of your blame and your shame and your anger and your hate and all your judgments and you begin to recognize that those are not helpful. They are not helpful. Every time you are willing to argue, guess what? You let go of the Love. OK? See? It is that real in that sense, or practical. People used to really criticize me for not being very practical. This is the most practical thing I can ever say to you! OK, I have said enough. I like coming here, by the way.

Q: I am still hanging onto this idea of what you are saying. "Yes, there is something to do, be more loving."

R: No, that's how you interpreted it.

Q: Make a good effort.

R: No, that's how you interpreted what I said. I said, "When you stop doing what you are doing, you will be what You have always been. What You have always been is loving."

I am asking you to stop doing what you are doing. Which is arguing, complaining, being angry and hurting one another. Stop doing what you are doing and then the path of Love will move through you. I am not saying anything different than I have been teaching all night long. But there is a difficulty hearing what I am saying because the ego doesn't want to stop. So, it hears what I am saying and it goes, "Are you saying...?" It knows exactly what I am saying and it doesn't like it. Since when does the ego like you being loving and helping people? What do you get out of that? Ego doesn't get anything out of Love.

Q: So, this split we are talking about, I am bringing that forward now and saying, "OK, I am seeing the split." And I am doubting that, because I felt a doubt. I must be wrong thinking that way. I have been hearing what you have been teaching. So I say, "How can I get my help with it now?" I don't want to wait again. Because when I was sitting there last week, I waited and I said, "I am not going to do that again."

R: No, jump in, the water is fine. You can be loving right now. You can let go of every grievance you can possibly dream of, you can just do it right now! Just practise it right now! "Let me see, how will I do that? Hey! That was nice. Oh, there does that go. Oh, well, then I wouldn't need that. Bye! Let me see, anything else? Oh, and that. Oh God, I don't know, shall I let go...?" Yeah. Yeah let it go." Does that kind of stuff happen in your mind?

Q: Yes.

R: "Yes, I see where I think about things; where thoughts come into my mind about people and so on and so forth. And I am tempted to believe them. But I don't have to, neither do you. Don't be concerned." See, this is another thing that I have discovered with those spiritual people.

They think they are really guilty, because the thought goes through the mind, and that is not so. They are not your thoughts, first of all. They are just thoughts that went through your mind. You can make them yours if you want to, and suffer!

Q: I don't get that part, whose thoughts can they be if they are not mine?

R: Well, good, listen to me again, they are nobody's, they have nothing to do with Life. They have nothing to do with The Eternal and That is All there is. They are nothing. There is no world, there is no you. Thoughts that say there is, are the thoughts you let go right through your mind, and you let them go. And if you want to have a wife, you can let your wife go too. And if you want to have a Rananda, you can certainly let Rananda go. And then, What You are, and What Your Wife is, What Rananda is, will be all that is left. And then you will be OK with That, because That is The Eternal, Which cannot go anywhere. It cannot disappear, It cannot go anywhere. But, you will stop holding those images of me, of you, of her, and if you stop holding them, they will disappear from your mind and What is left in your mind is What God put in your mind. And that is a lot of fun according to God. I mean, it was His idea to begin with. I hear He knows Everything, He has got Something going for Him. You don't know what it is like to be with Someone who knows Everything, do you? Pfftt... You are going to start to say something and He will go, "Yes, I know." "Yes, but I want to tell You..." "Yes, I know." "So, You are not going to let me talk?" "No." "So, I am just going to have to be..." "Yep." "Well this is fun." "Yes."

"Why do You think I created You like That?" "Well, I want to talk to You about That." "No, You don't have to." "Oh, OK." "So, I can just go create today?" "Yep. Have fun with the other Kids, just go create, go, go. Give Mum and I a night by Ourselves. How do you think We get more Kids?" One Christ is not enough, how many creations do you want? One? Or do you want lots of creations? Tricky question, hey? OK? So, I am asking you, encouraging you to be involved in an undoing. And in the undoing the Love that You are will come forth. And see, the ego is going to tell you that, "Yes, but what the Love does, is a doing," and I am going to say, "No, Love doesn't do anything, It is What It is." And What It is, is not a doing. It is a Being, and Being doesn't do. It just Is. That is the difference, just Be You. Be the Love, let the Love be What It is. Stop doing all the things you do.

You know, I think I have told you this a long time ago. One of the early conversations that I had with Jesus, in this lifetime, was him telling me... Well, actually it was kind of an interesting conversation. He said to me, "You do a lot of things to try to be loved, don't you?" And I got really embarrassed, you know, because, ppfftt... because you know, being exposed is what you think you don't want. You don't see it as healing, you see it as fault-finding. However, when you are with a Master that is not fault-finding, it is healing. But, I didn't know that at that time. And he said, "You do a lot of things to be loved, don't you? And all those kinds of things you do before you want to admit it." And I said, "Yeah, yeah, I do. Yep, yep, I do. I find myself doing and saying a lot of things because I want to be loved." Which indicated that I thought I am not loved. So, a lot was happening when he asked me that question. And he said, "You know, it is going to be really funny. In not too long a time you are going to find everybody loving you and you are not going to know why. Because now you are doing everything to encourage them to love you and you don't think they do. So it will be really confusing. You are going to stop trying and they are going to love you and you are not going to be able to figure out what you did, because it is not about what you do, it is about What God did, when He created You, that is what The Love is all about. And it is natural for The Love, when you stop doing what you are doing for that to be a constant." So, that was a nice conversation.

Now you have it, you've got the ball. Stop doing all the things you think you need to do to get people to love you. You are already loved. And when you stop doing all those things, all The Love will just start to be there, because you will not do those things any longer. And if that takes trust, have a moment of trust. If it takes more trust, have as many moments as it takes, because that is what you want. OK? Be The Love that You are.

* * *

I am not going to do any Golden Energy tonight. So if you want some, just close your eyes and breathe it in. There is never a moment that It is not available to you anyway.[17]

I have been giving a real lot. You have already received more than if I put my hands on you anyway. Whether you are aware of it or not, I don't know, but I can tell you, that is true. So thanks for coming. And I hope I inspired you to be The Love and not be so concerned about the concepts, but be really vigilant being The Love. And letting go of those moments where It doesn't seem to be happening. You have no way of judging yourself. So all you have are these shitty opinions, and opinions are not worth anything at all. You cannot judge, because you don't have enough information to really judge. Your opinions are based on lacking

---

[17] *The Golden Energy is the frequency of Oneness. During Remembering Events Rananda and Suzanne instruct participants to work with this Energy so they can pass it on to others.*

information. So stop. Just be with The Love, that is enough! Let Love do all the judging. Just go, "Oh, Love, oh yeah, Love, oh yeah, Love." It might get a little boring, but it might put a little excitement in your life too. OK? So, thanks guys. Those of you who are not coming to the three week program, I will see you in December maybe. [18]

Q: 21st December?

R: Just before we go, "Hallelujah, Jesus was born" and all that stuff. On the 21st we will celebrate the Christ being born in You. Not in some other guy 2000 years ago. How about that?

Q: Good idea!

R: OK, I am counting on it. Was that OK? Did I do OK?

---

[18] *A few times a year longer retreats or Remembering Events are scheduled in which the focus is entirely on joining with Rananda and Suzanne in the frequency of Oneness, in The Light and experiencing the True Self.*

11

YOU'll NEVER WALK ALONE

The Choice for Love / The Disappearance of The Illusion / Awakening / Accepting the Help / Forgiveness

R: We have all been let down, by our families, by our countries, by our churches. We all have grievances running all around in our heads, haven't we? And forgiveness is the key! Without forgiveness you'll die once again, the same way that you did the last time around! You don't really want that, do you? And forgiveness is the key. You can trust me on this if you want. You'll be a lot happier if you begin to let go of all that sadness and all that anger; all the disappointments that you have been carrying through so many different lifetimes, bringing them into this one. It is OK to heal now! The walls that you have put up around you are not protecting anything. It is the open heart and the open mind that will bring you what you really want. This world has had a dramatic, extreme example of one who believed in Love beyond everything else that can possibly happen in this world. And because of his dedication to that, he succeeded in the experience of Resurrection and Ascension. No one is asking you to follow the same path. But you are asked to join in It, you don't have to be crucified to join. In fact, when you join, the crucifixion has been finished; so has your Resurrection. And the only thing that awaits is your disappearing act. Isn't that exciting? Isn't that an exciting idea that you might be able to disappear from here and death has nothing to do with it? Does that excite you? Or do you think it is a fantasy? Hello?

Q: It is a great idea.

R: It is a great idea. Yeah. Maybe it is an idea whose time has come! Maybe it will be fulfilled in You! That would be exciting! Why wouldn't it? Why would that not be possible for You? Do You not have the same Creator? Does that Creator love You any different than He did the one who has demonstrated the extreme example of Love? Don't you have everything going for you that he had going for him? If there is a difference between someone like Jesus and someone like you, the only difference that could possibly be, is that he chose Love in every moment that it was possible and perhaps you choose something other than Love from time to time. That would be the only difference. But that is a choice, isn't it? It's a choice, it is a choice; you choose, you choose. And you can choose Love if you want to, isn't that good news? Anybody can choose pain and suffering, can't they? Isn't that what everyone does? Isn't that what you see going on every day? And in that story you think that not everyone can choose Love.

Hello? You think not everyone can choose Love, and you are mistaken. Everyone can choose Love, and you can choose Love! That's your choice. Take a look at what you call your life. Don't you think you would be better off had you chosen Love more often? That's a fair question, isn't it? For anybody, for everyone? It is a fair question. Don't you think you would be happier had you chosen Love all the time? Is it too late? No?

Q: No.

R: No? OK. So, if you want to you can make this moment your declaration – that in all your moments you are now going to choose Love, recognizing that if you don't, you have more of the same. Are you happy with what you've been getting? Are you happy with not choosing Love? Then everything argues for you to change, doesn't it? Everything argues for you to change. Everything wants you to change. Everything wants you to be embraced in the Love of your Creator, everything wants that. The expression of that sometimes might not look like Love, right? But it is a call for your Love. Don't interpret it as a call or justification for anger, or retaliation, or attack, it's a call for your Love. Did you hear the call?

Q: Yes.

R: Welcome. If you walk away from here tonight with anything, please walk away with the feeling, the recognition, the thoughts that you are completely set free from your past. That your sins are forgiven; and sins are nothing more nor less than choosing something other than Love. You're mistaken, that is all it is. If you walk from here tonight in that recognition that you are free, then you can choose once again. And you'll have lots of help. Because everything argues for you to be Love, everything does, absolutely everything does. You've been mistaken, nothing more, nothing less! Everything wants your Love! I don't know if I can say that strongly enough. Everything wants your Love! Everything does! It's a mistake to think otherwise. OK?

Q: I don't understand. Does it mean to have a compassionate attitude to things, or is it a way of thinking, is it a way of acting, is it a way of giving? What is actually meant by choosing Love?

R: It is being What You were created to be. It is not an attitude; I don't teach attitudes. There is too much attitude going on in this world already.

Q: That's right.

R: It is not an attitude, it's a Beingness. You were created as Love, by Love. It is just the willingness to be What You are, instead of trying to be what you can never be.

Q: So, is it kind of returning to what I once was? Beingness? Am I created from this Love, being a product of Love and expressing what I really am?

R: Yes. And What You really are is Love, so That is all that You have to express. And, that is what our brother Jesus demonstrated. He demonstrated only Love and his Love had nothing to do with circumstances. It had to do with his recognition of Who He is. And that is available to You, it is available to every Child of God.

Q: So, instead of an attitude it is rather a state of existence, of being?

R: It is an acceptance of What You already are. Can you accept that You are Love?

Q: Well, when I...

R: No, right now!

Q: I am not sure.

R: OK. See, then you'll have more of the same. And this is exactly what I am saying. You have an opportunity for freedom and to choose now, not based upon the past in any way whatsoever. The past is gone. Where is it? Why would you base something on the past? It is not even here. It wasn't so great to begin with. Look at all the mistakes that you and everyone else have made. Why would you want to base something on the past? Why wouldn't you want to base it on Something Perfect and Pure and full of Light, now? Why wouldn't you choose That now? Doesn't That make more sense?

Q: Yes, that I understand, if you have an experience of the Divine Light...

R: Yes, right now!

Q: ... then you cannot help.

R: Yes, right now!

Q: Yes, right now!

R: There is nothing to wait for and the past cannot keep It from you. It is your choice. What do you want to choose right now? What do you want right now to be like?

Maybe tonight you'll go beyond theory and you go into the Knowingness. Wouldn't that be something? Is it possible? Is it possible that tonight you go past all the theories? Is it possible? Be careful! Be careful, because once it's possible, it must occur! If you open up to the possibility it must occur! What do you think I've come here to offer you? A bunch of words? Haven't you had enough of those? Or do you want to know? ... and they all got quiet...

Q: You talked about disappearance. How does it work?

R: You'll disappear when you have no value for that that is valueless. It is a Law of God.

Q: Could I pursue this a bit? Last time you were here you said, I assume referring to yourself, "It could be that this body suddenly is no longer here. And the reason for that has nothing to do with the body."

R: That's right. However, I was referring to you! I was referring to all bodies!

Q: And if I disappear, what is it that disappears?

R: Nothing, that is why it can disappear. That is what nothing deserves, to disappear. What you think is something, is nothing that you've made into something. And when you're done playing around with it, it will disappear.

Q: So, the nothingness disappears...

R: Yes, back to nothingness.

Q: And what appears is...?

R: What has always been, which is hidden from you while you are playing around with nothingness.

Q: That's good news.

R: More good news, I like this place. It's a place of good news!

* * *

R: Can I read you something? I just discovered this book recently. It says, *"You'll Never Walk Alone-Your Resurrection is your Reawakening."*[19] Your Resurrection is your Reawakening. Does anybody understand that? Why does Jesus call it a Reawakening?

Q: Because you will awake from your own sleep?

R: Well, then, why doesn't he say, Resurrection is your Awakening?

Q: Because you were awoken in the first place?

R: Awoken? Oh, you mean You were created awake?

Q: Yes, that's what I meant.

R: Ah. So You were created awake, You were created aware of Everything. And your Resurrection is your Reawakening. Interesting idea isn't it? You're going to reawake. Where were You when You went to sleep, by the way?

Q: Nowhere.

---

[19] *Rananda is referring to the book 'You'll Never Walk Alone', in which he compiled quotes from 'A Course in Miracles, 2000' – The Manuscript of the Hugh Lynn Cayce Version, 'Jesus' Course in Miracles' – the complete Hugh Lynn Cayce Version, 'The Modern New Testament from the Aramaic' and 'A Course in Miracles' to shed light on the life and meaning of Jesus of Nazareth also called Jesus Christ.*
Published by MOM-Nederland – ISBN 978-90-78582-03-8.

R: Everywhere! You were in the Mind of God, You were in the Mind of your Creator Who thought of You. Where do you think you'll be when you are awakened, reawakened? Where will you find your Self when you are reawakened? You will call it a disappearing act perhaps. Where will You find your Self? Where were You when You went to sleep?

Q: In the Mind of God.

R: Oh, then, where will You find your Self when You awaken?

Q: In the Mind of God.

R: OK. So, You awaken to find your Self in the Mind of your Creator. That's exciting. I wonder what it's like to run around in The Mind of my Creator. I wonder what that would be like. See, you have no idea, do you? You have no idea what it would be like to be a Thought in The Mind of your Creator. You have no idea what the Mind of a Creator is like and you have no idea What has been created. All you're familiar with is a bunch of mistakes, right? Things that come and go, that die, things that go bump in the night. Don't you hate that when you get up and there are no lights on and you stumble around and your toe hits something that doesn't move? You know what I mean? Oh man, not fun! Nothing like that is going on in God's Mind, nothing to bump into. Isn't that great news? You don't have to turn the light on, because The Light is always on. No sleeping, just all that lovemaking though. "I don't know, that is kind of scary, making Love all the time, isn't it? Pffft... boy." Imagine that, no cigarettes, nothing, just lovemaking, that's it. No breaks. No. Just constant ecstasy and that is not a drug. Oh, OK, there you'll go.

"You'll Never Walk Alone [YNWA]." This part of the book is called, "God, You and Love". [YNWA, Chapter III, page 43]

"No course whose purpose is to teach you to remember what you really are could fail to emphasize that there can never be a difference in what you really are and what love is. Love's meaning is your own, and shared by God himself. For what you are is what He is. There is no love but His, and what He is, is everything there is. There is no limit placed upon Himself, and so are you unlimited as well."

And, so are You unlimited as well! And, so are You unlimited! Is anybody in here willing to admit that?

Q: But I really think I am limited.

R: Would you like to be mistaken?

Q: Yes.

R: Is that a choice?

Q: Yes.

R: Yes, it is! Yes, it is! Nothing makes you be here. It is a choice. And, it is a choice that you make in every moment. Either that or Jesus is a really good liar and he's got a lot of people convinced of some really amazing stuff. Like his disappearing act. That has confused a lot of people, hasn't it? They are still angry over that, aren't they? Hello? There is a debate going on. Did he really resurrect? Did the apostles come back and roll the stone away and steal his body, so they could make the story about him? What is it with this world anyway? There is just a real reluctance to be unlimited, isn't there? And then, what do you do? You make all these incredible statements about the brilliant minds of your scientists, don't you? Like, what is this guy's name...? Einstein. You just really praise him, don't you? Einstein, the greatest mind the humans have ever known, Einstein.

Q: He was a religious man.

R: Yes, what did he tell you? What was one of the main things he loved to tell you?

Q: God doesn't play dice.

R: Yeah, as if he knew, right? He said, "You cannot go faster than the speed of light. If you do, you won't exist." And so he advised you not to do that. And what did Jesus advise you? If I remember he said, "Follow me!" And then he Resurrected and Ascended. And he was doing this before Einstein. It's a good thing Einstein wasn't around at that time. He would have said, "No, no, don't do that!" Jesus said, "No, I don't mind, I don't mind going faster than the speed of light, ciao amigo!" And then he did his disappearing act. He is not the only one, you do know that, right? There are others that have Ascended. Hello?

Q: Yes.

R: Oh, OK. So, he goes on to say,

"Love is not learned."

Let me see if I get this clear. Somebody help me here. My Creator is what Love is, is the Source of Love, and creates more Love by creating, so the only Thing that has been created is Love. But Love cannot be learned, right? Then, what are you teaching yourself?

Q: Love.

R: But you can't learn It. Love cannot be taught! Why are you working on yourself then? Why don't you just accept it? Why are you working on yourself? Why are you trying to be a better person? Why don't you just be What You were created to be? Why don't you just be Love? Is that a valid question? Not everybody thinks that way, I can see. That's interesting. I've gone too far, haven't I? You like it when somebody talks about how you can learn these different things, don't you? That's what you like. You don't like the challenge of being Home in Heaven right now, right? You want to work on things. Right? Hello?

Q: Not any more.

R: Not anymore? That is a good answer. Come on, give me a break!

Q: In what?

R: You are Home in Heaven right now, dude.

Q: Yes.

R: Yeah. And it would be really, really nice if you would accept that, not as a theory, but let yourself be undone. You've analyzed this teaching from every possible angle. As a matter of fact, you've made up a couple that weren't there before. And no angle is going to do it, you know. The only thing that is going to do it, is flat out, full on forgiveness. That is the only thing that is going to make it happen for you. You can't do it yourself, it's impossible. But you can allow the forgiveness to overcome you. That is possible. Like a little child. Do you remember what it was like when you were a little kid?

Q: They aren't the best of memories.

R: So, that's the part you've been holding on to. That's why I said forgiveness. See? It's time! It's time! There are a lot of people waiting for you. In your teachings, do you teach anything about body language?

Q: No, beyond that.

R: Really? Are you ready to let go?

Q: More than ever.

R: Can I ask you a question?

Q: Yes, of course, please.

R: What would it take to get that last bit. What do you think it would take?

Q: Help.

R: No, you've got the help, are you willing to receive it? And I think that is saying, the time is now.

Q: The time is now, yeah.

R: The alarm has gone off. Don't do that again! So, the help is here. That is the first part. And the second part is, once the help shows up... Come on, your turn... Once the help shows up...

Q: Share... a lot.

R: Receive it! Let it have its way with you! See, and that is where the forgiveness comes in, you know. Otherwise you'll fight your help.

Q: Most of my life I have been trying to learn to forgive others, and I forget myself.

R: Well, not only that, when you attempt to forgive others, there are others then, aren't there?

Q: Yes, of course.

R: So, you have to be careful whose program you're running. Do you want to run this program?

Q: Yes.

R: Yes? OK. Then, don't do that. Stop trying to forgive others. You think you can do that?

Q: Yes.

R: Yes. There you've got the whole program then. I am going to forgive, but I am not going to forgive others, because forgiveness shows me there are not others. I only need to forgive what I think I see; those are my mistakes. I release them from what my mind is telling me is going on with them.

Yes? You know the program. See, there is nothing that I can say that you don't know. But, there is a lot that I could say that you haven't been willing to apply. But as soon as I start to say it, you say, "I know, I know, I know."

Q: It's true. Definitely.

R: It's true? See, and that is not receiving the help. Remember our friend Jesus, when people were asking him, "Why do you hang out with those people?" he said, "The saints don't need me." Are you a saint?

Q: I'm a sinner.

R: Then maybe it is time for you to accept this. Stop trying to be a saint. Who wants to be a saint anyway, man! Talk about boring. All the passion, all the fun, is in the transformation. It is not in being the saint. Who would want to be a saint?

Q: Well, I've tried.

R: Yes, I know. And failed, by the way.

Q: And failed, yes.

R: So, look. I mean, you know how the phases go. First of all you have no idea of what is going on and you're just kind of angry most of the time, trying to find the way of happiness in this world. And then you reach a point where you go, "Man, I just don't want to keep doing this anymore. There have got to be different ways. There has to be some kind of help in this whole thing." And then the help begins to show up. But when the help shows up, the one being helped has to receive it and has to let himself be helped; otherwise, how could you even call it help? It just would be someone giving you a hard time. Is the Holy Spirit giving you a hard time? Or is the Holy Spirit giving you no time?

Q: I've been giving the Holy Spirit a hard time.

R: Yeah, that's clear, that is clear. And that's why your teacher says to you, "Don't do that!" And then you go, "Don't tell me what to do." You want help, right? "Yeah, boy, I really want help." Don't do that. "Don't you tell me what to do." It's funny, isn't it? I mean, it is funny; it's also sad, you know. It's funny because it doesn't make sense in the mind, but it is also sad, because while it is not accepted there is a lot more pain and suffering. Not only as an apparent individual but others that know you don't get your full Joy and your full Love, and that's sad, you know, that's sad. People want your Love. Everyone wants your Love; they don't want it to be hidden. They don't want to have to do something to deserve it. Everyone is so fed up with having to do things to deserve to be loved; that's not the way of our Creator. You don't have to do anything for your Creator to love You. Why would you have to do something with one another to be loved? It just doesn't make sense. Stop! Don't do that, don't do that to one another. And this is what forgiveness is. Forgiveness is, we don't do that to one another. Isn't that good news? And if you have to practise, practise. If you don't go, "OK, this is it, boom! I'm done." If in your mind you can't find the place where you can do that and have a complete shift, then I suggest that you practise. How often? Twenty minutes in the morning and twenty minutes in the evening?

[YNWA – continued.] *"Love is not learned."*

You are not going to teach yourself Love. No one is going to teach it. No one is going to do that. The only thing that is going to happen is, you're going to admit what you are doing in your mind to not know that You are already Love. And you're going to look at that and you're going to go, "I'm not willing to do that anymore, because when I do that I don't get to experience Love. And neither do the people I'm living with, neither do the people I work with, neither do the people that are at the grocery store, where I go to buy groceries, they don't get my Love. They get a smile, they get a hello, they get some politeness, but they don't get my Love." And there is a big difference between being a nice guy and being Love. That's really good news.

Q: In my case, yes.

R: Yes, in the case of everyone who thinks they're human it's really good news. Being Love is so much more outrageously beautiful than being a good guy, a nice person. You know, nice persons die. I know a lot of nice people that have died. But I haven't known one Spirit that has died. I don't know one Son of God who has died. Which would you really rather be?

Q: Spirit.

R: Is that a choice?

Q: For me, yes. But in general no, of course.

R: But while you think you have choices, it is a choice. Yes. So, if we are talking about theory, no one has a choice, because You were created that way. But when you look at what you have been thinking and doing and experiencing, then you certainly have a choice. And while you have a choice, you know what? You'd better make it. Because if you don't, you just go around again. How would you like to be born and do this all over again? And maybe next time it'll even be worse to get the message through to you. I mean, how do you know? How do you know? All that you know is that you are making a mistake and you want to learn. You don't think you would make it tougher next time in hopes of learning? Wouldn't you? Because you really want to learn! And you see how stubborn you are. So, let's make it worse, maybe then I'll get it. Why do you think it was like that this time?

Q: Because I'm very hard-nosed.

R: Yeah, right.

Q: It was hard.

R: It was, I know. And all that can be healed now! To me that's the really good news. It can be healed now. And you know like with alcoholics... have you ever known an alcoholic?

Q: Yes.

R: Well, the best help for an alcoholic is someone who has been an alcoholic and quit. They're the best help for an alcoholic. So, the best help for somebody who is being addicted to being a human is someone who has been a human and is no longer a human. If you keep turning to humans, you know what you'll get?

Q: More humans.

R: Yes, you get their advice that they have learned, based on their past humanness. So, that's what you'll get. So, if that's your choice, choose wisely. Hang out with whomever you want, but choose wisely.

[YNWA – cont'd.] *"Love is not learned, its meaning lies in itself. And learning ends when you have recognized all it is NOT. That is the interference; that is what needs to be undone. Love is not learned because there never was a time in which you knew it not. Learning is useless in the Presence of your Creator, Whose acknowledgment of you and yours of Him so far transcends all learning that everything you learned is meaningless...,"*

Everything you learned is meaningless. Now, would you like to fight with God on this?

[YNWA – cont'd.] "... *replaced forever by the knowledge of love and its one meaning.*

Love is One. It has no separate parts and no degrees; no kinds nor levels, no divergences and no distinctions. It is like itself, unchanged throughout. It never alters."

Wow, Love never alters. Your relationships that you have with one another, does Love alter? Hello?

Q: Yes.

R: Hmmm...

Q: What do you mean by alter?

R: Changes. More or less.

[YNWA – cont'd.] *"It never alters with a person or a circumstance."*

Now, that is an extreme example. Love doesn't change based upon circumstances, or people. And this is what Jesus came to teach, didn't he? And most people say, "Oh man, I could never do that," don't they? Hello?

Q: Yes.

R: It's interesting isn't it? Do you say that? "I couldn't do that?"

Q: Not anymore.

R: That's a good start. But this is not magic. It is not just saying the words. It's active forgiveness that reveals the Love. Hello? Active forgiveness reveals the Love. Hello?

Q: Yes.

R: Right. Because, not forgiving means you're holding on to something that is not loving. And, if you're holding on to something that is not loving, then you can't know What Love is, because you can't know Love partially. Like you can't know God partially. If you're going to know God, you're going to know All of God. And if you're going to know Love, you have to know All of Love. Because, God is Love. If you want to have your Awakening to Who You are, you are going to awaken to Love. "Man, I just want it to be The Light and all that kind of stuff, you know. Rockets going off, and stars and stuff. I didn't want to do the love thing, brrr... Love! Brrrr..." Funny, isn't it? Because you have funny ideas about what Love is. Love is What holds Everything together, is what links Everything together. That's what Love is. Wow, amazing.

[YNWA – cont'd.] *"It is like itself, unchanged throughout. It never alters with a person or a circumstance. It is the Heart of God, and also of His Son."*

Wow, that's nice, isn't it?

[YNWA – cont'd.] *"Love cannot judge. As it is One itself, it looks on all as One."*

Do you look on everyone as One? No? Then you don't know that You are Love. And when you don't know that You are Love you have a tendency to judge, don't you? And that's how you get circumstances.

[YNWA – cont'd.] *"Its meaning lies in Oneness."*

You guys like the idea of Oneness, don't you? Is it possible for you to leave Oneness? Hello? If you left Oneness, would there be Oneness?

Q: No.

R: No, there would be oneness, missing one. That's all there would be left, -ness. You would just have Nessie. [Pet name for the monster of Loch Ness in Scotland.]

[YNWA – cont'd.] *"And it must elude the mind that thinks of it as partial or in part."*

Well, Oneness and Love both would elude the mind that thinks of it as partial or in part. Do you think that you can partially love somebody? I mean, don't you say you love somebody, but you hold something back? You call them, what, like private thoughts and stuff like that. You just wouldn't fully love them, would you? You wouldn't just fully love them, right? You would have a somewhere where they can't go. "You can't talk to me like that. You can't do that, not in my house." Somewhere you would have to stop, wouldn't you? Somewhere you would stop, wouldn't you?

Q: I'm wondering. So, ask me.

R: Are you ready, are you really ready for this?

Q: Probably not.

R: Yes! You were acting so sincere there for a minute I thought I was going to get you, you know. But then I looked and I went, "Oh, man, that will scare the shit out of him, better not go there." OK, are you ready? Are you ready?

You are The Savior of this world! And this world needs you to be the Savior and stop playing your games. Now, that is the most loving thing that I can ever tell you. Because when you accept that, You will be the Love and the Love that You are will save everything that is in your mind. Save it from having to demonstrate less than Love. And that's what makes You The Savior. Can you accept that much Love?

Q: I can.

R: Yes? So, you are going to let everybody now know that you are The Savior? By being the Love. I don't care about verbs.

Q: I understand that.

R: Be The Love.

Q: I will.

R: OK, that's a deal now. And Everything in Heaven has heard this deal. Including those angels that keep flopping around there behind you.

Q: Angels too.

R: Yes, they've heard it.

Q: OK.

R: OK. So has your wife. She's heard it, too.

Q: She is an angel.

R: Yes, yes, but she heard what you said. And she is going to hold you to it. Because she wants you to be the Savior...

Q: She wants me to be The Savior?

R: Absolutely! Because, if she doesn't see You as the Savior, you know what, she doesn't get to be the Savior. See, we really do need one another. And what Love really is, really needs to come and be alive. And It can't be alive without forgiveness. If you're not going to practise forgiveness, how will you possibly ever going to be The Savior? Are you with me?

Q: Yes.

R: OK, I totally support you, do you know that?

Q: Yes.

R: That's important. OK.

[YNWA – cont'd.] *"There is no love but God's, and all of love is His. There is no other principle that rules where love is not."*

Wow, did you hear that last sentence? *"There is no other principle that rules where love is not."* Wow! So, Love is the key. And while you don't know what Love is, forgiveness is the key to Love. Isn't that great? Isn't that great? Man, you can just forgive all day long, isn't that incredible? You only get one job.

That would be easy, right? Don't you think your Awakening would be a lot easier if you only had one job? "There is only one thing I have to do." And it is not boring by the way. Forgiving is not boring at all. You start to forgive and you go, "I am not going to forgive that person! Come on, I remember how much pain I got out of that. I'm not going to do it!" Do you ever get that kind of feeling? And forgiveness takes care of all of that. And if it's a practice, it's a practice. The thing is, sometimes we get in there and we come up against things where there is no way we are going to forgive that person, because they really did hurt us. Hello?

Q: Yes.

R: You run into things like that in your mind. That's why it's a practice. Sometimes you might run into that and you'll find the unwillingness to forgive. And so it is a practice, but don't run away. Don't run away, practise. Because The Love is right behind it. What you really want is right behind it and all that you actually ran into were thoughts. That's it, thoughts, that's all you were looking at. Thoughts in your mind. Listen, if I say to you, "When I was a little boy I had a red wagon," you don't have any problem with that. You don't go, "Oh, I'd better forgive him." That was a thought, "I had a little red wagon as a boy." "But when I was a little boy, my father really hit me when I didn't do anything wrong, you would think I'm going to forgive him for that?" Now I had thoughts and I took thoughts to energy, didn't I? I gave them a certain meaning, didn't I? And I had no intention of letting go of them, did I? And so it's in there where Love ought to be, having an effect in my mind. It is just a thought. It could have been like a little red wagon. "I had a little red wagon when I was a boy and my father did something when I was a boy."

Hello? They are just both thoughts, aren't they? But one of them I think of differently, don't I? And I have energy associated with it, haven't I? Because of the way that I choose to think.

Q: In a way this still is the easy one, but now, when your father hits you now, then of course there is the same answer.

R: It's still the same choice, isn't it? There are still thoughts and there are still... And that's why Jesus becomes so amazing for anyone who truly wants to awaken to the nature of Self and Creation and Creator. He is an extreme example. He is telling us we don't have to go through the same things. But he showed that Love is stronger than an illusion. Not only stronger, but more desirable.

Now I get to the outrageous part, the most outrageous part of all. Are you ready? Jesus said, "You know, I discovered something when That happened to me, and It really surprised me but I want to share It with you. When It happened to Me, It happened to You.!" If you have not accepted that, all that you are waiting for is your willingness to accept it and when you accept it, you will find it as true. The totality of the illusion is happening in One Mind. And that Mind has been healed! And, it awaits your acceptance of that healing, and that's forgiveness; that's the real forgiveness, right there.

And that'll take care of all of our dads and our mums and the people we have worked with, all the stuff, the kids at school that beat us up, all that kind of stuff. It is taken care of when you forgive the big picture and it'll include all of that. I mean, how many lifetimes do you think it'll take to get all the billions of things that went wrong in this lifetime? And all the other lifetimes that you're still holding on to that you're not even letting yourself be aware of?

There has got to be a faster way. OK? Is there one idea that would kind of get all of them? Is there one idea that they kind of all link into? If we can get that one idea, like pulling the thread in the sweater, everything comes apart. Is there one idea? And that's really personal, isn't it? That one idea is really, really personal. It has something to do with You and your Creator. "Mmm..." very personal. "Mmm... Mmm... Mmm... Boy, mmm..." Boy, that would be a healing, wouldn't it? "Boy oh, boy, let me see. I can't blame my Creator, oh. Let's see. I have a relationship with my Creator and I've just decided that half of that relationship can't be blamed. Who does that leave left? So, if I can get past the blame to the forgiveness, I'll be OK. If I can get past the guilt, through the forgiveness, I'll be OK. Now, mmm... if I relieve the other half of that relationship from the responsibility that I have placed upon it, can it play a different role for me when I do that? Mmm... What kind of a role would my Creator play for me then, if I didn't make the Creator responsible for all the problems I have? Let me see, what kind of role do I like my Creator to play? Let me see. Mmm... OK, which one am I the most afraid of, that's the one I should choose. How about... pffft... no, that might be going too far." Right?"

Perfect Love, that's the part I want my Creator to play, Perfect Love. I want a Creator That thinks of Me as I Am. Wholly loveable. "Go God, I am wholly loveable!" Oh, and totally loved. Not good enough to just be loveable without being loved. Holy loveable and totally loved. That's your part.

12

A FISH OUT OF THE WATER

Knowing and Loving / Faith and Certainty / Accepting The Truth of You

Q: You said, if I remember well, that in Love, True Love there are no degrees, no differences. But, isn't it necessary to be aware of Love, to be conscious of Love, to experience Love? Then there is a difference. Because, for any experience of consciousness there has to be a difference. Otherwise, if there is no difference, how can we experience something?

R: What you're saying is true, but what you're forgetting is knowing.

Q: Knowing and loving go together?

R: Knowing is what Love is! Not knowing is what consciousness is! Consciousness is about things you can perceive. Knowing has nothing to do with consciousness, it has to do with Being. And Being is what Love is. It's not about observing circumstances and interactions between people, you're just seeing yourrelf. You're seeing an expression of your Self expressing Itself as Love.

Q: Sorry for my stupidity if I continue, but I get the impression that the way you describe Love is like a fish that has always been in the ocean. It doesn't know what water is.

R: Exactly. Because it is the water!

Q: But, if it's never been out of the water it's not aware of it.

R: No, there is no out of the water! Being a human is being a fish out of the water. Why do you think you feel uncomfortable most of the time? Why do you think you are trying to adjust to most everything you do all day long? Why do you think there's nothing natural that goes on here? Why do you think you feel so strange about yourself? Because you're not being You. I'm offering you not only a recognition of what is True about You, but I'm offering you the release from all your sins, from all your mistakes, from all the necessity to continue to do what you have been doing. I used to not like to say the word sin. Now I really love to say it because I see people go, "Grrr," you know. "Oh, I hated sin. I hate it when the Christians talk about sin. Just makes me bristle." Good. I'm showing you right where it would be nice if you practise forgiveness. That is the program, isn't it? So, where you find things that come up, that's were you heal. And Lord knows, Christians really need to be forgiven. Along with everyone else. But, they're not exempt from the forgiveness category, just because Jesus was the head. No, everyone who believes they're separate from their Creator and they think their Creator made this place, need to be forgiven. There is a lot of forgiveness required. How can you know Love in a place created or made not to know Love? Exactly, how? How, how? Ik hou van jou, ik hou van jou. [Dutch for I love you, I love you.]

That's how. "Ah," said the blind man, "now I see." To know Love you would have to know "not here". And, as you connect with "not here" and you begin to realize the nature of Self, the nature of Oneness, the nature of Love – which is all one and the same – you then begin to demonstrate That here. Why? Because, as you learn that, you learn what I just read to you, which is, Love does not change by circumstances and people. So, you begin to just be You. You just begin to be Love and no matter what situation you find yourself in, You don't have a different you, but a different situation. You have the one You, which is just being there, being loving and recognizing that Love is what is missing in that moment. If It's not missing, then you share It. If It's missing, you bring It, because you are connecting with It. It's being revealed to You, you're remembering. You then have It to give, to share. It's just what's natural.

R: Is that helpful?

Q: Yes.

R: I was talking to you by the way. It would be nice if you heard the message that I've come to bring. If you didn't hear anything else the whole night, at least hear the message that I've come to bring. Forgiveness is the key to happiness! Can you say that to me?

Q: Forgiveness is the key to happiness.

R: Yes.

Q: I think...

R: No no, just stop for a moment. Just say it and be with that statement for a moment and see what happens within you. Just do what I've asked you to do. Make the statement, be quiet for a moment and see what happens. OK. Don't let your mind go so fast that you run on to other things. Just be with it for a moment. Go ahead. Say it and just see what happens.

Q: Forgiveness is the key to happiness. Forgiveness is the key to happiness.

R: See, its already starting the change in you. You see it? Look at him, he's got already more light coming out of his face. Believe me, it's just simple, little things and being willing to turn toward your Creator and the Thoughts that your Creator would be willing to share with You. Believe me, even the physical structure of your body begins to change as you turn towards The Light and The Love. Physical transformation happens every time you turn. Face The Light.

Every act of forgiveness moves you, some of you anyway, lifetimes. Removes lifetimes of what you had intended to do in your future.

Q: Can forgiveness also imply that you do not tolerate certain things?

R: It has nothing to do with that. Forgiveness means it never happened! See, there are ideas that I talk about tonight, that are so radical to what you call normal thinking here in this world, that it is really easy to just set what I'm saying aside and say, "I could never be like that here." With that I agree. Because, if it's like that, fear would disappear. The question is, which would you prefer? What I'm talking about or the way that you have known the world to be? That's the real question you should be asking yourself. Do I want what I hear being said to be true or do I prefer the way I experience things right now? That's the question you should be asking yourself. And, then the really bright ones say to me, "Yeah, but how about if you're wrong and I spend all that lifetime following what you're saying? How about if you're wrong?" You know what I always say at that point? I would say, "What's the worst thing that could happen to you if I'm wrong?" And then you'd scratch your head, do your chin thing, you know, then your ear kind of thing, then your nose and then you'd say, "I'd probably die." And then I say to you, "Well, you were planning to do that anyway." It's what all humans do anyway. So, the worst thing that could happen if I'm wrong is you're going to get what you've intended to get anyway. But if I'm right, which I am, then you are released from all your pain and suffering. It's not a bad deal. I'm not offering you a bogus deal. I'm offering you happiness instead of all your problems.

I've never met anybody who told me, "You know, I don't have one problem. They all just disappeared after listening to you." Instead, somehow they became aware of a lot of problems. Which means that they've been hiding them and not wanting to have the Love solution take care of the problems. They've been hoping for some magical thing or some financial thing or some handsome man or woman to come and change everything for them. That's the way of the world, that's what the pursuit has been here. And, I'm not offering you that, I'm offering you something different. I'm offering you full responsibility, full ability to respond. I'm giving you all the power and glory that is possible. I'm just reminding you that's The Truth of You and you either like That and accept It or reject It and continue your daily, pitiful activities that just sometimes you're OK with and sometimes you're not. Most of the time not, because you have all these wants that don't seem to be fulfilled. You find a great lover but somewhere in that whole love affair it's not enough. You find the faults in your lover. Anybody here not find fault in their lover? – not one hand went up – amazing. So, these are the people you really love. You love them more than the others out there in the world. Right? Or maybe you find more fault in your lover than you do out there in the world. What's that all about? Why is it that you love them so much if you find all those faults? It's just a strange world. Maybe I'm strange. That's probably pretty true, isn't it? Yes, I knew that you would say that. But it's true, I don't get what goes on here, I really don't. I don't get when you're married why you are always arguing. "Well, that's what married people do." So, you got married to argue all the time? You have to get married to argue? I see people on the streets do it all the time and they're not married. "Well, it just goes along with the territory." Why? "I don't know, Rananda. I don't know. I just don't know. I don't know. That's what we do here." Ha, ha.

* * *

R: Any other topics you like to talk about?

I always hit a nerve when I talk about your humanness, you know. When I talk about your humanness I really hit a nerve, because everybody goes through this. Everybody wants to find somebody that they can love, that they can never find fault with. It's not what you want. You really don't want that, but you do it and then you justify it instead of stopping. And, this is what I mean. When I go, "Stop!" I literally mean that you can stop. When I make that declaration that I literally mean you don't have to continue, that there's such a Power and a Love available for You, that you don't have to keep doing that and that you're being taken care of, hardly anybody believes me. They would rather rely upon their past. Which means, I am not trustworthy enough yet, in your eyes, to guide you. But, that's a choice. That's a choice. And we know, even when somebody as outrageous as Jesus walked on your planet, people didn't agree with what he was saying. So, even a great Purity can be denied here in this world, because it's the same Power that gives you Life. You can be intent on darkness just as intent as you can be on Light. The Power is the same, it's just where it is applied. Your saving grace in all of this is that God won't let you do this eternally. Pooh. You would prefer that God would just say, "OK, that's enough. Can't do it anymore, that's it. Home in Heaven. Get Home. Go on. Don't play with these kids here anymore. They are just illusions. Go Home. Bad neighborhood!!!"

Q: In this process of becoming loving, is there any basic role for faith?

R: Yes, one moment. One beautiful moment of faith.

Q: And in that moment, what happens?

R: Certainty comes in.

Q: Jesus often said to people that they were small in their belief.

R: Yes, have you noticed that?

Q: Yes, so I think there is a basic role for faith.

R: Yes, one moment.

Q: Does one moment mean one second in time or one time?

R: Whatever, one moment. However long it takes. My point is this, when you look at the world, whatever it is that you look at, you go, "Something is not right here." Then you recognize nothing from within the framework as you see it corrects it. OK? Then you say, "There must be something outside of that that can correct it." That's faith. There's something out there, that's outside of the situation, that can correct it. That's faith, because you say you don't know what it is. If you knew what it was, you wouldn't hang around here.

So, you have a moment where you want something outside of that situation that can take care of the situation. But you don't know that it's there. Otherwise you know the situation is taken care of. But you don't know that. You want something to be there to take care of the situation. Yes. Say yes. That's faith. But because there is something there and you turn to that for help, it did help you. And you got the help. Now you're certain that there is something there to help you. You don't need faith any longer. You have certainty. You know it's there. You turned to it with faith. It showed up, it helped you, you know it's there. No faith necessary anymore, because now you are in the certainty. If you keep on going to faith, you keep doubting what you've already been shown. Over and over and over and over again. Why would you do that? Why would you do that?

Q: It seems pretty useless.

R: Thank you. Don't do that. You see it? It doesn't make sense, don't do that. Learn the lesson. "I don't do that anymore, I've learned, I see. I hear what you're saying. It makes sense to me. OK, I don't do that anymore. I'm learning the lesson." Ah, cool. This is the way it works. Show that you've learned your lessons by being that. OK?

* * *

R: How's everybody doing? Are you having a nice Christmas gathering here? Celebration of your Christhood? Do you understand that what I've been talking about all night long, is that You are The Christ, You're Spirit? That the Love affair between You and your Creator establishes You as that relationship with your Creator, which is what The Christ is? And that Jesus became The Christ, because he became so identified in his own mind with The Christ, that he realized That's Who He is. So he talked that way because he had a moment of faith, he had a realization and then he was willing.

"Was he tempted?" Yes, like you, yes. "Can I use that same mind that he used?" Yes. "Well then, what's my problem?" I don't know. "I don't have one." Well, that's what I've been telling you. "Well, thank you very much." Now, go give it away. Stop acting like you've got a bunch of problems. Don't you have a Creator? Is this the group that has a Creator? Did I come to the right group? Hello? You're the one that has a Creator? Then you don't have problems, right?

Now, you can think otherwise and act otherwise and get the result of doing all that, but it wouldn't have anything to do with The Truth. The Truth is, You do have a Creator and You don't have problems. And, all of time is to be either your rejection of that message or the acceptance of that. Now, which one do you think will bring you happiness? So, if you want to be wise Dutch people and beyond, go beyond your

Dutchness, then you would choose... If you want more of the same, no one, no one can stop you. If you really are happy with the program you're running, with your problems, no one can stop you. Absolutely no one, not Jesus, no one, not Buddha, no one, not Mohammed, no one, not Rama, no one, not Krishna, no one. Too busy playing the flute. Dancing with the cows. They won't stop loving you, but it's not enough to change your mind, evidently. So, somewhere that recognition – I have had enough – has to hit. And when that hits, then looking for another way or a different way can kick in. And then, once you're looking for another way, then you think you've got all those different roads. Right? The Christian road, the Hindu road, the Celtic road, the Muslim road, the Sufi road, the... I don't know, the sex road, the money road. See, these lead down to this way. And then you go, "Ini mini miny mo, catch a program by the nose, if it complains then let it go, ini mini miny mo." It helps when you have a sense of humor to do this stuff. Everybody is so serious.

* * *

Q: Can I ask you a rebellious question?

R: Ah, you can ask anything you want. This is our Christmas celebration. Your celebration of the birth of the Christ in You.

Q: Maybe it is a rebellious question, but how do you react if people say there is no Creator? It's a theory of Charles Darwin.

R: I just say, I hope you're happy.

Q: You hope that?

R: Yes. I wouldn't want them to think that way and be sad. If they are, they've got to give it up. What have I just got done saying? Somewhere you have to come to the realization that it's not working, that there has to be another way. If somebody is not at that place, they don't want to hear what I have to say. You know, I'm not here for the saints. I'm here for the people that recognize that something is not working. Because, until they recognize that, they don't want to hear what I have to say at all. Even when they hit that point it's hard enough to hear what I have to say.

Q: Can I ask another question? About The Christ. You say that if he did, I did.

R: No, I said when. And I've said Jesus.

Q: When Jesus did it, we did it.

R: Yes, that's right. Isn't that good news?

Q: Yes, it's very good news. In a sense, then, you could say that Jesus changed the human essence.

R: No.

Q: It's like that because...

R: No, there is no essence to a human. It's an illusion. There is no essence to an illusion! That's why you call it an illusion. What Jesus did in his mind is let go of the illusion of self and allow the real Self to reveal Itself. And that Self was The Christ. It's called The Christ. The True Self of Everyone is called The Christ. Jesus allowed himself to recognize It, so identified with It that the illusion of something other than That disappeared from his mind. And then you have the analogy of light and dark, right? When The Light is there the darkness is dispelled. So, when you identify with The Christ, your identification with you will disappear. When? When? When will you so identify with The Christ that you will disappear? When? Is that not a choice? It's a choice. We recognize it as a choice. Do you recognize it as a choice? Do you see it as a choice?

Q: I want to give an honest answer.

R: Yes, definitely be honest. Honesty is what comes from God. So, let's make sure your answer comes from God, because you want to be honest.

Q: I am not aware of that choice.

R: It's a choice that you make.

Q: I don't think it's deliberate.

R: It's definitely deliberate.

Q: So, it is inevitable?

R: It is inevitable that you make that choice. The question is, when? I've been saying this all night, haven't I? And I say it to you, to you, to you, to you and to you. We all have that choice and we decide when we are going to make it. Everything That is Perfection, Everything That is Love already supports you to make the decision.

Q: Can I ask to get a clearer picture...

?

R: Yes, but I want to know when you're going to take the decision. You keep trying to avoid my question. Just listen for a moment. When? That's the question.

Q: You want to know it now?

R: Wouldn't you want to know now? OK, let's look at this for a moment. If everything continues the way that it is, it means a lot of pain and suffering. Or, I can choose for no more pain and suffering. Let me see. When should I choose for that? When?

Q: If you put it like this...

R: I will.

Q: Right now.

R: OK, that's what I'm expecting. Why would I expect other than that when you're The Savior of the world? And, if you don't step up and be The Savior of the world it continues to be a place of pain and suffering. Why wouldn't I ask it of you right now? You think I want this world to go on with more pain and suffering, because people are too... reluctant to stand up and say, "Holy mackerel, all of that is available to me right now? Wow, I didn't know that. Of course I'll take my place." I'm getting a little excited here! But I don't understand why you wouldn't. I don't understand why you wouldn't get excited hearing this message. "You mean, really, you mean, really, if I just take the responsibility, no one would have to suffer anymore? That sounds magical." That's because of what you taught yourself. That you have nothing to do with this. Some God did it. And, in fact, you're being punished for it. "Wait till I've got a hold of this God!" It is about forgiveness!

Q: Could you give a clearer picture of it?

R: That was pretty clear.

Q: Could I ask a question?

R: Oh, you can do it.

Q: If I would have lived before Christ was on earth...

R: You did.

Q: Could I have made the same choice then?

R: You didn't, did you?

Q: Probably not.

R: So, then, let's move on to right now. Are you making the decision right now? Or are you letting your mind go all over the place with all these other things instead of just being the Savior?

Q: Too good to be true.

R: OK. God's like that. God's too good to be true. Right? God is All-Understanding. Too good to be true. That's right. That's exactly what the ego would say. That's exactly the position of the ego. Don't go there, it's too good to be true. You'd probably just die anyway, you know. And then you miss out on all the good things you could have had, like women, drugs, drinking, houses and bicycles. Not necessarily in that order.

Q: Dying can be a fantastic experience.

R: Oh, it's fantastic, you keep coming around and doing it over and over again. It's so good. OK, tell me how good Eternal Life is.

Q: Better than eternal suffering.

R: Because, there's no such thing as eternal suffering. It would have to be better than that. You give me the easy one, man. I give you the hard one; you give me the easy one.

Q: Choosing it actually has to do with valuing it.

R: Yes, it has everything to do with valuing. Let's look at that for a moment, valuing. OK? Do we know anybody that we could trust in there, helping us finding value in anything?

Q: You mean somebody that I know?

R: I just want to know, is there anybody you can trust? Completely? Always? Yes, and who would that be? God? So, if we value what God values we're in good condition, we're in good shape? Yes? So, what do you think God wants for What God creates? What does God want? I mean, what's He doing? What does God do? Create? OK. He doesn't make up illusions, He creates? So, then God helping You, is going to help You create, yes? This is an illusion, this is not creating, so God does not tell You to hang out here. God is going to tell You what? "Create," and there's no creating going on here. Creating is extending Love and Love is like a virus. It just spreads and spreads and spreads and touches everything, and the moment It touches it, because of Its Perfection, It changes it. It changes everything that It touches. Because Love is Perfection. Love is not a concept. Everything It touches – like if I reach out and touch your heart – you'd have a really hard time being a human again.

Q: I have a hard time being a human.

R: That's good, that's called transformation. The question would be, why are you still trying?

Q: That's a good question!

R: Yes, I have great questions. I've been given a great array of questions. Your question is all about, how do I find value? Well, to me the wisest way to find value is to join in That that knows Everything, knows what value is and, in fact, is the Source of value Itself. So, if I share with That, I am sharing What is valuable and I can never go wrong because It's the Source of value. OK? Now, mmm... that Creator created you? Mmmm... So, what value do You have then? That my Creator created Me... Mmm, so you are valuing yourself that way too? If you don't, you are bound to believe you have problems, because you are trying to experience something that your Creator will not experience with you. It just has to show up that way if you don't value what God values.

I can walk anywhere around this world – you and I have traveled most of the world, not all of it but most of it – and everywhere I've gone I have asked questions. You've noticed I'm really good at asking questions. I ask people if they have problems, and they all say, "Yes." And the ones that are trying to hide, they go, "But, you know, not really bad or anything, just a little here and a little there." And, then I'll ask them a really simple question. Do you love your Self... like God loves You? And then I would say, "Why not? He's The One that gives value to Everything, why wouldn't you love your Self the way God loves You? Why wouldn't you?" So, there is no good answer, I understand that. But do you understand that me asking these questions and you looking at them is revealing something that can be healed? That doesn't need to be avoided or be an excuse or a justification for why it is the way it is. Do you recognize we have opened the door where healing can take place? OK. That's the most important part because now we practise...

Q: Forgiveness.

R: Why? Because we have believed something we cannot share with our Creator. We have been mistaken. It's not true. That's what forgiveness is. That it is not true! I'm not what I have been telling myself I am. That's not true! What God tells me I am, That's what's true. I'm mistaken. My forgiveness is, "I'm mistaken, I accept Your value of Me." And this is where I get upset with some of the Christians, because they get into this, "You have sinned and it's a terrible thing," and so on and so forth, rather than, "Yeah, the sin means I've made a mistake, that's all that it means, I've made a mistake. But my Father is only Love, He's only Love, and so I can let go of my mistake, which is like the story of the prodigal Son. I can come Home to my Father. He's going to throw a banquet for Me. He's not going to beat Me on the head, give Me a spanking, send Me to bed without dinner, and then make Me, you know, sweep up everything for ninety-two years to atone." Imagine that, being out in the field where all the sheep are... trying to sweep up all the... Man, what a job that would be. Can you hear what it is that I'm saying?

Q: Yes.

R: Yes, so Everything is arguing for you to accept The Truth of You, The Christ of You, to accept your Sonship, You being the Effect of God being the Cause; rather than the person you've been trying to fix and satisfy with stuff that has no value whatsoever in the Mind of God. There has to be a switch, or the happiness that you seek will never be recognized until you get into such a deep and painful place that you will finely say, "I quit. I can't do this anymore. I don't want to be me. I want to be What You created." That is a really good place to be. Everyone is trying to avoid it as best as they can because they think something is wrong with them. And I'm telling you, you won't know what's right about you until you reach that place. Because you still have hope for your program, rather than the acceptance of God's program for You, which is, "You are My Son in Whom I am well pleased. Of course I'm pleased with My Son, I'm the Creator! I'm only Love. How can I not be pleased with What I create? I create only loving Things. Why wouldn't I be pleased?"

This is good stuff. This is good stuff! You're being forgiven, I forgive you for all your sins! Am I allowed to do that? Can I forgive you for all your sins? Well, I just said I did!

Q: Thank you.

13

IT JUST OCCURS TO ME

Holy Instant / Seeing The Christ /
Separation / Thoughts / Holy Spirit

Q: What I don't understand is, if you look at some of the teachings in the world like the Vedic teaching...

R: You know that I don't do that.

Q: Yes, I know that you don't do this. I know, I know. You take your own experience of course. But then you have the entity that's called Brahman. Brahman is the absolute unbounded awareness...

R: That is an idea.

Q: You could call it an idea, but...

R: I would if I were you. You are an idea.

Q: Alright.

R: Brahman is an idea too.

Q: So, God is also an idea?

R: Yes.

Q: Brahman is described as unmanifest, omnipresent, bliss, consciousness, intelligent...

R: Also as something that cannot be defined.

Q: Yes! On the other hand you have the manifest world, right?

R: Yes, that's what definition is.

Q: The illusion?

R: Yes, that's what definition is.

Q: It's difficult to concentrate when you do those things.

R: Well, you told me you wanted to join. I did knock![20] See, what you're discovering right now is that you actually prefer the experience to the words. That's what I keep trying to say to you. And then the ego keeps saying, "But how? How is that going to happen? How is that going to, how?" Well, you tell me, how did that just happen?

Q: Now, I know you're right. But, of course, this is an intelligent satisfaction...

R: Exactly, and you know what? It's never going to satisfy you. There is no satisfaction in it. It still leaves you with the longing, because the longing was put there by God. Only God can take care of that longing.

Q: I have some... let's say some difficulty in trying to understand that you're pushed into illusion and you have to...

R: That's a thought.

Q: OK, that's a thought.

R: See, there's a thought, that you are something that is in an illusion.

Q: I understand.

R: Then there is a thought that says, because you are something that is in an illusion, it's no longer an illusion. See, these are thoughts. And, I keep telling you when you verify those thoughts you're going to get the results of them. And if somebody is completely being undone, you still think they are in the illusion with you, because that's what you think. Like when Jesus went through what he went through,

---

[20] With a wink to Emma Thompson as Nanny McPhee in the film of the same name by Kirk Jones.

people say that he could not have been free of the pain and the suffering... But if he knew he was not a body, he was free from the pain and the suffering. And that's what he teaches. Resurrection.

You think he went through a lot of pain and suffering, because you think if that happened to you, you would have a lot of pain and suffering. And, then you project it onto him. Just like you have ideas of meditation and so on and so forth and you project them onto me. You're doing the same thing to me that everyone does to Jesus. And you do it to each other. And so, somewhere, when somebody awakens, you have to realize that They are actually not like you. And then hear them teach you You're the same Thing They are. And when you're undone in that, that's when You will reclaim What has always been real. That's the way it works. It doesn't make any difference whether you like it or not, it's still going to be that way. It doesn't depend upon your liking or disliking. It doesn't depend upon your saying it's hard or easy. It's that way because it is that way! Because that's the way of Perfection. That's the Way of God!

The sooner you come to a conclusion in your own mind that you'd rather be true to the Ways of God than to your own ideas, the sooner that idea of progress, acceptance or realization will dawn on your mind. Otherwise you're constantly thinking you're something that needs to figure it out. And if you need to figure it out, you know what, you'd be working on yourself. Now, that idea is that something that is not perfect can become Perfect. That's why you're working on it. And I am telling you, that's impossible and you don't like it. You don't like it when I tell you that's impossible! That something not perfect cannot become Perfect. You don't like that idea.

Q: But I think I am somebody who forgot that I am Perfect

and that I am in the process of remembering.

R: That's a thought in the mind. And that's a thought that's coming to you from Spirit, so that Spirit can get you to start listening to Spirit. But that's not Who You are.

Q: OK, but I am in the process of remembering then.

R: That's right. And so, those words and those thoughts will help you to remember, because the purpose for you is to remember. In that sense it's valuable, but it's still not true.

Q: Working on myself is more like I am trying to remember?

R: Well, you have to start hearing what I am saying.

Q: I try. I am in the process of...

R: Stop working on yourself!

Q: But working on myself is the remembering!

R: If that is what you want to tell yourself, then that's the way it will be.

Q: Don't you agree...? No...?

R: No. I am telling you, you cannot work on Perfection, which is What You already are. The only thing you can do is train the mind to value the thoughts that are brought to you by Spirit, so that Spirit can lead you into the realization that all of that is an illusion, all of it. Even your need to work on yourself is an illusion. But it's the part of the illusion that has value. So, I am not taking the value away, I am trying to tell you what's really going on. And you don't like it. There's a lot of resistance to what it is that I teach. I know that. I can understand that. I was totally resistant in my Awakening. Believe me, when you try to awaken, when it's time for you to awaken, you will do everything absolutely possible to not wake up, because you are that thing that believes in laws of death. You believe you die in your Awakening. That's why the Hindus, for instance, will teach it that way. They teach you God is a destroyer. Destroyer of what? What, what does God destroy? What ignorance does God destroy? What ignorance? What ignorance did God make? What ignorance is part of God's Creation? See, there's the problem, because that thought system says that God made this. They even teach you that evil was in God. He tossed it out of Heaven. See? I don't teach that stuff. You have to understand that you are trying to hold onto a thought system that I am not teaching. And, then you try to reconcile what I am saying with the teaching that you're not willing to let go of. That's not going to happen! You cannot reconcile The Light with darkness. It's never going to happen... Ever.

So, the most you get are these incredible bright reflections on the inside of your skull from your meditation experiences. You made the whole universe out there and you go look at the lights. How about the sun? Don't look at the sun too much or it will damage your eyes. You think that you can't make these experiences of what you call beauty inside your own head, so you can have a nice feeling about yourself? I guarantee you it's happening a lot...

What words can get you out of here? You call them mantras. What words can make the world disappear? Disappear, disappear, disappear, disappear, ohm, home, home, home, ohm, mommy home, home, ohm, daddy home, home, home, home, home, home, home. What words? I just don't get it. I am sorry. I did it for years and lifetimes, so believe me, I know what I am talking about. I don't get it now, because something has happened to me. You understand what I am saying? There's been a revealing, there's been a connection, I've been lifted out. And after that happened I looked at all the things we've been doing as a human species and all I could do was laugh. But between here and there I was devastated, crying, in pain. You know, worse than depression. You know depression? Worse than depression. I mean, I was just like... In English we have this phrase, beside myself. I was totally beside myself and in the recognition that everything that's ever happened in time and space only ever happened to me.

You don't know what that's like, and until you know what that's like you hear the words, but you have no idea what it's like to be aware of Everything. That it is an illusion, all of time, all the beings, all the humans, all the animals, all of it. You have no idea what it's like to find the realization, that it's all just playing out in One Mind and that That is your Mind. For me that was totally devastating. I was sad, devastated, crushed beyond every word you want to use. It's just like the most terrible thing you will ever experience. And that moment my Savior came. And that moment the One Who was to take me across came, because finally I wasn't denying any longer that nothing outside of me was making me make choices and have experiences. I had finally come into where I was willing to be The Source of Everything that was going on in the illusion.

Q: And this is necessary?

R: Well, how can I say it's necessary? All I can tell you is what happened with me.

Q: Is it the same process as the life of a Buddha or...

R: Well, I can tell you that I met Buddha on my way out and I didn't stop where he did. And Buddha didn't stop, later when he was no longer Buddha. But in the lifetime you called him Buddha, he had a point where he stopped. And I didn't stop there. I was taken beyond that.

Q: If this has been the way for you, it must be the way for me, because we are One.

R: Only if you join in the Oneness of It. Otherwise you'll demand it be the way that you want it and that's what you've been doing. Because, how long have I been offering you this? I just look like a regular guy, don't I? I even make mistakes from time to time, don't I? And, so you miss Who I really am, just like you miss Who You really are. But making mistakes in an illusion doesn't mean that You are not Perfect and Pure and Whole and still What God created and That is What you're looking for. You look for teachers and everybody Who is Perfect. And you look through the filtering of your mind, through your judgments. You don't let anybody be Perfect. You always look for a fault, because you think there are faults about you. And so it's just a natural thing that happens in that sense. It is natural in that sense that you get the results of your thoughts. You know what I am saying?

There's a certain law that plays out for you. I mean, I show you guys your Perfection sometimes and you get so close to It you start to look at It and then you freak out. If you spend too much time with me, as soon as you're not with me you start to lose everything that I was showing to you. You start running your old patterns again and then you get really guilty and you wonder, what the hell happened to my experience? Where did it go? And, then you'll finally ask me that question and I say, where can it go? Where can your experience go? It doesn't go anywhere! You choose to place your awareness on whatever you want. You go. The experience doesn't go anywhere. Reality, where's Reality going to go? Where can It go? It's not like a twinkling star. Now I am here, now I am not, now I am here, now I am not, now I am here, now I am not.

The illusion does that. The illusion literally has to be held in every moment. And if you hear what I am saying, it means it is disappearing in every moment. And, it happens so fast, that you don't know it's disappearing. And, you hold it back again. And, that's what makes you so tired that you have to go to sleep at night. Because, all the time that you call yourself awake you have to fight to keep Reality from getting you. And you do that by holding on to the idea of a subconscious and the idea of laws – like the sun, night and day, food, that you're inside the body – all these different laws that you accept. You have to think about them all day long. You accept them all day long, and just act through the acceptance of them. And that holds off Reality. You know how the eyes work, right? You know that there are things that you can't see and there are things that you can't hear. So, you can't really rely upon them. And, when I say this thing is blipping in and out so fast that you're not aware of it, you say, "Well, what good does that do me as I am not aware of it?" And then you try to use your senses to be aware of what I am talking about. They are not capable of that. The senses are not capable of knowing Reality. They are not capable! Not possible! It's not possible! Perception is never going to reveal Perfection! Not possible!

While in association with the body you will never know Reality. You will have to lose the association with the body and to have a moment of recognition of Reality. And that's the one thing that you've never really wanted to happen to you. You never really wanted no body in association with what you're experiencing, because that idea is death to you and death you plan for later. But, when you've had enough, you know, when you have a hard time getting your body moving, then you go, "OK, I'd rather die than be like this." The stuff's dripping and somebody is trying to feed you, because you can't do anything, then you go, "I'd rather be dead then be like this." OK? And that's the way it works. At the end you are a kind of like you are at the beginning. And all that stuff that happened in between, what was that? "You know, Rananda, its life." Life??? Birth to death is what life is? Wow, what a deal this is. In English we call that getting a raw deal. Birth to death and that's life? Pffft. I can't wait to get a hold of that God.

Q: Is it fair to say that all the time I have my awareness not on God, that is what ego is?

R: Ego never has awareness of God. That is true. However, it doesn't mean that there are not moments in which you're aware of God.

Q: I don't get it.

R: Well, you can think about it a little bit if you want to. Jesus will teach it like this. There are moments where time and space are not a part of your Awareness, the Mind. In the mind the ideas of time and space are not active. He calls it moments of holiness or holy instants. In a holy instant there is time nor space. When you experience that holy instant, your mind is altered. OK? And, if you can collect them you'll have enough verification in the mind to turn toward What is being revealed. And that's why he has lessons to help you have holy instants.[21] So, when you practise these lessons and you have those holy instants, you begin to realize that what has been said is actually true, which is different than accepting the concept. You'll know that It is True, because You'll be It; It will be revealed to You. In between you might have to find some acceptance or liking of the concepts. But it's not necessary. After the holy instants begin, you probably start to like the concepts. For instance, you like

---

[21] *Reference is being made to the Workbook in 'A Course In Miracles', which contains 365 lessons, meant to free our mind from the conditioning that prevents us from being in touch with Love and Truth.*

that you didn't defile Heaven while believing that you were separate from God. You like that God doesn't know about this world. At first that's disturbing, but you will come to like it. You'll be glad at some point that all the things that you have been holding about yourself and people are not true. At some point you will be happy about that.

Q: But ego is the idea that I am separate from God.

R: That's right, that's why, when we have an experience of outside of time and space, ego is not a part of it. That doesn't mean it is gone from the mind. It means, it is gone from that experience, because the mind is not focused on the thought system that is presented to the mind through the idea of an ego.

Q: So, the experience you're talking about, the one you had...

R: Had no ego in it.

Q: The one, when you were beside yourself...

R: Oh, that kind of an experience. That's ego.

Q: But, it is necessary to see that this is nothing and that all the time I have been in God.

R: That is a part of your Awakening. Recognizing that this is an illusion is what your Awakening is. In that sense I actually teach there's more than one Awakening. And your first Awakening is to the fact that this is an illusion. You see it's an illusion. You awaken to that.

The second Awakening is the realization that You are The Source of it. Now, they can be all at the same time and it can be one Awakening, but many people experience it as separate insertions of Light.

Q: And, it's not that if you see that you are the Source of it, you at that same moment recognize You are the Son of God, because that's another experience?

R: You know, the way it works in the mind is really interesting, because it doesn't. Until it recognizes It is the Son of God, it cannot make instantaneous recognitions. It seems like there's a sequencing to it, which is what time and space are. Because, that's the way the mind has been thinking about self. But, the reality of it is, the whole entirety of the illusion, the whole entirety of time was but one moment, one thought.

Q: And the whole remembering is...

R: Is also within that one moment! See, but to the mind it looks like progress and evolution. It looks like certain steps are following one another. But, you do recognize that that is an illusion, that these things are following each other. Because, at some point along the line you begin to have experiences that don't fit cause and effect. All of a sudden things start happening that are not logical based upon the laws of the world. For instance, you're coming head-on with a car and all of a sudden find yourself at the other side of it. You didn't have an accident.

See, because it's a dream, it's just like it's malleable. All kinds of things can happen with it. And you've been doing a very specific thing with it, brought lawfulness to it and so part of your dream is you cannot abuse these laws. That's why you call them laws. Right? For instance, you cannot go faster than the speed of light or you'll die. You're following what I am saying?

Q: Yes.

R: All of that will be abused.

Q: When you thought you were about to hit a car, were you practising? Not wanting this to be true? Or did grace take over?

R: Well, at that point you don't know Who You are, so you don't know how it worked. This is why people keep practising things like meditation. Because they think there's a technique to get to It. And I keep on saying it doesn't work like that. It happens when it happens, because it happens through The Will of God. No one awakens that God doesn't know of. And no one knows when the moment of their Awakening is going to happen, but everyone chooses it.

Jesus says, "I don't know until I am told." And, he says that he is the first one that knows for everyone. And, then he sees you through that. And, he's not talking about just Christians. He said everyone, because he was the first one that completed it.

Q: But you can't collapse time.

R: Yes, time can be collapsed, because there is no law to it.

Q: But it has nothing to do with a moment you choose or have chosen...

R: It does, but like now you get back to somebody saying, "What do you mean, choosing unconsciously?" Well, it's not magic. OK? Everybody say, I am Home now. Perhaps everybody say that, I am Home now... You're not in time and space any longer? Hello, is your awareness that you're not here any longer?

Q: No.

R: So, it's not just saying something. Well, how about you say, "I am Home now," like you did a mantra, would you then be Home?

Q: No.

R: Or, would you at some point be so tired, you go, "Time to go to work now, the hell with this I am Home stuff. I come back to that later."

* * *

R: I am really a tough guy to deal with, am I not? I keep taking all these pearls away from you, don't I? I keep on trying to give you diamonds to replace your pearls, but you really love your pearls.

Q: One thing in this is that you can meditate or you use a mantra to get rid of it.

R: Use a mantra to get rid of what?

Q: To get rid of the mantra.

R: You use the mantra to get rid of the mantra?

Q: Yes.

R: Whose idea is that?

Q: You know whose idea that is.

R: It's not one I have anything to do with. Do you want to know what ideas I have to do with? Listen to what I say. That's what I have to do with.

Q: But you also want to get rid of the illusion, that evil come out of it.

R: No, I don't want to get rid of the illusion, I want to get rid of *you*!

Q: Thank you. I agree with you.

R: You see, I'm trying to tell you that the illusion does not exist. Not existing is what you call an illusion. So, I don't need to get rid of it. It's like I'm not going to destroy something that does not exist. That's my point about God. He is not a destroyer. You don't destroy something that is not there. God is so busy, Perfection is so busy being Perfection, It could care less about an illusion. It's never going to enter into Perfection. The idea is never going to enter in there. It always remains separate, because that's what it is. It's an idea of separation. It's not going to enter into Perfection, because Perfection cannot embrace it in any way whatsoever; that's where your saving grace is. OK? Now, all I am saying is, there is a necessity to admit that the you that is perceiving, must be the illusion. There is a need to admit that. And, it does no good whatsoever to deny that you're dreaming, while you're dreaming. Because that won't help it be undone. That's the difficult part that you have. Because, once you recognize and begin to hear this message, you want to be the innocent thing. "I am really glad I am Home in Heaven. Don't talk to me about problems, baby. We are all Home in Heaven."

And then you keep doing the things that you do to maintain the illusion and that's not helpful. What do you do? You keep saying, "Other people are doing things to me. If so and so did not do that, I'd be OK. If so and so didn't do that I'd have a better job, I'd have more money, I'd have less kids or more kids," or however you want to do that. It's always something. It's always because of someone else. You don't want to take the responsibility yourself. And of course, if somebody runs into you, you can say, somebody ran into me. And I say, well, why do you want that? Why do you want that to happen? And he goes, "I don't know why, I don't know why that guy did that, he's probably drunk or something. I hate it when drunk people get out on the highway."

And then you tell your story about how you're functioning in the world and what you like about it and what you don't like about it. And then you expect a person you're talking to, to just join in, right, because it's their illusion too. Hello? And then, if they are friends, they are supposed to talk about their part of the illusion, because that's what friends are for, right? The ones who help you verify the illusion. The more willing they are to do that, the more friendly they are. But, meet somebody that won't do that with you, you don't want to be around them. Not fun being around them then. "I can't even talk about the things I like to talk about, because they are not even there to talk to me about it. I know where they think they are; they probably think they're not even here or something, you know. I talk to them and they just sit there. And then, when I got done talking, I wonder what did I talk to you for, you don't even talk back. Can't you at least tell me what you think about it?"

Yes, I did and it's an illusion.

"Oh God, here he goes again. How do I deal with you?" Don't deal with me. "No, come on, really, tell me, how, how can I deal with you?" Don't deal with me. I want to see Reality. Use me that way and you will succeed. It's inevitable. But use me as a part of your problems and you will be guaranteed to have more problems, because you get the result of your thoughts. The difficulty is when somebody does something that, obviously, is not loving. But how am I going to see that as a loving person? That's the difficulty, isn't it? Like, take for instance, we'll use Jesus again because he's really a great model, isn't he? OK? Who looks at the soldiers that did all that and sees The Christ? Because, when you hear the story, you're looking at guys that didn't know. They weren't nice guys, were they? And they did this thing. Who sees them as The Christ? You follow what I am saying? Well, Jesus didn't actually see them as The Christ, but he relieved them from the idea that he himself is a body. So, he relieved them from what they thought was going on in their minds. Because, what they were thinking is, that he is something that they can harm. He didn't see that they were actually The Christ, until he knew Himself the fullness of being The Christ, which didn't occur until his Resurrection was fulfilled in him, when he realized that the body is nothing more than an illusion. Until then he knew that it was not The Truth of him, because he had been shown that this is an illusion. But, he didn't know until then that the idea of having a body and not having a body was of his own making. He knew what he was told and he knew what was revealed and he knew the Power of the Creator.

Q: Are you saying that part of the practice for me is to see everyone, all the time, as The Christ?

R: That's called forgiveness. Right? If you don't, you see them as something they're not and that's not forgiving, because you're the one that asks them to play all those parts. See, everybody has to come to the point where they see that it's only ever happening to them. But, that's like saying that everybody has to know there's only One Mind. Yes, at some point you'll have to know that there is only One Mind, because That is Reality. Does it have to play out the way it played out for me? I don't know and, in fact, I don't care. What I care about is that everyone comes to the point of accepting. Right? That it's only happening to you. Everything that is happening is only happening to you. So that you stop saying, "Yeah, but how about that and how about that?" And then you get into, "Well, I am doing OK, but how come they're not doing OK if there's just me?" And then you have to remember what you have thought you have accomplished. You think you've accomplished being separate from everybody. Now, you think they have their own free will and he has his free will and she has her free will and how am I going to deal with all these people with their free will? I don't mind letting God get me, you know, grasp me by the throat, rip me, put me back into Heaven again, but how about all these other people? See, there's still the idea of all that separateness in there and you suffer because of that. What does Jesus tell you how it is that you become a teacher of God? What does he say?

Q: One moment, for one moment you realize that your interest and those of others are actually the same.

R: You become a teacher of God the moment that you have an experience where what's in someone else's best interest, is the same as yours. Then the idea of the gap between you has been closed. And, you actually see. It's kind of like saying, you know… How about when you see somebody in pain. Do you feel the pain or do you feel there's somebody in pain?

Q: I feel the pain.

R: OK, isn't that the same, when you feel your brother's pain, you're not separate from your brother? How about the joy? How about when you feel your brother's joy? Or…

Q: It's very hard for me…

R: Yes, "Get out of here with your joy. Hey, hey, I want my crap. Hey, hey, I hate it when happy people come around. You know, I hate happy people, because they're so happy. They are just happy. How come? I don't get it. Don't they know about all the problems in this world? If they had my problems, they would not be so happy."

It's kind of like that, isn't it? No, it's exactly like that. It's funny, you see, and that's the temptation. There's a necessity to recognize that, just because there's a thought in your mind, it doesn't mean anything. You think because the thought is in there you have to do something with it. Accept it, reject it, whatever. It doesn't matter, but you think because it's in your mind, you have to do something with it. And that's not true.

Q: If I feel hurt because I think that somebody is doing

something...

R: To You Who is Something That can't be hurt!

Q: To Me Who is Something That can't be hurt...?

R: Yes.

Q: If I just let that be, will it disappear?

R: Of course it will, if you just let it be.

Q: I don't have to fight against it?

R: Oh, definitely, don't fight it!

Q: That's a relief.

R: I don't tell anybody to fight with anything, that's not my program. You don't fight with your thoughts, you don't fight with images. This is an image, you're an image. You're a thought. Why would I want to fight with that?

Q: I can just have another thought?

R: Well, you will have another thought.

Q: Yes?

R: That's a guarantee; that's what happens in minds. Thoughts come, thoughts go, thoughts come, thoughts go, thoughts come, thoughts go. They hang around a little bit longer in time when you do something with them, but if you don't do anything, they'll just come and go. And they'll come and go and they'll come and go and they'll come and go. You choose what to do with those thoughts when they enter your mind.

Q: Can you choose to follow one thought or the other thought?

R: Yes. That's what I am telling you.

Q: So, you wait for the thought of forgiveness?

R: Well, when you're practising forgiveness or you're

practising wanting to be with Spirit, Spirit's Thoughts. You hear thoughts that you know do not come from Spirit. You can even recognize where they're coming from and then you just let them go. It works like a magnet. It'll draw your attention to the Thoughts that are coming from Spirit. This way you begin to have an active relationship with Spirit that leads you out of the illusion. You have to understand... I mean, listen to this guys, you have to hear what I am saying. Spirit will put Thoughts into your mind and bring your awareness to them, because its intent is to lead you out of the illusion. What I mean by leading you out of an illusion, is that It's going to lead you into an experience where you recognize you're already out, because You're not something that's in an illusion. OK? It's going to bring you to that Awareness. If you don't listen to that Voice, if you don't listen to those Thoughts, you will not be thoughtless. You'll be listening to another system of thought, that is doing nothing but verifying the illusion, and you choose in every moment of time which one you're going to listen to. There is not one moment of time that you're not choosing which thoughts you're going to value.

That's why I am saying, if ego's thoughts come through and you don't give them value, they will be replaced. Maybe by another ego thought and if you don't do anything, maybe another thought will come, maybe it will be another ego thought. You have to remember also that Spirit doesn't give you thoughts about action. I can tell you how many people want to argue with me about this. Spirit only gives you Thoughts that God would share with You, because that's Its purpose. Its purpose is to have you turn to what you can share with God, because that's the True You. You share Everything with God. Can you hear me? Spirit wants you to remember You are something that shares Everything with God. Its intent is not to get you into activities of the illusion, because It knows when You share what You can share with God, You will be Love. And when You are Love, whatever you do in the illusion, while you're still there, will come from Love. So, It's not concerned with what you do here; ego is.

You know how you love to say Spirit told you to do this and that in the world? Crap! Not true. No, Spirit tells you what you can share with God. When you're with That, if you need to do something here, from that clarity, from Love, you do whatever it is that you do. If you do crappy things and say Spirit told you to do it, it just means you need to get more clarity on the voices that you're listening to. OK? And that's why it's really good when these things come up and you're tempted, that you just take your hands off. Just ask yourself, is this something that God will share with me, something I could share with God? Is this something God will share with me? When you get deeper into your transformation, you're more vigilant, present for what's going on with your mind. And then, as these thoughts come in – whether it's temptation to be angry with somebody or upset with somebody or friendly with somebody or whatever – you'll literally have a moment where you're asking that question of yourself, is this something that God would share with me? And that's your guideline.

Q: Does it mean there are no thoughts anymore and you're just filled with Love?

R: There still will be Thoughts, but Love will be the Source of that Thought. It could be as simple as what I said last night. Any time of the day this energy package that you call Rananda can get this Insertion, this Thought. There is no reasoning with It; It's just a Thought and the Thought says: put on your coat and go out. Or it might not be wintertime, so it's not a coat, it's just: go out. OK? And then I'll do it, because I have learned to be true to what occurs to me, because that's the way Spirit begins to have freedom to allow you to really undo the illusion. So, it could be any time of the day, meaning three, four, five in the morning, it could be raining, snowing, it could be whatever, but when it happens it happens and I just go with it. I could be lying in bed under the covers, all nice and warm and it's really cold outside and all of a sudden a Thought occurs to me, and I go, OK, because I've learned. And then, when I do it, all kinds of amazing things happen. Usually the first thing that happens, I go out of the front door and I can only go right or left, because there's a building right in front and I don't know which way to go, because I don't know where I am going. So I wait for the feeling of where I am going and then I have to remember how to move my legs, which is not always easy. People see me as I stumble down the streets. I probably kind of look like I was out drinking all night. But I am not in a trance or something like that, I am just waiting, allowing myself to be led. And that's a practice and I can be brought to all kinds of people. There are people out on your streets at all kinds of hours and sometimes, when I walk down the streets, there'd be people who are just crying and crying and crying. And somehow I got led there. And sometimes there are people that are really sick, you know what I mean? Really sick, cold, pneumonia, whatever and they're out on your streets. I get led to these people only because I listen to the Voice that wants me to be helpful. But if I was running my own program I'd say how cold it is. I'm in bed and it's warm, can't you get somebody else? I mean, take one of my angels or something, you know, I'll be OK, I am just here in bed and I don't need an angel for a while. Take two if you like, but I am not going anywhere.

This is the fun of having the Holy Spirit be able to communicate through your mind, because, you see, in my mind I am dedicated to my Creator. And I remind this mind,

Father, into Thy Hands...; Father I am really only here to be helpful." I remind myself, you understand, even with those words I remind myself that that's why I am here, because sometimes I have no idea why I am here. I don't look to ego, because I know why ego thinks I am here. And so I turn to Spirit and I say, "What is it, why I am here, what do you want, what's this all about?" And then the memory package comes in and then I begin to function in that way again. That's the way it is every morning, or if I was up early in the middle of the night.

That's the way I function. I don't know how you function. I don't particularly care how you function. You shouldn't care how you function. I am suggesting that what you should care about is your connection with your Creator and then it will all unfold in whatever way. Don't try to imitate me or Jesus or anybody else. It's not about the imitation, it's about the realness of that connection and then how that connection plays out in you specifically. But remember, it will be Love or you're listening to the voice that you're hoping is Spirit, but is not.

Q: I want to be sure I understand this listening to the Holy Spirit. I do it over and over again. I practise listening to the Holy Spirit for what I am supposed to do, so I just ask and wait. The other day I asked Holy Spirit, "Am I supposed to visit my brother?" A really direct question and the answer was, "No." And I asked, "Why not?" Because my brother really likes me to visit him. And there was this thought, as long as you see him as some lonely guy, you won't be helpful, so don't go. I am not sure if it is Spirit or ego.

R: Well, things can be almost anything. You also have what you call Masters. Those are parts of You that are no longer bound by the world, and there are angels that can also connect with you and they represent entities that are all of your goodness. So, when you turn for help, you can have input from many different ideas. All I am trying to tell you is that the Holy Spirit does not tell you to do something in the world. Its sole job is to connect with you as to what is shared with God. Then you have Masters like Jesus and so on and so forth and they can tell you where to go get the underwear you are missing.

Q: Is it helpful to turn to...?

R: To find your underwear? Sometimes!

Q: To Masters or angels for help?

R: Yes, of course it's helpful. The thing is, you have to know which is which, because the ego is going to tell you it's a master, too. It's just not going to say it's master ego. See, you can have all kinds of voices. Go to the hospitals, there are people that hear voices all over the place. You probably have a whole section of the hospital for them.

Q: So, what you're saying is that when it is specific it cannot be the Holy Spirit.

R: That's right. Not specific. If it is encouraging you to go into an activity of the world it's not the Holy Spirit, that's what I am saying. But I am not saying that it can't be an angel that's doing that, or it cannot be a Master that's doing that, or it cannot be ego that's doing that. But I am saying, it's not the Holy Spirit.

Q: So, what's the best practice then for me? To just wait a little longer so that I am sure it's the Holy Spirit?

R: Well, if you're talking about that the Holy Spirit told you to go out the door and you go and wait around to find out if the Holy Spirit really told you to go out the door, that's a waste of time. I just told you, the Holy Spirit is not going to tell you to walk out the door. But, the Holy Spirit can take you into a recognition of your connection with God, and then, from that place of Love, you might walk out the door, because Love Itself, You, your Self are connected with everyone. And in that connection, through your subconscious in Everything, you literally get the feeling to get up and go out. And then, who knows what's going to happen?

Q: So, it's on the level of feeling, not on the level of thinking?

R: Well, you know, I use the word "feeling", but I really shouldn't. However, that's the way you guys like to talk. It felt like I should do that, but it's not really a feeling. If you really want to try to stay clear with the words that you are using, you wouldn't use the word "feeling". But there's a recognition. See, the way I explain what happens with me is exactly what I said earlier, it occurred to me. That's the only way that I can express it, because I don't know any other way of expressing it. Things occur to me and I have learned to be true to that. And it is easy to tell when the ego is doing it. So, the majority of what's occurring in your mind is just occurring with your connection with Spirit. And, as you get these different moments of inspiration, what occurs to you is what will happen. And you don't have to look for reasons, because that's what the ego does. It wants to know, why did you do that, tell me your logic so I can understand how to come to that conclusion, too. My mind is not working that way. It occurred to me, that's why I did it. My logic is, I pay attention to what occurs to me. And you might or might not like what occurs to me. That is not my concern, what you like or dislike; it's not my concern in anyway whatsoever.

My concern is that I keep paying attention to Spirit. And somewhere I know that you'll join me in that, because you won't be happy until you do. So, somewhere you're going to let go of everything that's causing you pain and suffering.

You'll begin to be with that too, because what occurs in that sense is always of Love, because everything that's not of Love is always justified. Can you understand what I mean with "justified"? You always have a reason for why you do it. That's the ego. But Spirit never has a justification, because It's always just encouraging you to share with God. It needs no justification, because sharing with God is the full justification, the act of it. Can you hear what I am saying?

Q: So, when you're with other people...

R: What other people? I only do one thing.

Q: Follow...

R: Yes, but I only do one thing with the people. I remember Who They are.

Q: And then is their healing natural?

R: Absolutely! All healing is remembering Who You are.

Q: But then it's actually your healing...

R: Of course it is! If I didn't need to be healed I wouldn't be here! It's the willingness, you see, that's all that's required. Who's willing to get up in the middle of the night, because there is some urge? Some urge to go out and find out why you have the urge to go out. Who follows that? How about if, now you heard the story, you went out and you didn't see anybody? Would you start looking for somebody, because you did do something with that urge? How do you know? Maybe your energy, your presence just needed to walk by somebody's house. See, how do you know? How the hell do you know what's going on? There's so much more going on than what you're aware of. I just don't do any of the judgments on that anymore.

14

GOD IS A FACT

Your Presence is Enough / Football / A Course In Miracles /
Part of the Solution / Change of Mind / Learn through Love

R: So, it is surrender, in the face of something saying it's very hard, in the face of something telling you, yes, what gain are you going to get out of it, or, what is somebody going to think? or... You know, in the face of all the reasons, it's being true, that's what it's all about. And sometimes you are mistaken as to what you're being true to. Well, just learn, forgive and learn and move on and don't let it happen again. And if it happens again, just learn, oh man, it happened again, I was mistaken again, somehow I keep getting into this pattern. Right? So, I was really sure It was Spirit, or whatever. OK, so you're being trained to know what is Spirit and what is not. But learn! Don't waste all your pain, your suffering and time by not learning. Don't waste it. Right? Hello? Don't waste it! Let it be a lesson that you learn, so that you don't have to learn from your pain and suffering any longer and you can just follow the path of Love and let Love teach you. Learn the lessons of Love, not the lessons of pain and suffering, which eventually are going to tell you to learn the lessons of Love. Hello?

Are you OK? Isn't it nice when you're with Spirit? Spirit doesn't worry about anything. Spirit doesn't go, "Oh, I hope there's enough Light here." Right? Spirit doesn't think, It doesn't say, "Move your head a little bit more to the right there, up there, no, a little more, up, up, there you go, you got it, you got it, OK, that's it." Spirit doesn't do any of that kind of stuff, Spirit just radiates full on. Spirit is really cool like that.

Q: [Laughs.]

R: Spirit says, "You can't do anything wrong, I'm with you!" How about that? Would that take a little trust? All the people that believe in techniques will teach you that there's a right way and a wrong way to do the technique, won't they? Hello, is that true? Is that true?

[Audience.] Yes. Yes.

R: Yes? OK. But Spirit isn't concerned about any of that. It just wants your willingness. Do you know what I'm saying? It's so strange that you have got to do it right, you know, and there are limitations on it. And it's so defined, isn't it? It's so structured. Reality is not like that at all. Reality is complete Freedom. Complete Freedom! And, complete trust that in that Freedom nothing can go wrong, because there's no such thing as wrong. There's no such thing as something that can be harmed. There's just the joy and the freedom of creating. Here everybody wants to tell you the right and the wrong way of doing something. "No, don't meditate like that, no, no, no, that's not right, no, do it this way." If you are going to ride the bicycle, don't try to sit with your back to the front.

[Audience laughing.]

R: It's fun to play around with the world. Did you guys ever sit on your bicycle backwards and then, then... See? It's really hard to keep your balance; that was the hardest. Without hands was not so bad, but sitting on backwards, that was really hard. That way I fell more than with anything else.

Q: Can I ask something?

R: Oh, yeah, yeah.

Q: Yeah? [Laughs.] What can I ask of the Holy Spirit? You said no things in this world. Can I ask to remember God?

R: It's the Holy Spirit's job to lead you inward to a meeting place, where it will be revealed to you that You are The Christ, You are The Buddha, You are Spirit. OK? That's his job. But you won't want to do that if you've got fear of God. So, part of his job in leading you to this holy place of communion is to help you let go of your idea of the need for fear in association with the realization of Who and What It is You are, The Truth or whatever spiritual concepts that you might use. Literally finding your Self in the Presence of Perfection. Releasing all the guilt that you hold on to, that you've accomplished something that you have not actually accomplished. But you believe that you do and have. So, Holy Spirit's job is to help you with that. Well, what better way of knowing that You didn't accomplish anything than having You share ideas with God, because God doesn't see You having accomplished anything. See, that's why it's not about doing anything in the world. It's about You realizing that what You share with God has nothing to do with the world. And as you begin to value that, you'd want to meet in a holy place with The Christ. You would want to know that that is true, these ideas, that Relationship between You and God. See, that's why the focus is on that. As you begin to focus on that, and you recognize how really beautiful it is to be loving and kind, then you just act that way in the world, because it's natural. Not because somebody told you you should, or because it's more Christian-like, or part of the ten commandments, or what the Koran says, or what the Bhagavad Gita insists on, or something like that. It's just..., you find it your natural expression because you've been dipped into the frequency and recognition of Love Itself.

Then it's great! It's preferred. So, you become natural, and natural is what God created. It just happens. That's why I say it occurs; it just occurs. It's like if you had a waterfall, you wouldn't go, "Why does that water fall?" It just does, because that's what waterfalls do. Here there's this thing called gravity, right, and you would try to explain it. But for me it is just because that's the way it is. And you're going to find out that that's true about You, you're just going to be the way You are, because That's What You are. And that's enough; You don't need more than That. And eventually, what you will learn is, that in any given moment your Presence is all that is required of You! Your Presence is required! It's all that's required of You in any given moment! It's enough, because You are What Love is and all that's required in an illusion of pain and suffering, is for Love to be there and it will change everything. Your Presence is enough!

Q: And Your Presence has nothing to do with your body?

R: Well, it does if you think you're inside of one. But, you know, my Presence is enough because I'm not inside of a body. So, I can do things like watch television, hurricanes and all these different things happening, and some strange guy pulling a gun and shooting all these kids in the school or whatever. I can watch this on television and I'm there with my Presence, not in the belief that people die, but in my Presence, and many people have the value of my Presence being there. I don't sit there and go, "Oh, yeah, this is a terrible thing and oh, yeah," looking at all those people dying and so on. They're telling me, they're telling the world that. I'm sitting there going, "Oh, man, they're still telling this story, and I tell a different story." Because, if I don't, who will? It's my world! So, you can be an agent for healing or you can verify the illusion and get the result of that. And, it's a choice. OK?

You can either play the role of the problem solver or you can be the Son of God. But those are the only two roles that you get. That's why you have a choice. To solve problems all day long day after day, see problems that need to be solved day after day, or be the Son of God. And the Son of God is not solving anything; He's just being What the Son of God is, just being That. Not out looking to solve problems, not looking for problems to solve. He's just being What He is. And whatever is happening, He recognizes that What He is, is What's been called for. So, it's natural. Not working on Himself, just being Himself. He doesn't have to figure out What that Self is, because Holy Spirit is constantly revealing It. Isn't this a nice program? I mean, if you like some other prime kind of program, don't get involved in this. Because this is a very specific program. This is the one that relieves you from all the things that you think you need to do to be what you hope to become, because You already are What You hope to become. This is a very different program. It's very fast too; it's a very fast program. You think it's going really slow, but I guarantee you, man, you're passing through lifetimes of stuff. Until you have no more need for lifetimes. That's the program. Isn't that good news?

Q: Yes.

R: Eh?

Q: It's a good program.

R: It's a good program. It's the only one that worked, in fact!

Q: So, tune in?

R: Yes, tune in. It's broadcasting 24 hours a day, seven days a week, every year. Year after year, till there is none. Isn't that good news?

Q: Yes.

R: Yes.

R: So, remember, Holy Spirit is there to lead you to the recognition of your Perfection. And Jesus has demonstrated that the path that the Holy Spirit leads you through, is a path of Love. And through that Love there is no judgment about your brother being anything other than What You are. It's revealing to you that What You are is Love and therefore That's What your brother is, too. So, if your brother is not demonstrating Love, then he's calling out to You for your Love. And, judging him as being less than loving, is not a response to somebody who calls out for Love. And that's perhaps something that you need to learn. And if he's not doing that, then he's sharing his Love with You; he's just telling You, I'm willing to share Love with You. And those are the only two things that are ever going on. Your brother is there loving and you're sharing; or he's telling You how he needs Love. That's your job. It's simple. It's when you start seeing something else going on that it gets complicated. That's why I can watch television and either see that something is sharing Love with me, or it's a call for Love. I see people that come to my apartment sometimes and I've got the news on – because that's mainly what's going on. If it's not news, it's football. But that's because I've heard the news over and over and over, because they just keep repeating it. So, every now and then I have to see people just kicking a ball around, you know...

[Audience laughing.]

R: ... let it become playful. And not only that. I get to have contact with thousands of people at one time that way. It's kind of really nice. I like it when they all gather 30, 40, 50 thousand people in a stadium like that. It's concentrated. I can really reach a lot of people all at once...

Q: Are you watching football for that reason?

R: Of course! What do you think I'm here for? Why do you think you find me in your dream? What do you see me doing in your dream? What purpose have you given me? And for you I can't be more nor less than what you think. I haven't just come for Holland.

Q: But why are you in Holland, then?

R: For you.

[Audience laughing.]

R: Wouldn't that be enough? I mean, wouldn't that be enough if you actually thought, gee, he's here for me! Wouldn't that be enough for you?

* * *

Q: Can I ask a question? You are talking about the Holy Spirit, about Jesus, and you're also teaching out of *A Course In Miracles*, but many of the stories of Jesus are in the Bible. Why are you not teaching from the Bible instead of from *A Course In Miracles*?

R: Well, do you want to know The Truth?

Q: Yes.

R: I don't like the Bible.

[Audience laughing.]

R: The reason I don't like it is, because there are too many ideas about it that I don't need. See, when I teach that my Presence is enough, I really mean that. And I'm not interested in people going to what they call the Old Testament. Why do they call it the Old Testament, by the way? And why do they have a New Testament? And why do they have the latest testament, which is not in the Bible? That's in *A Course In Miracles*. It's the modern day testament of Jesus Christ of Nazareth, that's *A Course In Miracles*. Why should I go and deal with all of that stuff when you've got the modern day teachings available to you? Every one of them had a corrective pattern in it. The Old Testament corrected the mind of man at that particular time. And it was really primitive in the sense that men were out raping women and burning villages and pillaging, and stuff. So, you needed stories and morality to try to get people just to stop killing one another, you know, and settle down a little bit, so that you can be at one place, so that we can reach you. That's the Old Testament. And then you have the New Testament, which is, you know, the necessity for one of us to demonstrate in the illusion the completion of it. That became the story of Jesus in the New Testament. OK? When Jesus went through the completion he had an incredible surprise. When he was completed, You were already there. But he didn't tell you that, because he didn't know at that particular point. So, there was a need for something like *A Course In Miracles* to come in for Jesus to say, "Hey look, I completed this; when I did, You did. Of course I didn't tell you that then, because I wasn't completed then. But I did tell you I was going to send Somebody to help you after I left, because there were even a lot of things I was aware of that you didn't want to hear at that time. And here it is." So, that's the modern day testament, *A Course In Miracles*. I'm much more at ease using the New Testament with whatever corrections needed to be made as far as understanding is concerned, and *A Course In Miracles*, in which I have found nothing that needs to be corrected. And believe me, I spent years looking for it! It's true, I spent years looking for parts that were mistaken in *A Course In Miracles*, because then I could be OK being what I thought I was and would not have to accept that then, because there were errors in it. And I spent years trying to find the loopholes in *A Course In*

Miracles! Eventually I surrendered! Because I couldn't find any!

Q: Thank you.

R: There were days when I used to teach the *Bhagavad Gita*. Yes, this was before I woke up. The only thing that I did not teach was the Koran. But of all the major religious works, I've taught a lot of them, because there is the need to connect with God in all of them. And that's really what I want to teach. I want you to know that GOD IS A FACT, not a fantasy! Not a hope, not a wish, but a fact! And that the path of Love, because God is Love, is The Truth. It is the way and it is what life is. In fact, and this is another thing that I've been emphasizing recently, because it occurs to me that there's a need to emphasize this, I think you get brought into an experience that is really going to surprise you. OK? And it goes like this: GOD IS LOVE! See, that's such a simple statement, isn't it? Three words. And you actually think you know what that means. I'm telling you that you don't. Because, when you experience Love, you don't think you experience God. And, you keep saying, "I don't know God, I want to know God." But, you insist you know Love. And if I ask, "Is God Love?" You say, "Yes, God is Love." And then I say, "Well then, why do you keep saying you don't know God? When you know Love, you will know God, because God is Love!" There's not some God somewhere and Love is not there. God is Love Itself, God radiates Himself as Everything that He creates. God radiates Love and all of Creation is Love. Can you hear what I'm saying? But somehow that gets lost; it gets lost in how you function from day to day to day. God is Love! Holy Spirit wants you to connect with What You can share with God. What can You share with God?

Q: Love.

R: Love.

Q: Because That's What You are?

R: Because That's What You are and That's What God is and there is nothing else. That is all of Creation, It is all of God, It is all of Perfection. That's why you think you know what Love is here, but you don't, because this is an illusion. And I tell you, when you experience Love, you do not experience time and space. And you do have experiences of how you've connected with another being and time and space were suspended and you weren't really aware of what was going on in the world any longer; you were so connected with them. That was the closest you got to what Love really is. And believe me, I keep telling you, you can't know God alone. I don't care what your mantra is. You need to join with what you're separate from to know God. Because that's where you know Love.

Q: That's why you remember someone else as Love?

R: As Self, as Love, exactly! That's why it's about joining; not hiding in your closet with your meditations and stuff. It's about the passion of joining, where Love is! You guys are so afraid of everybody that you try to stay by yourself as much as you can. And, it's not about whether you are with people or not. That's not what I'm trying to say. I'm trying to talk about that openness to join, to go beyond your bubbles of self-identity and definitions, because God is Love. If you really want God, you let Love in. If you really want Love, you cannot leave God out of it. And if you want God and Love, you're going to have to stop your judgments upon yourself, your brother and God; otherwise it's never going to happen. And apparently, since we say we're lost, we have to remember. And the way you remember is by practising, training your mind to remember what you want. And as you remember what you want, and you turn to the Holy Spirit, the Holy Spirit shows you. All It's doing is waiting for your willingness and then It's right there to show you. And, as you connect with It, You be It. And, as You are being It, that's how you stop using the world and circumstances to define You. You bring You to all of that. And, as you do that, that will be rearranged, because it is the result of your thinking, And as You bring Love to it, it will change as a result of your thinking and in this case your Being, because your Being is Love. Then You become the solution and You're no longer part of the problem. That's something that you guys need to begin to learn. Once you start walking this path that I'm teaching, you're no longer part of the problem. You are part of the solution and you need to see that. You need to embrace it and you need to allow it to begin to be radiated from You. You're not part of the problem any longer. You're on the path that is the solution. You're on the path of Love. You're on the path of Remembering The Truth. And, don't be concerned about moments of losing faith, losing the idea that you're on the path, not being completely loving. Don't worry about any of that. You're on the path. Part of the path is that you come off and come on and come off and come on and come off and come on, until you're done doing that. Don't be concerned about it. Remember you are the solution. That's the program, you remembering You are the solution. You're not the problem any longer. OK? Can you hear me?

Q: Yes.

R: Is it OK to be part of the solution instead of the problem? It's really important that you hear that. Because that's where guilt and all that stuff comes in the problem. But, when you begin to associate yourself as the solution, what you verify strengthens. So, more and more you will be willing to be the solution. And we know what the solution is, don't we? It's Love. So, you find yourself more and more being The Love. Then all you need to add to that is what I already have given you, that every moment is either somebody willing to share that Love with You, or the calling out for your Love. They're in pain and they're in suffering and they're hurting; they're in anguish and they're calling out for your Love. That's not the time to turn your back on them. That's the time to remember Who They really are, to love Them. And that's the way You love Them, by remembering Who They really are, rather than seeing them as somebody that has a lot of problems, is in anguish, in pain and suffering. You see that your brother thinks that, but you're not supposed to think that. You're supposed to remember Who They are, you're supposed to remember Who You want them to be. Don't be confused by what they're telling you. Be connected with what Spirit is telling you. That's what gets you through. OK? It's really a simple program, isn't it, when you look at it. Right? It's really simple. Not a lot is being asked of you; very little is being asked of you. But that very little is supposed to be applied throughout all of time. So, you don't have a lot to remember. You just have such a little, little thing to remember. So, the idea that it's hard doesn't make sense, because you've got so little to remember.

[Audience laughing.]

R: It's the willingness to be with that little part. Because, the big part is being played by God. Holding it all together, Source of Love Itself, the big part is already being played and being played really well. Your little part is the one that you need to get trained in. "I have to remember that this is not real and that I'm the Son of God, and the Son of God is Love! OK. So, I have to remember this is an illusion and I came to bring Love here." It's just really simple. Don't worry about all the other intellectual stuff that everybody loves to get confused about. Just let it be really simple and you'll find the answer to all of that. But it won't be in words. It will be in your own Presence of The Truth of how awesome You are to be Everything. Don't you think, being aware that You are Everything would be much more fun than trying to figure out the answers of the illusion? How did this happen? How did that happen? What's going on on the other side of the universe? Well, you are going to have to be there to know. "Yes, but I can't get there if I'm going to die on the way there." Yep, that won't work, you'll have to be something different than that. "Yes, but this is what I am." OK. See, you're going to have to change your mind if you want the entirety of Eternity, Which is the only thing you can have if you want any Eternity. You will have to have a change of mind! You cannot get there following the laws that you believe in. Including the ones that say you can die and then get there. That's not going to happen either. Death does not get you entrance into Life. Hopefully you're finding that good news.

Thank you for coming. It's been another one of those enlightening evenings, where we get to look for greater and greater clarity. What you hear me doing here this evening, is what I used to do for years all by myself in my bedroom. I talked to the walls, just like I'm talking to you. I would look at ideas and I would see, and I would just talk, I would talk to the walls, and I would say, "Well, if that's true..." I was searching in my mind for What Truth would have to be like, you know, and you can only go so far until you reach the point where you go, "Yes, but these are still just thoughts about It." So, no matter, for all those years that I was doing that, I was getting clarity on concepts, but I was still devoid of the Awakening. Until one day my teacher said to me, [Rananda laughs.] "You can leave this world right now, right?" He called me Clark and he said, "Right, Clark?" And he looked at me like that and I'd go, "Yep." And then he said, "Death doesn't make it possible, right?" And I'd go, "That's right!" Absolutely sure of that teaching. And he'd kind of look at me for a moment, and then he would go on. And then, eventually, after the second day when he looked at me I realized he was challenging me to undergo the experience and that, until I did, I wouldn't be happy. It's not enough to just know those words and agree with the concept. It's the fulfillment of it, where what you want is fulfilled. And then it started to happen. Why? Because there was willingness to go beyond accepting the concept, to undergoing the experience. Did the fear leave me? No, in fact it got worse. [Rananda laughs.] As it was happening, it got worse. I even tried to die, to prove that there is no such thing as Life Eternal. But the beautiful thing about that is that once you have accepted the teaching, the teaching is there. This is what Jesus calls the borderland, where the attempt to die is there, but The Truth that death does not exist, is also there with it, in concept. OK? Because death is just a concept. You think it's real, but it's just a concept. Just like the idea of Reality is just an idea. There is a place in your mind where both of those ideas, both thought systems are available. And, not until then do you actually see that there is an alternative, that all of the ideas of differences is just one idea. There's not lots of ideas. One idea; it's an idea of differences. And then there's an idea and that idea is Perfection. So, until then you don't see that there is an alternative. You think all the alternative is in differences.

Q: It sounds like it is very easy to let go of differences.

R: Once you see. But, without seeing, you don't even think you're letting go of anything, because it's all differences. Then you still have all those other differences. You don't see that you're letting go of one thing and when you let go of that one thing, all differences are let go of. Until then it is what you call difficult, because of what you're doing in your mind. That's one of the ideas. So it has to play out for you. But when you see it's no different than anything else, then you see that your self-identity and everything else are all the same and all just come forth from one thought system. The only alternative to that is the one that says that You are Eternal. Now you can see. Because, when I was trying to die, the thought kept coming to me, you can't die. And the body was dying, it was saying, "Oh yeah," and then the thought was, yes, but there is no such thing as death! They just wouldn't stop, you know. Spirit didn't stop. Thank God, it didn't stop. But the body continued to try to prove it. But, because it's not provable, Spirit was always going to win. But the body did its thing. All the way to the point where it was done and knew it had lost, it tried something else. It said to me, "You know what, there's something worse than death! Yeah, yeah, that's right. You could be crippled and not able to die, how would you like that? Crippled is bad enough, but how about not being able to die, so that you're forever in the pain and suffering of being crippled?" And then I laughed. Yes, because I had been warned. I had been warned that there is no such thing as eternal in an illusion. So when it tried that, I just laughed. But my body – you have to understand – my body was trying to fulfill that thought, because that was the pattern, right? You have thoughts and you try to fulfill them. That's the pattern. Try to be a human and there you are, you're trying it. So, my body was playing it out and it was an extreme agony, a pain. And then it just stopped; it just finished. It had tried it's best and it lost and all that was left was Spirit. So, how that will look for you, I don't know how it will look for you.

Q: Can I ask a question?

R: Is it an important question?

Q: I was just thinking about what you were telling. We can turn disease into a lesson, for instance.

R: Yes, it's a lesson that it has nothing to do with Reality, and then, who will be threatened? Just the ego.

Q: Yes.

R: Yes, you can learn from your pain and suffering. But the only thing you're really going to learn from pain and suffering is that the path of learning from Love is a lot more pleasurable and faster, and, because you're learning from Love, full of Love. With the other one you're full of pain and suffering. "Full of pain and suffering, full of Love, hmm, which one will I want to learn from, pain and suffering, Love?" Wow, what an incredible hand. Do you guys have hands like this? You guys have hands? You do, don't you? Aren't they amazing! Full of pain and suffering or Love. Is that a no-brainer?

[Audience laughing.]

R: So, if you have chosen pain and suffering, please learn, don't waste it. This is what I'm saying, don't waste it that you have chosen that. But if you learn, learn that choosing Love is a better path. Learn that pain and suffering is not a great path. So, if you don't have to learn that way any longer, learn from Love. OK? Practise Love and let that teach you What Love is all about. You don't need to practise pain and suffering any longer to learn what pain and suffering is going to bring you. OK? This world has been practising the path of pain and suffering long enough! Two thousand years ago there was an advent, a Light factoring that came upon the human species that the path of Love is the path that God supports. Not the pain and suffering any longer and that's what the Resurrection is all about, the overcoming of pain and suffering and death through Love. That's the path. I'm not a body, I'm...

[Audience.] Free!

R and audience: I'm still as God created me!

R: OK? So thanks guys.

[Audience.] Thank you!

R: And I hope this has been helpful. Don't worry about your failures. The pathway to your Enlightenment is built on failures. Can you hear me? The pathway to Enlightenment is built on failure, not success, it is built on failure! So, let go of your guilt and everything about your failures. Let go, so the Enlightenment can dawn upon you. OK? Don't hold onto them like a badge of honor. Man, I failed the best.

[Audience laughing.]

R: Yes, we know you have already failed the best. The Best is What You were before You thought you could fail. You were the Son of God, You are the Son of God. You failed in trying not to be the Son of God. Your Awakening is built upon your failure. Be glad that you have failed.

Learn from Love, because that's what your failures are going to show you; trying anything other than Love will not work. Follow the path of Love now and let the entirety of your mind be healed, so everything will be undone. See everything as a call for Love or an opportunity of sharing Love with You. It's all the same message. I keep using different words, but it's always just the same, simple message. I've come to indicate to you: GOD IS A FACT! You can do with that whatever you want. I'm telling you, God is a fact! If God is a fact, I guarantee you, you don't have problems. If you think you have problems, you are denying that God is a fact. Accepting that God is a fact is the path that will heal you and all the world of pain and suffering. That's the path of Love, accepting God. OK? I want you to know you have a relationship with your Creator. If you don't know that, if it's not alive, it's only because you have not valued it and instead have been valuing pain and suffering and have not truly valued Love. All right? And, it's time for a change. We know it's time for a change because we're all sitting here talking about it. That's how we know. OK? You'd rather be here than somewhere else, evidently. Well, at least you thought that way at some point. Maybe that will get stronger, too. What you're verifying gets strengthened. If you verify that this was helpful, it will strengthen within you that being here is helpful. And, when you're here, if I'm talking about You being Love, then You, and You, and You verify that. You will be more helpful wherever it is that you are in every given day wherever. And you'll just be giving that Love. And when you give that Love, people will recognize you as a very kind and loving person and they will like that. That's them verifying that Love Is... and now It becomes stronger, you see, and the next thing you know is your species are going to be reached and they're going to find the acceptance for the path of Love. Now, it looks like it's going pretty slow, but that's what time looks like. There will be a point where you will be filled with enough Light to see that it's already been completed and that you don't have to be concerned about when or how long or who in any given moment, because it will include everyone. No one will be left, no one will be left out, everyone will be found and everyone will be converted to Love from the path of pain and suffering. There will be no allowance for following the path of pain and suffering. It will all be healed. Because of You. Do you understand that? Because of You. Because you're going to give up the path of pain and suffering, the pathway will be brighter and recognized by those who've been following the path of pain and suffering. But they can't get it until you do, because you're the ones that are supposed to get it now. They're waiting for You, so that You can show them the way, can demonstrate the path of Love is preferable to continuing to learn from pain and suffering. We know that the path of Love has not been followed on this planet, don't we?

Q: Yes.

R: Yes. We do know that the pathway of pain and suffering has been followed on this planet and it doesn't work. There should be a clue right there. It's always been tried through pain and suffering and it hasn't worked. There is an alternative, it's Love, but it's never been tried.

Q: Jesus did.

R: I'm talking about us as a species. I'm not saying that the message of Love has not been presented. I'm saying as a species there has not been willingness to try to follow it, to allow it to show us. And, maybe now is the time to begin the path of Love! And, as you guys begin to remove yourself from the source of problems and be a part of the solution, you will be demonstrating that that path of Love not only can work, but is working; it's working in you. It's like Jesus saying, "Show the world I did not die because I'm alive in you." It's the same message. Show people that the path of Love will work because it's working in you. All right? Amen.

So, thanks guys, and I'll see you soon! Why?

[Audience laughing.]

R: Because I love You. Ik hou van Je. Believe me, if I didn't love You, there is no way I would stay.

[Audience laughing.]

R: No way. No. Once You know that this is an illusion and once You know that Love is not here, you would have to be centered in that Love to be able to remain doing this. Otherwise it's just, I know that I don't have to be here, I don't have to be here. I know that I choose to be here and I know that I choose to be here for you. You might not know that. You might not know why you're here as well as why I'm here. I know that. And if I didn't know that, there is no way I could continue to do this. None. So, we meet in our Love. It's the only place where we can meet. There is no meeting in pain and suffering. Pain and suffering is a denial of the joining. We can't meet there. But you can meet in Love! It's the only place. OK? So, go forth and multiply, no, no, that's a different...

[Audience laughing.]

R: That's a different talk. More Love.

[Audience.] More Love! More Love!

15

THE SEVEN SECRETS – PART 1

You Do This But to Yourself / God Loves You /
Forgiveness is the Key to Happiness

R: In this world there seems to be a secret. And since it's a secret you seem not to know it. Sometimes you might say there is something missing. Do you ever have that feeling, there is something missing? You might call that a secret, because it's missing for you, hey? Somebody is keeping it a secret from you, aren't they? And you've heard that somebody knows about that secret. Hello? You have an idea that someone knows a secret that you don't know. But when the secret is revealed to you, you have difficulty believing it.

That's why in the eastern religions they talk about the pearl that's right under your pillow. You go seeking for it throughout the whole world, asking everybody for help to find this pearl, whether you call it the pearl of wisdom or something that will change all of what you call life. And you seek for it. You seek for it in meditation, you seek for it in many different ways. And apparently it's a secret, because you don't know it. Tonight it can be revealed to you if you want. But revealing it is not the difficult part; the difficult part would be you accepting it.

You see, if you were a farmer and I had a rough diamond in my hand and offered it to you, you might think it wouldn't help you grow food at all and you'd be correct. And so you wouldn't really value it. But if you were a gemologist and I held it in my hand and offered it to you free, you'd look at me and you'd go, "Mmm, such a deal." No? So, it's really about recognizing what is offered, isn't it? So, tonight I'll offer you the secret that you've been seeking through many different lifetimes. But if you don't value it, it will be useless to you. What is that secret?

You do this but to yourself

You do this but to yourself! That's the secret. And, you choose the experiences you're going to experience, you choose the feelings you're going to have and nothing happens that you did not want to happen. That's the secret! Doesn't that make you happy?

Do you understand that you've just been giving the freedom of all freedoms? You've been empowered as much as you can possibly be empowered. You've been given the key to release you from all the pain and the suffering and death that you've been pursuing lifetime after lifetime. You need but accept it. To reject it, certainly you'll get more of whatever you've been getting. Or just somebody is doing something to you, somebody else is the problem. If only they would change, you would be OK. Did you ever hear that in your head? If only they would change, I would be OK. Is that not a rejection of the secret? Now you know why it's been kept a secret.

Because, every time it has been offered it has been rejected. You say, how can a person like me, who is so powerless and weak and small, have that be The Truth? And you'd rather have The Truth be mistaken than your idea of yourself. That's why it's still a secret. So, is that wisdom more worthy than your most expensive mantra? Only if you value that more than you do your most expensive mantra. How much did you pay to get in here tonight? I think you paid the wages of sin. Because you thought you're here; you thought there was a place to come to and you thought there was somebody not you that was going to say something of value.

And certainly you are wise enough to know what you should value and what you shouldn't value. Yet, you're still seeking to be awake. Hello? You think you can decide what is valuable. Yet, you seek to be awake. Is there a clue in there? How are you going to find the wisdom to know if you are not awake? Is there a secret here somewhere?

Q: Apparently. Unless you are awake you cannot choose for being awake. Unless you are awake you have no clear idea what to choose to become awake.

R: That's probably why you have students and teachers.

Q: That's why you go to somebody who seems to be awake.

R: But if you consider them to be awake, why wouldn't you listen to them?

Q: I don't know the answer. I'm not awake.

R: It's a secret. And as long as you say, "I'm not awake," you're not awake! Who do you want to represent? Who do you choose to represent? What are you telling yourself? What is the secret again?

Q: I do this but to myself.

R: I do this but to myself? So, you're telling yourself the story and you're getting the result of it.

Q: … to see a teacher and then I decide not to listen to him.

R: It sounds like it. I don't know why you would want to do something like that. It wouldn't make sense would it? "No, it wouldn't." Don't do that. Temptation is one thing, but buying into it is another. See, thoughts just come through the mind, don't they? They just come right through your mind. They don't seem to ask you if it's OK. They just come right into your mind, don't they? Thoughts, they are just there, aren't they? Right. And they will actually leave if you don't do anything with them. You have to feed them by valuing them or they will leave your mind just like the way they came.

They will just pass through you. And, in fact, if you don't feed them, there will be a moment where they don't come back any longer, because there is nothing to feed on. Is that a choice? So, you do this but to yourself?

Q: Is that so?

R: You could make a song out of it. The first line is, I do this but to myself and the second line is, be still an instant and go Home. Do you remember that song? Be still an instant and go Home? How long is an instant? As long as it takes for you to know you're awake. And who chooses how long it takes for you to be awake? What's the secret?

So, you choose when you're going to awake. You're in charge of time. You're not in charge of the material, the content, are you? That's Eternal. You're not in charge of That. But, you are in charge of time, aren't you? Because you do this but to yourself. So, when you choose to be awake is up to you. When you decide to stop sitting around saying, "I'm not awake," that would be helpful. It would be more helpful even to be awake.

Q: Because with it comes the responsibility.

R: Because you do this but to yourself. That's the responsibility.

Q: As long as it is there.

R: The Eternal is already Eternal, isn't It?

Q: Yes, so when you're aware of your Awakening there must be help with it.

R: Yes, the part of You that already knows is helping you. You represent the part that doesn't know and we know that because you keep going around saying, "I'm not awake." You keep going around telling stories about your problems, as if you don't do it to yourself. So, the seeker is revealed and to reject that you're awake you use, what? Perception, the world, what your body tells you, what you tell your body to tell you, what you decide your body is telling you as to what is real and what is not real and what is valuable and what is not valuable. You do this but to yourself.

And, when you want it changed, you will allow a change. If you don't allow a change, it means you don't want a change. You can say, "I want a change," every day until you die, but the day you allow a change, there is no death as far as your Awareness is concerned.

Q: I heard you say it would be helpful at least to say, "I am awake," and this is just so… It's because I think that the thought must go before the experience. So, though I seem to think I'm a body, I am awake. I don't want to deny that any longer and I still see myself denying it the same moment. So, supposedly it brings up a lot of fear, but it doesn't. It must be what I want at this moment. It's strange.

R: Is it possible for you to change your mind?

Q: It's a new possibility to look at. So, yes it is.

R: I recommend you look. When you practise saying, "I am What God created," if your intent is to deny or escape what it is that you are actively representing and manipulating and manifesting, then that is an unworthy form of denial. But when you assert to Truth, because you want It to be The Truth and you want It to dawn on your mind, then It has all the power of The Eternal in association with that idea, that can unfold within you instantly. So, you might say, there is a need for honesty.

But, remember, honesty is that you're Home in Heaven right now! Honesty is not, yes, I'm here and I need to awaken.

That is true to the illusion and apparently is your present condition as you describe yourself, circumscribed by a world of pain and suffering. Hello? So, it is unworthy of you to deny that that's where you find yourself, because if you did, then there would be no need for you to undergo the healing of your mind. But the declaration of The Truth of You is worthy of you, because It is The Truth and It aligns You with What You share with your Creator. So, you who play around in the trickery of your mind so that you don't have to heal, can talk about Oneness all you want, can talk about The Love of God all you want, can talk about the nature of Love or kindness or compassion or gentleness all that you want and continue to kill everybody in your mind, because of your own unwillingness to be What God created, and your own willingness to let your brother be What God created. All you will do is continue to foster your own fraudulence, imaging of separation, of anything that you can determine as more than One or not You. All you need is one thing that's not You and you have your identity as other than what Perfection is.

With Perfection Everything is the same. In Perfection Everything is Perfect. Perfection is the same. Who would try to make differences in Perfection if Everything was Perfection? It doesn't make sense, does it? You can't have parts of Perfection, can you? So, what do you declare? What is your declaration? How do you represent you and what results are you getting in that willingness to represent a self you believe in? What's the secret?

Q: I do this but to myself.

R: I do this but to myself.

Q: Could I ask, just for the sake of verification, why you used the word assertion and declaration in opposition to, well let's call it thinking.

R: I don't think in terms of opposition, but that might be the way that you think.

Q: Well, one can reason endlessly about the concept of Awakening, but a declaration seems to be something different. So, to put the question in another way, what do you actually mean by having your inner declaration and assertion, instead of thinking?

R: Are you aware of The Truth?

Q: I think so, because you cannot be aware of untruth if you are not at the same time aware of Truth.

R: Whose teaching is that?

Q: Well, it just came up in my mind.

R: So, it's yours then.

Q: It came out of me.

R: Yes. But that's not what I teach. I teach that Perfection only knows Perfection, and it's impossible to know more than Perfection, because Perfection is Oneness and there is not more than Oneness. That's why you call It Oneness. However, that that believes otherwise experiences otherwise. So, you can say those are my experiences if you want to, but that does not make it The Truth. It just makes it your ideas and your experiences.

Q: A declaration, to make a declaration, what does one exactly do or undo?

R: Declaration in my mind is nothing more than the willingness for what Perfection declares to be The Truth in my Mind. In other words, Truth is true and nothing else is true, It is What It is. I just let It be That. I don't have to analyze It, I don't have to reason It, I have to do nothing. All I have to do is accept It. It is What It is already. What problem can you have with Perfection? What would you be if you had a problem with Perfection? If Perfection is Oneness, what would You be? Try to reason that. It doesn't make sense, does it? See, so there are a lot of ideas in your mind that are actually very insane and they're insane, based upon the idea that there are ideas in your mind that are true to The Truth or represent Perfection. And when you embrace those ideas, when you find value in those ideas, what you call Happiness and Joy are a part of That. And when you don't, you believe in opposition to That. And the belief in opposition is what separation is and then you have heartaches. Does anybody know about heartaches? Some people make millions of dollars on them. You have a whole industry in the music business called the blues. "Is that what's bothering you, booby? You had a hard day? Your wife ran off with your best friend? It's been raining for seven days and seven nights. Your roof is leaking and the water is falling on the electricity and you have sparks everywhere, and your dogs and your cats, they've just left defecation everywhere in the house and you went to your telephone and you tried to call for help, but the telephone was dead."

Q: Somebody did something to my credit card!

R: "Is that's what's bothering you, booby?" What does that have to do with Perfection? What does that have to do with your Awakening? What does that have to do with Happiness and Joy and Innocence and Love?

Q: At least it can inspire you to seek for help.

R: Well, if you were that insane, then hopefully you would be inspired by your pain and your suffering to have no more pain and suffering. However, that path is not what I teach. I teach the path of Love. I do understand that you can learn from your pain. I do understand that's possible. I also do understand that you don't always do that. However, my teaching is that Love can guide you, because Love is What

You are and Love can guide you to realize that You are What Love is. Pain can guide you that you've made a mistake. Love can guide you to The Truth, Love. And then you will recognize, as you begin to allow Love to manifest Itself in your mind and through you, what is not Love. And as you see what is not Love and you apply the secret, you will change your mind and there comes your freedom. Why? Because you're no longer doing what is required to not know Love, because You are What Love is. Then, What It is that You are, just manifests for a moment. And as It manifests, the illusion in its entirety begins to be altered, even on the molecular level. It will begin to be altered until you find the willingness for the entirety of it to disappear. And, when you find the willingness, which is not a huge thing, for the entirety of it to disappear, it will because of the secret.

When you're no longer doing it to yourself, because you have no value for it, it must disappear. It must, it's a law! But, I'm not talking about, I don't like that part, I don't mind that part disappearing, but please don't let this part disappear because I like chocolate ice-cream or Dutch cheese. What would I do without my cheese or bicycle? Can you imagine the Dutch without bicycles? You would be in a mess, wouldn't you?

I know another secret. Do you want to know my other secret? But, don't forget, it has no value unless you accept it! Do you remember that from the first secret? Are you sure you want to know? Because once you carry this knowledge, you know you're responsible for it, don't you? You do realize that, right? You are now responsible, because I gave you the answer to the secret, You do this but to yourself. You are now responsible for the awareness of that. Are you sure you want to know the second secret? You're absolutely sure?

OK, you're going to be responsible for this! I will hold you responsible! Are you ready?

OK, the secret goes like this:

God loves You

But remember I asked you to accept God's Love, and you said you would and that you would be responsible for accepting the secret, didn't you? So, you are responsible for accepting God's Love, that God loves You. You don't have to do anything to become worthy. God loves You. You do this but to yourself, but God loves You!

Finally! So, can you find a place within you where you can become aware of God loving You, is that possible? Is it possible? Would you like to do that tonight? I mean, when would be a good time to accept God loving You. Do you hear God whispering, " *Ik hou van Jou. Ik hou van Jou…?"*

You see, if it was like that and you couldn't hear, then God would be a really cruel God, wouldn't He? People that don't have hearing would not have God available to them, if hearing God's Voice had to do with your ears. But, You can hear. You can be aware of God's Love. You can hear a Voice That speaks for God. And, this you can learn. You can learn to value It and you can learn to let It guide you and if you do, It will show you the secrets.

The secrets will show you that you do this but to yourself and as you see that, you'll no longer want to do that to yourself, because you recognize it's insane to want to kill yourself, to want to die, to want to suffer and to be the cause of pain for your brothers. You just wouldn't want to do that if you saw that that's what you were doing. So, you hide it from yourself that that's what you're doing. And you pretend that you're innocent and perhaps even that God made it all that way, so you don't know what to do with it, because God made it that way. So, you hope He comes along some day and changes things for you and pulls your butt out of this terrible place.

"Now, I really want Enlightenment. God, do It to me." You are responsible for the story that you tell yourself. How about if the story that you told yourself was, "I don't have to tell a story anymore. I can just let myself be shown by Perfection the way to let go of my story and accept The Truth, Which is not a story, but the Presence of Reality Itself, or Perfection Itself." Maybe there is a twist to your story. Maybe one day someone from what you thought was your illusion, came and sat with you and helped you look at your story for a moment and gave it a different ending. And, as you looked at it, you went, "Mmm, I like that ending better." And from that moment onward you begin to let a different ending or a different goal or a different purpose be what guides you from moment to moment to moment. Is that possible? I mean, are you sure that's possible? Do you want that to be possible? Because, once it's possible it must occur!

So, you're telling me now, there is an end to pain and suffering and it is not death. Is that right? But you can't get to the end unless you accept the truth of the secrets. You cannot reach the end without accepting that your Creator loves You and you can't reach the end without realizing that you do it but to yourself and so that's how it stops, when you don't do it to yourself any longer and you stop blaming your brothers for what's going on instead. I really love where Jesus in *A Course In Miracles* says there is only two things that can happen when you meet a brother, when you meet anyone. Right? One is, they share Love with You. Right? That's what he says, they share Love with You. And the second thing he says is, if they're not sharing Love – it doesn't matter what they're doing – they're calling out to You for Love, no matter what it looks like, it's a call for your Love. So, how are you going to get around being loving? Your brother is either there sharing Love or he's calling out for your Love. What other role have you been given? You're supposed to be a lover. Can you admit that you've been mistaken about your role? Can you? Can you say, "I'm mistaken. I am mistaken. I no longer want the results of my mistake." That's pretty empowering, isn't it? I no longer want the results of my mistakes.

Then, what would you want instead? "I want What my Creator wants for Me," because in your confusion it would be difficult for you to be clear about what to say. But you know your Creator is not in confusion and you're never going to be misled. So, wouldn't you want the One That's going to bring Perfection, rather than you trying to figure it out? I'm not going to figure this shit out! No, God, whatever you want to call It, Yo, Yoho, Almighty One, whatever. Those words, they absolutely mean nothing, When what you're saying is, "You show me." That's the important part! "You show me. I made a mistake. I'm not going to tell You Who knows Everything. I made a mistake. I made a mistake. You show me!"

Q: I have the results of my mistakes.

R: See, and that makes sense, doesn't it? It makes sense. Now, you know what I mean? It makes sense.

You certainly have gotten more than you wanted. I have given The Truth back to you by being willing to represent It for you. And when I say, represent It, I mean be the Voice of the Holy Spirit that speaks for your Creator and speaks for The Truth of You, The Love of You. That was more than you wanted. You wanted to sit and listen to a teacher for a moment, but you are given much more than that. Now, that's good news.

Q: Thank you.

R: Now you can sit and judge this if you want to, but I don't know why you would want to do that. You can sit and analyze what's being said, but I don't know why you'd want to do that. Or, you can look at that and hear how everything that is being said supports Oneness, supports the Love of You, speaks of your Perfection and then accept That, because you've admitted that you made a mistake.

The identity that you thought was yours is a mistake that you've been doing to yourself and you don't have to do that anymore. I release Thee, I release Thee, I release Thee.

[Audience laughing.]

You don't have to do that anymore. You are not bound by some strange spell that I put upon you when I dreamed up this dream and said, "Hey, would you mind coming with me?" And you went, "Yes, let's go, dude, let's have fun. It is fun, right?" And I went, "Oh yes, you'll have lots of fun pretending you're not Home in Heaven." "You're sure?" you ask me, "You're sure? You're sure it's going to be fun, right?" And I'll say, "Yes, remember evolution?" And you went, "Yes, illusion! It has a kind of a sound to it, evolution…Yes, let's go for some of that." And then we got here and I went, "Oh man, what was I thinking?" And Holy Spirit, you know, from out of a cloud said nothing. And I went, "Boing!" And then I looked in and there were all you guys. You didn't hear The Voice. And then I had to come back and go, "Hey, excuse me, I made a mistake."

I got You into this. I've been doing all this but to myself. I got You into it. Now, mmm, if you're willing to accept that idea, that I'm the One that got You into it, which you're probably struggling with, all that you would actually really have to do is practise forgiveness and we could take care of that. But, if you want to be pissed off at me for all the pain and suffering you've gone through all these different lifetimes, then you'll find it extremely difficult to be involved in forgiveness. However, there is another secret, that you have to understand. It would be really valuable if you would hear this and let it enter into your heart and your mind, so that it can begin to activate what's required to be activated to fulfill the purpose that you are now giving this world, which is the ending of the world. It would be really, really simple if I could only remember what it is. This happens from time to time, it just comes in and it just gets pulled out of my head and I just kind of, you know, may sit around for a moment. Maybe it will come back, maybe not. But it was there...

OK, I remember, thank you. Yes. The other secret is,

Forgiveness is the key to happiness

The only way that you can get to the point where you remember Love, is when forgiveness removes from your mind what you put in the way of Love, because it's impossible to teach somebody What Love is. It's impossible! You think you guys can teach your children What Love is. You're mistaken. But you can teach them forgiveness and to practise forgiveness, and as they do, which actually many of them are already good at, they'll find it very natural.

So, forgiveness is what allows you to recognize Love. The idea of not forgiving is the idea of holding onto a grievance. So, when you hold onto a grievance, you don't see The Light and you don't see The Love. But when you practise forgiveness, then the doorway to Love opens up. Right? And then, when you love more, you're willing to forgive. And then, when you forgive there is more Love and it just feeds a nice pathway. But, if you're not willing to forgive, it will lead to a lot of grievances.

Have you noticed that? You really grieve over a lot of things. You don't like this and you don't like that and you'd really like things to change and there is not enough love and if only... You just have a lot of grievance going on, right? So, if you were willing to let go of your grievances, then the Love that you want will be there. But, you're not so sure that that's a smart thing to do, because you equate Love with pain. You say, "I love and that hurts." So, now you're saying, "Something that can be hurt can love," and that's insane. But, you have demonstrations here that that is true and you don't question that.

You say, "That's the way it is." But you forget secret number one. So, you are the one that told yourself that you are something that can be hurt. You are the one that told yourself that something else can be something that can hurt you. Then you had experiences and you said, "See?" But those experiences were not of Spirit, they were of perception. So, you want perception to be your reality and you support that and as you support that, which is your choice, because you do this but to yourself, you get the result of this being reality. You will be able to be hurt, love can hurt you and somebody else whom you love can be the object that can hurt you. And that's the way it would have to be, unless you were mistaken and then things could change.

But, without the willingness to be mistaken, things will continue the way they are, because those thoughts are still there in your mind, continuing to bring to you the images that you put out there to bring to you. OK?

So, the third secret is forgiveness. It's the pathway to Love and allows you to release the perception that you have received and determined to be reality. You forgive that activity of your own mind or your brother's, whom you said is doing it to you, by activating secret number one, I do this but to myself. OK? Now, when you put those three together, I do this but to myself, God loves Me and Forgiveness is the key to Love or Happiness, however you want to say that, you really have such a powerful message that it can change everything, everything being you, your mind. It doesn't change The Truth of You, but it changes the mind that pays attention to thoughts that represent non-perfection, anything other than Oneness. I'm sorry, I just...

Q: No, mostly it's the answer to all questions, really. But my question is, when I am talking to a friend or somebody who goes through a lot of trouble and pain, I sometimes see that I kind of feel the pain rather than being Love, you know. So, that's again believing perception and the truth of the pain and then, yes, then I guess it takes forgiveness to know that that is...

R: You know, when you get into the nature of how miracles work, you really want to look at what you're saying right now very, very closely. Because, one activity there that you were looking at would allow a miracle to enter in and the other, although it seems to be kind, doesn't.

Q: Which one, that seems to be kind, doesn't? Feeling the pain, you mean, and believing that it's real?

R: Yes, and believing, what? The story that they're telling you. See, if you said to yourself, "OK, I'm going to listen to your story," you'd really have a shot at it, because you called it a story and now, in your own mind, you're keeping it clear.

All I'm doing is listening to a story. I know my brother is in pain, because he believes the story is real. Now, I know my brother is not that story, neither is he actually the one who is telling the story. I want to remember Who my brother really is. Now the miracle can come in. But, when you get into the story... "Yes, that's happened to me too" or whatever...

Q: Yes, but also I'm getting the frustration because of this person not listening, you know...

R: There is a clue, frustration.

Q: But, you know, it's what you're teaching us now. I could teach her and sometimes there is total rejection, but then what can you do?

R: I talked about this last night in Utrecht and actually I've already given you the answer to that. When? When I said that Jesus said there are only two things that can ever be happening. Either they are sharing Love with You or they're calling for your Love. So, if you get frustrated or whatever, you're forgetting that they're calling for your Love.

Q: Yes, that is my difficulty, because I'm going back to the beginning of the evening. That's the difficulty when I'm faced with all this pain and the rejection of whatever.

R: Which is every moment of every day!

Q: Yes, and that is the challenge.

R: Yes, but don't forget, God loves You, You've got the Power!

Q: Yes, but how can I love her all the time?

R: You've got the Power, God loves You, that's how. The moment you let God out of this, you're on your own. The moment you're unwilling to let God out of it, you have all the help that you need. Even if you can't figure it out, God is there, bringing whatever it is that is needed, whether it be clarity to your mind or your brother's. All of a sudden that person just kind of, you know, does whatever he does.

Now, here is the thing that I've recognized has been really important for me and I see very little of. So, I want to bring your attention to it, because perhaps you'll begin to embrace it, recognizing what I'm going to say. I know that you'll find difficulty with it, because I did. But I know that when I overcame it, You did! And that's why I'm going to say it. OK, here it comes. So, you do with this whatever it is that you want to do with it, alright? It's extremely powerful in changing your mind and seeing the world differently, so that you can find the ease with which to be true to the greater calling, alright? And it goes like this. Thank you for being the thorn in my side, because it made me look even deeper within me for the Love in the face of my temptation for me to be angry or frustrated.

Thank you, it's a thank you! It's that gratitude that some fool is acting like a fool, because it made me go deeper to see The Truth! Because of the way we judge one another we say, "It's much easier to be with you than with you." You know what I'm saying? We're like that. We think that way and that's part of our problem. We get the result of doing that.

Q: We have the tendency to think we are the victim of some situation.

R: There is a danger of being addicted to anything in this world, that's absolutely true. But I tell you what, when you don't leave God out, be addicted to God, that's a winner. If you're going to be addicted, be addicted to God and you'll be OK, you know. Those who are addicted to techniques will all be healed, too. Everyone is going to be healed. You can't do this stuff forever. So, there are those who play the role of, oh, I'm so weak, and there are others that play, that's not me. There are so many varieties of roles of illusion that you can play, but you can't do any of them forever because of The Truth of You. Sooner or later you're going to be tired of being you. You're going to being tired of being upset with everybody, but, oh man, do you ever hit that place where you were just angry with everybody? Everybody! Your best friend, Jesus, "Get the hell out of here and leave me alone." And Jesus said, "That's what I've been trying to tell you, get the hell out of here," but you won't listen. Wise guy.

Sooner or later you will fail at pushing everything away from you, because you want to hold onto the idea that you will be hurt, unless you have a safe barrier between you and everything or everyone else. See, and this is where the third secret comes in, the forgiveness, tied together with number two, God loves You. You think God loves something that doesn't have value? Do you think God, the All-Powerful would love something that's weak? Do you think He would create something that's weak? What would weakness have to do with Something that's All-Powerful? Wouldn't it be an opposite? Wouldn't weakness be an opposite to All-Powerful? And there is nothing opposite to Oneness!

So, it's impossible that you could be weak! You're just taking all your power and trying to hide it behind an idea and you use all that power to hold the idea. I know you're insane, you're silly, I mean it's laughable. It truly, truly is. Although, don't do that in a hospital or something like that, because they're dedicated, you know in hospitals, to being sick and weak. If you do that in a hospital they might hurt you, if you believe you're something that can be hurt. Am I making any sense at all here to you tonight? Is this of value to you? Yes, so we've got three secrets out in the open here tonight and you've agreed that you're going to accept those secrets and you're going to be responsible for The Light and for the knowing of those secrets. Right?

You do this but to yourself, God loves You and Forgiveness is the key to Happiness and Love. Through forgiveness you will know Love and You are Love Itself. That's nice. You've been given three very powerful ideas that will be a part of you changing the ending to your story. Now, as those three begin to dawn upon your mind as a Light factoring, you'll be led through what some people call Enlightenment, which is really nothing more, nor less, than recognizing What has always been and also recognizing what you've tried to make to replace What has always been.

16

THE SEVEN SECRETS – PART 2

The Holy Spirit Always Knows Only and Supports Only The Truth of You

R: In your Enlightenment You will see What has always been and what you've tried to replace it with and finally, for the very first time, you will see there is a difference. Hello. You'll see there is a difference. You'll see that the ideas of differences that you held, are really all one thing. So, the only thing that's really different from all that one thing is Reality. But you didn't see Reality before. You were trying to choose between the best and the worst of the differences, right? You wanted the least amount of pain for instance.

You thought that was doing things right. You were more interested in right and wrong than in Truth. You were more interested in morality than you were in Eternity. But, that moment comes into every mind, because of the nature of your Creator. Therefore, the nature of You will come into every mind the moment You see, You recognize. You even understand for a moment, before it is all completely transcended and you come into the knowing – you can even use the word being at that moment – You're actually being The Truth. You're actually being Reality. You're actually being The Eternal. You're not seeing It because that takes two. But You're being It, You're knowing It. The Divine Essence is just expressing What It is. That's your destiny.

Now, maybe that changes the ending of your story, should you accept what I'm saying. Maybe it changes the ending of your story. Maybe you were thinking there was a different kind of story going to happen for you. But, even though I tell it, if you don't accept it and carry The Light of that, you can come around again, start all over again and you know what I say about that, right? Don't do that! That's a declaration. Find where you're willing to accept the message that speaks of your Perfection, of the end of all pain and suffering and death. Find a place where you can accept that. If you can't accept it, find a place where you're willing to accept it and don't be concerned about the time factoring as to when that is fulfilled in you. And then you will find yourself practising. If you reject the message, practise until that moment where you won't have to practise anymore.

Or, you can gladly and gleefully – oh, what a word, gleefully. God, I've never used that word before, gleefully. That's really funny, thank you. I was given a giggle.

You can gleefully accept The Truth, instead of grudgingly. "OK, You're a God and all that, You know. I really did want a new bicycle and a nice house and a family and someone to love and children that didn't give me a hard time, but, You're God and All, I mean, pfff..., OK..."

Q: What would gleefully look like?

R: Gleefully? Gleefully, what would it look like? You're going to have to answer that question. Let it happen and then you can share it with everyone. But, see dude, the party is going to happen on the other side of time and space. You guys have been partying here long enough. Your parties have always ended up in death. And when somebody dies, party, party, let's not get all morbid and everything. Let's party, party, party, yes. Just, give me an excuse; let's party, but let's not go Home! No, let's not get out of all of this, I mean...

That's the way it's been, you know, because it's so tough on us. We've made this thing so tough it hurts. From the moment that you begin to look at how babies come into your illusion. [Rananda starts coughing and crying.] Whaahhh!!! Does that sound like happiness? Is there a clue? It's a clue. And how do you get out of here? Boink!. Do you understand what I'm saying? And in between that whaah and the boink, you're hoping that there is something here of value and you're so disappointed.

As a kid, I was having amazing things occurring in my mind from the time I was around five. And I remember by the time I hit seven or eight, I looked for everybody who was really old. You know what I'm saying? I looked for old people, because I had this idea in my mind that old people ought to know what's going on here, because they've been around for a long time. They ought to know! But, what I found out was that they've been doing the same things longer. They didn't learn, they just did the same things longer than the younger people and I went, "Mmm, so it's not about getting older then." Because, when I went to the wise guys – you know, the wise guys – and I asked them questions that should not have been coming out of somebody who was five years old, they said to me, "You'll learn later."

I was very disappointed! And there I was, you know, having all kinds of communications with Masters and Stuff and I was learning and being taught and guided, you know, and I was really, really upset because Jesus wasn't here. That was the first really big upset that I can remember. I'd heard he was the Savior of the world. Did you ever hear that? Yes? And I'd got to meet this guy. Five. I was five! I got to meet this guy.

And then they said they had churches where Jesus was honored and stuff. So I figured that's the place. Five years old! So, I convinced my parents they should drop me off at this church building. So, they dropped me off and I walked in and I found out what was going on in there and I waited around for the guy that had the nice robes and all that kind of stuff and who did all the talking. So, I waited till everybody left as much as possible. I went and I tugged on him and I asked him these really important questions to me like, "I hear he's coming back." And he said, "Yes." I said, "How come you don't have a chair for him?" "Whose kid is this?" That was the response. And I'm thinking in myself, ha, they really don't believe what they're saying.

That was one of the first things I recognized. They say he's coming back, but they don't really prepare for him, not even in their own hearts. Now, I can either judge them or I could recognize there is something going on here that's not quite right. Hello? That I couldn't necessarily believe what was being presented. Hello? That's a little difficult on a five year old kid, if you're really a five year old kid. Right? Who can you believe if these elders, who are responsible, are not being responsible? So, just like you, at a very early age, we knew something is not right here. But we didn't quite know exactly what it was and we really didn't know what the solution was. So we started looking around as to who is already here who might have been pursuing that same idea before you and could help you.

Hello! That was when you began your student phase of your Awakening. You were supposed to progress beyond that, you know. You weren't supposed to make a career out of studentism. You were supposed to not collect information, you were supposed to let the information guide you to The Knowing. You've been making the mistake of collecting pieces of information and then interpreting them based upon what you wanted Reality to be like. Aha! However, tonight you've heard me say, don't tell Reality What It is!

Don't tell It how to be What It is. Admit that you have made a mistake and ask for Perfection to show you that you have let go of That in your arrogance. The ego, that thought system, that self identity or non-identity, is doing everything it can to make you do something. And it sounds so noble! Yes, I'll do this and yes I'll do that and certainly that's helpful and I say, *nee*, step back and let Spirit teach you.

Step back, take your hands off, open up and let yourself be shown the way. And then, when you're shown the way, own that responsibility, because That that's guiding you is going to reveal It to be You, You to be It. But, only in that revealing do you then have that responsibility of that Light factoring. Until then, step back, no matter how bright it gets, step back. But, when You know You are That, You will also know, through your own Beingness, the willingness to just be and then, if you carry this message, you will carry the message. If You carry the frequency, You will carry the frequency. If You carry the frequency and the message, that will be that way. You know what I mean. You don't necessarily have to talk, but maybe You should. But You will know, because it will be your Essence. It will be your Beingness that is just being, You're just being What You are.

See, like me for instance. It's so easy for me to talk, have you noticed that? It's really true and I've been like this for a long time. Well, maybe all of time. But I can talk, I have no problem talking. I can talk in big groups, little groups, one person, nothing; it's Me, it's too late, I'm only talking to Me. You get in there and you go, "Oh man, they're not Me, I wonder what they'll think of Me. I wonder what those who are not Me are going to think of Me. I hope I don't make a mistake." See, you have all these questions, you know, but when you awaken, that stuff is not there.

All you're doing is being You. And sometimes that You is a cook and through the cooking an incredible amount of Love comes through and for people, in eating that food, all of a sudden there is something different going on rather than sustaining a body. All of a sudden there is a Love factoring that's happening that they don't quite understand how and why it's happening. But the cook does, because the cook puts so much Love into that, that The Love is being recognized by people. But it might not be their job to do any of the talking. It could be the same with gardeners or anybody else, except for liars. Liars don't make it there, can't play that role.

Q: But you have to play a role?

R: You will, because you're already doing it. You are already playing a role, so, you're already guilty or you're already fraudulent in your attempt to present to yourself what you're not. So, trying to be innocent won't work either. You might as well admit, I made a mistake. Have you ever heard that before, I made a mistake?

Q: I no longer want the results.

R: I no longer want the results, because the results I've been getting have been pain, suffering and death. Why would I want to continue to have those results? There is an alternative available to you, isn't there? So, you can prefer that. I like it when roses smell like roses.

Q: When I was ten years old, there were no elder people around, so I started to go inside.

R: There was nobody eleven or twelve, is that what you're saying?

Q: Yes, but I'd no contact with them. Anyway, I was alone and I learned myself to pray three or four hours or even all night and I discovered at that age that I could do miracles if I prayed long enough with a loving intent and a loving heart. If I repeated the same subjects, they would happen.

R: This is true!

Q: And this I discovered as a child. But nowadays I think I'm too lazy for this.

R: End of story! I learned something and now I don't care about it anymore.

Q: But in general, I would like to learn to destroy the false image of Reality that I have and can prayer be helpful?

R: Yes, pray for what you've already been given!

Q: Yes.

R: So, you'll be aware of it. Don't pray for something you think you don't have, that's a mistake.

Q: But, when I was ten, I prayed for somebody, let's say, it's not The Truth but let's say, I prayed for an event to happen.

R: Yes, God is merciful.

Q: And it did, to my surprise.

R: It's a surprise because you forgot secret number one.

Q: Yes, I did it to myself.

R: Hey! You still think the one that got healed wasn't you?

Q: Yes.

R: OK, then suffer that. So, they got healed so they could die later?

Q: I was only surprised that through prayer things happened which are against all laws of nature.

R: Yes, it's a beautiful thing to learn that prayer is the medium for miracles. Yes, it's a beautiful thing to learn, however it happens, it's beautiful.

Q: But how does it relate to declaration and willingness?

R: It's all a part of the same thing. Prayer is the medium for miracles. Miracles alter the time sequence and when the time sequence is altered completely it disappears. When time disappears you'll know The Eternal. When you know The Eternal, You'll be What You've always been because that's What Eternal is and then You'll go, "Hallelujah." Can you practise now?

Q: Yes, if I remember.

R: OK, right now. How? It begins with an H.

Q: Hallelujah.

R: Yes, there you go. That wasn't hard, was it? Hallelujah. That's kind of like praising God, isn't it?

Q: Yes, that's not how I felt my contact with God was at that time.

R: Yes, but we're talking about God now, we're not in the past any longer.

Q: I seem to have lost it.

R: No, you don't, it's right there, you just say it. Will you try it again? I bet you're really good at it.

Q: It doesn't have the intensity.

R: Come on, give some intention to it then. Come on, just pretend, let's see if you can do it.

Q: You want me to pretend? Hallelujah!!!

R: Yes.

Q: But that is not the thing which I experienced when I was ten.

R: Let me show you something. This world in its entirety is pretending.

Q: Fake it until you make it.

R: OK. See, here is the thing, here is another secret. God, what's going on here tonight? Secret number four is like this, yes, yes , yes. Boy, I'm going to charge for this. Wow! Secret number four, what was it? I hate it when this happens. I've got it. See, it can't go very far, it's just in your mind. It goes like this:

Q: Hallelujah.

R: It's working already. You're not going to believe this but I'm going to tell it anyway. OK. Secret number four,

The Holy Spirit always knows only and supports only

The Truth of You

Holy Spirit doesn't care if you're faking it. If you say, "I love God," He's going to go, "Yes, Yes, Yes!" If you go, "Hallelujah," he's going, "Right on brother, right on." Because Holy Spirit knows that that's The Truth of You. Holy Spirit knows that You love God. You might not know it. You might have chosen to forget it or to hide it, but Holy Spirit knows that's The Truth of You.

So, if you try to fake it, "Oh, I love God." Holy Spirit is going to go, "Yes, you're damn right, you do." Or something like that. Probably something in Dutch.

Listen to what I'm saying! The Holy Spirit is going to support That in You, even when you're not in what you would call what I think is sincerity. I know when I'm sincere and when I'm not. Holy Spirit says, "I have no idea what you're talking about." It's either The Truth or it's not. And when you say, "I love God," and you think it's not true, it's still true. So, Holy Spirit supports that in You. Man, if you can hear that! Even when you're not sincere – although sincerity would really be helpful in this – even when you're not sincere, you still have got all this help, because Holy Spirit knows The Truth, The Truth of You.

Now, if you're really hearing what I'm saying and you look at secret number two, maybe you'll put that together with secret number four. God loves You. That's why the Holy Spirit always knows only and supports only The Truth of You. It sees these other things and It knows that You believe in It, but It stands only for that Truth of You. Why? Because God loves You! Isn't that cool? If you guys ever begin to hear this, you're not going to be Dutch any longer! You're going to get so excited with this message that you're going to really carry it forth through your own demonstration of what you're hearing here tonight. You'll come alive. Like you've been kind of dead, if you haven't noticed.

I mean, who would want to do all the things this world offers you to do? It's pretty dull. There is not a lot of excitement going on here at all, even bungee jumping, you know what I mean? You do it ten times and ten days in a row and then, where has all the thrill gone? Get a mate and have sex for ten years, then what happens? You know what I'm saying? It's just like there is an end to it somewhere, that's all that I'm trying to say. "OK, I know something I've been doing for fifty years." Well, good on you, mate. What happened in fifty-one? "Well, when I was ninety I couldn't do that anymore, bub." Well, then there is an end to it. "Yes, you've got that right. I guess I'll admit that before I die."

You know what I mean? Guys? The stuff you love the most is still going to pass, because that's the nature of this illusion. It changes, it passes, it's not Eternal. And you give so much to it, because you don't know what to do. And you can't find The Eternal to give yourself to It because you tell yourself you don't know It. You don't even know if It's true. I meditated for years and I didn't get what I wanted. I heard somebody once said they had a little something going on, a little tinkling going on in their body or something, but I don't know anybody that woke up from a mantra.

* * *

Q: How about doctors?

R: What about them? When do you go and see them?

Q: When I'm in pain.

R: OK, you say, "I'm in pain," and you'll get the result of that. You go to the doctor and say, "I'm in pain, you fix it." That's what you're saying and you know what? That's OK, that's actually OK, as long as you let him fix you. What's a bummer is, like you do it to yourself and then you say, "You fix it," and then you don't let him fix you.

Q: So, you shouldn't go to hospitals then?

R: See, that's what I just told you. If you believe in a hospital, at least let the hospital help you. It doesn't make sense to deny God and try to use a hospital and then you go and say, "Try, see if you can fix it. Go ahead! You're a specialist, right? I have to pay you more than the nurse and I still have got that problem on my toe. What kind of a specialist are you anyway?"

Q: So, you shouldn't have faith in the fact that doctors can heal?

R: I'm not telling you what to do. I'm helping you see the result you're getting of what you are choosing to do. You don't like to see the result you're getting. I'm not telling you what to do, I'm helping you see the results of the choices you are making.

Q: If you say God is Love...

R: He is.

Q: Then that's the hospital you believe in?

R: Oh, if you want to put it that way, that's very poetic.

Q: I mean...

R: I generally don't look at God as a hospital, but...

Q: No, but in this case?

R: No, in this case, if you really trusted God, there would be no need for a hospital, because God doesn't make sick things.

Q: If you have enough trust in God.

R: Listen, God does not create sick things. If you think you're sick and you turn to God and give up your ways and your thoughts of you, you will heal, because God does not create sick things. God does not even create minds that are asleep or confused.

God creates only Mind Awake, Eternally Awake. That's What God creates. You're not sick. You're mistaken. Didn't we go through this already? You're mistaken. Didn't you say, I made a mistake?

Q: Yes, it's a mistake to think the hospital can heal you.

R: Yes, or that you are anywhere near a hospital. Because God doesn't create hospitals or people that need them. That's an illusion, that's what I'm trying to tell you. You know that. You know that, own it. Let it empower you. You know that, you've been shown. Carry that Light, be responsible for that Light. You're not a whimp. Doctors will try to make you that. You're not. God will never make you that, neither will I. I'm going to empower you, you better look out.

Q: I tell The Truth.

R: Good, Truth, the whole Truth and nothing but The Truth, so help me God.

Q: I did meet God in a hospital and the next day the doctor said, "You can go."

R: Oh, my goodness. No wonder you were in the hospital. God is not in the hospital, He's in your mind.

Q: When my body was in the hospital, my mind had a meeting with God and...

R: You talked about the hospital?

Q: No, He didn't talk about the hospital.

R: No, He wouldn't, He would talk about your Perfection and how well you are and that He doesn't create shitty things and the next day you were well and you could leave.

Q: He showed Love and Infinity.

R: See.

Q: And then I met you.

R: Yes.

Q: It's true. It's The Truth.

R: Many disguises this God has!

Q: Aha.

R: Aha.

Q: I see the point. I thank you.

R: Oh yes, that's my job. I like roses that smell like roses, don't you?

It's really disappointing what they've done to roses, you know. I mean, really. Who did that anyway? If I can find them I'm really going to tell them. So, what is secret number one? I do this but to myself. Secret number two? God loves Me. Secret number three: Forgiveness is the key to Love.

Forgiveness is the key to Happiness and secret number four, Holy Spirit doesn't care if you're not sincere, it's going to support everything that you say that God will share.

Holy Spirit's job is to help you recognize in your mind What You can share with God. Those thoughts that you think are not sincere are still the thoughts that can be shared with God with sincerity. So, God, Holy Spirit supports the thought and helps you find the sincerity. Cares not how would-be you think you are. It will help you find the strength, not the religious falsity, not false humbleness, not religious prostrations through idols, but The True Love that exists between Cause and Effect, Creator and Created.

And this is the path that you're on. Well, if you hang around me you will be. Yes, you can be, even if you don't hang around with me, you know. Imagine people following you all day around, man. You wind up being a guru, wouldn't you? That's what they do to gurus, don't they? People follow them around all day long. They want to touch their feet and all that kind of stuff, because they're something you're not, right? Brrrr! *Nee.* Not going to give me that role. Been there, done that, sold the dotie. No, we gave the vibuti away. It's not spiritual to sell the vibuti.

OK? You guys, are you all right? You OK, man?

Q: Yes.

R: So, everybody is OK, right? You're all happy, is that right? Everybody is happy? If you're happy that means, you've been practising forgiveness, because forgiveness is the key to happiness. So, if you're happy, you have been forgiving. Hello? So, if you haven't been forgiving, whatever you're calling happiness must be something else. Because forgiving is the key to happiness. So, if you haven't been so happy, then you haven't been forgiving. So, know what practice you can do if you're not happy. Be forgiving, be more forgiving.

And lately, actually I've been doing it for quite a few years, but lately I'm putting an emphasis again for those who might not know this or might not have followed it when I presented it to you years ago. I highly recommend the prayer of Saint Francis.[22] The reason is that this prayer turns you around. Instead of trying to get things, you give. And, in the giving you find out that it's there. In the getting you think it's not there. So, the getting verifies it's not there. But the giving verifies it is there. And that prayer helps you to stay focused on giving, like, let me not seek for Love but let me give Love. Let me not ask to be forgiven, but let me forgive. See? It's really, really beautiful. It's a really, really beautiful prayer.

I highly, highly recommend anybody to get a copy of it and read it and just see how powerful it is in shifting you as to how you look at your world. Because, you've been trying to get something out of it that's not there. But, it is there where you can give and find The Truth of You in your giving. OK? So, those of you who work with that prayer, you know what I'm saying. And those of you who haven't, I'm not telling you to do it. I'm just telling you, if you're wise, you'll take a look at that and see if you think it can be of any help to you.

Because I don't tell people what to do, ever. Well, I do, sometimes. I tell them to go to Heaven. But no one listens! But some day they'll surprise me. Some day you'll surprise yourself. There will be one moment where all of a sudden this thing happens and You find yourself in the Presence of

---

[22] *For the full text of the prayer of Saint Francis see page 355.*

your Creator and You'll recognize there was nothing that you did to allow that to happen, made it to happen. Nothing that you do. All you ever did was get in the way.

You thought it was so innocent to be helpful and it wasn't innocent and you weren't helpful. God did everything, created You, gave You all the gifts, kept You safe within His Mind, loving You constantly while You were dreaming. You didn't do anything, it was all God. So, humbleness is accepting that You're in God's Mind as a beautiful, loving Thought of God, completely empowered with all The Love and The Presence that God has given You as that Thought. Arrogance is insisting that this world is real and you're going to have to die. That's arrogance. Humbleness is being All-Powerful with God.

I do this but to myself. All of my thoughts create on some level. Now, if you just are willing to get beyond levels, you'll get to the only creating there is and that creating is the extension of Joy Itself. So, there is only happiness and creating. This is your destiny, to be where creating is happening with You. Now, you find yourself in such a forgetting that you don't even remember all that You've been creating before that mad moment of believing that something can happen beyond the Will of God.

But, because of that impossibility, because of that paradox, it has to have an ending in your mind. It has to, it is not optional! That's your saving grace! You can depend upon that. As Jesus says, your tolerance for pain is quite extraordinary, but it's not infinite. It does have a limit. At some point you will reach that limit of willingness to continue to suffer the pain. You will reach a limit in your willingness to die over and over and over again and when you reach that point, you will turn for help. And it really will be at that point that you'll recognize something in you is trying to kill you. Until you recognize it's within you that's trying to kill you, God will not be the solution because until then God is trying to kill You. But when you realize it's something in you that's doing that, then God will finally be a solution for you. You'll finally be able to turn to God as the solution, not as the cause of pain, suffering and death. Hello? This is very, very empowering. Secret number one. I seek and experience as I have chosen.

17

THE SEVEN SECRETS – PART 3

Your Mind is Not In Your Body / What Could Possibly Experience More than God? / There is only One Awakening / It has Already Happened

Q: There was just this thought, I do this but to myself, and then you spoke of there is something in you that wants to kill you.

R: That's the one that does it to itself.

Q: And, since I do this but to myself, this is me. OK. Just to be clear. Whoops.

R: What most of you miss, is that you *are* the ego when you represent the ego.

Q: I am?

R: Do you ever say, "I have a problem." Did you ever say that? Who do you think is saying that? Does Spirit walk around in Heaven going, "I've got a problem. The angels kept me awake all night singing. [Sniffing.] I've got so much to do today!"

Nee, that's not going to happen. Right? So, who's got a problem?

Q: Me, thinking it.

R: Yes, me thinking there is a me that can have a problem, right, and we have a label for that. We call that the ego. But, if I tell you there is no such thing, you go, "Yes, there is," and I'll say, "No, there isn't" and you say, "Yes, there is," and I'll say, "No, there isn't" and you say, "Yes, there is" and I'll say, "No, there isn't" and you'll..., but who are you arguing with then? And I tell you The Truth, no one. And then you really get upset.

Q: So, nothing is trying to kill me?

R: That's right. The idea of nothing is what death is, because God is Everything. You're going to get this. But not intellectually.

At some moment your Heart is going to burst into the Presence of God. I don't mean the physical heart. I mean the part of your mind that receives Divine Communication. The Heart is actually a part of the Mind, right? There is not the Heart *and* the Mind. There is so much confusion in your world, so much confusion. It's like you think there is the Holy Spirit *and* the Christ *and* God. No, there is only God! Sorry. There is only God! You're a Thought in God's Mind; there is only God. Sorry. You're not happy being a Thought, I know that. And the reason is, because you don't like your own thoughts. You don't like yourself. That's why you need to know that God loves You, because you don't love yourself. If you loved yourself you'd never want to get involved in pain, suffering and death. What loving thing would do that? Daaah!!!

Q: Is it possible to know guilt?

R: See how fast? That's how fast the ego gets in there and moves you away from the most incredible message that you could ever hear. From the secrets to Salvation, the secrets to Truth, the secret to Remembering and Being what it is that God created You to be. Because I do this but to myself. It is so important. I mean, how do you forget? "I don't know, I haven't memorized it yet." You're not supposed to memorize it. You're supposed to *be* it. "Well I don't know, maybe I should practise." OK, start now. Hello? I do this but to myself, I made a mistake. I don't want the results of my mistakes any longer, I want the Love of God! Let's see. Give me a choice, the Love of God and yuck. [Rananda holds up his hands as a balance.] Let me see, Love of God, that has a kind of a ring to it and yuck. Mmm.

Jesus, this is a hard decision: yuck and the Love of God. Oh! Decisions, decisions, mmmm. Please. "Well, if you're going to look at it that way, Rananda." Yes, I do. I am going to look at it that way, yes. Why would you want to look at it some other way and get pain and suffering and death? Why don't you join with me in looking at it that way and find the Love of God bursting forth within You, into The Presence of your Creator. Why wouldn't you want that?

What do you have to lose that's so precious? Your bicycles? Your orange T-shirts? *Hup Holland Hup.* And I tell you where you can find me Sunday night. Watching the match, saying *Hup Holland Hup.* But if you think I'm going to watch that and think it's Reality, you're nuts. You're nuts! I do it to love them. Did you know there is going to be a bunch of guys out there who are going to be sad because they lost? I'm going to love them, I'm going to love them. No losers in my head. All winners, all lovers. Yes. Does that mean I don't want the Dutch to win? Of course I want them to win. You guys don't get it. You're fraudulent. You know fraudulent? You're not what you say you are. Yes. So, how are you going to get around it? In your mind you have two teams battling one another and there is going to be one winner, hello? Even if you don't watch it, that's what's going on in your mind. Then, how are you going to get around it, you're fraudulent?

It's going on, whether you say, you like it or whether you pay attention or not. It's going on in your mind. Hey guys, here is another secret. Secret number five,

Your Mind is not in your body

- 331 -

Your body is in your mind along with all the other illusion of a universe! You don't know where your mind is. You think so small. Jesus says in *A Course In Miracles* you're stuck in an infinitely small maze! The first time I looked at that I went, "Say what?" Can anybody comprehend an infinitely small maze? Can you? Can anybody conceive of what an infinitely small maze would look like? Can you? Well, Jesus said it's what you're in. So, you can.

This world of yours, this universe of yours, is an infinitely small maze. And The Realm of God, the Universe that God knows of, see, you can't even imagine what That must be like. In this universe you cannot even get to the other side, because you will die before you get there. It's part of an infinitely small maze, hello? What perspective does Jesus have? Questioning minds want to know. Maybe this dude has something I can learn from, this Jesus guy. Maybe he's on to something here, besides drugs. An infinitely small maze, you can't comprehend that!

I mean, you look at the stars and you go, "Wow, they are so far away, I wonder if there is other life in the universe?" There is not even life here! This is not Life! This is where things come to die. Life is Eternal. It's wherever God is. That's Life. This is not Life! I wonder if there is other life in the universe. No, there is death, just like here. Why wouldn't you want to be with What God and What You create and What's Real and What's Alive and What is Loving and What is supportive of joining and knowing? No hidden thoughts. No thoughts that you have to protect, that somebody else better not hear and know about. Imagine how free you'd be of all of that. Pooh! Boy, that'll be a load off your mind, wouldn't it?

No secret thoughts, wow. No more secrets. And we got five, didn't we? You'd have no purpose for the great five secrets.

Is somebody writing this down, because I need to remember these. It's hard enough to remember what I'm trying to say and... Oh, yes, recorded, yes. I forgot. See, how fast I forget? It's a thing tied to my chest. It's a good thing my head is not screwed on, because if it's screwed off, I'd probably lose it.

Q: I want to ask this question, because I've been sitting on it all evening and now I'm going to ask it.

R: You see, he thinks that's patience. Go ahead.

Q: OK. So, what I recognize is what you were saying. I can see myself identifying with that part, the one who wants to commit suicide and kill. Then, a couple of weeks ago I had this experience that I do this but to myself. It was like a revelation. If I do something to hurt myself, I immediately get the result of doing that and I choose for Love. Is that God or is that Holy Spirit? I no longer believe in the part that says I'm not good enough, that I'm not worthy, that I should suffer.

R: Right, you have already made levels out of Singularity. You have an idea of Spirit, of Mind, and then thoughts that are placed into that mind. OK, now, when the thought enters into that mind that there is something other than God, a whole system of thought was placed into that mind. So, you not only had the Thoughts that were coming from Spirit, which is receiving them directly from God, but you also have this whole other thought system that's there.

Now, you represent that demonstration of the mind having thoughts of separation. OK? And then all of this, everything that you can perceive through a body, that you say is yours, verifies that thought system. OK. Now, your mind, from which all of that is projected, is actually doing all the experiencing. You think you're doing it.

Q: If something happens now, I see I do this to myself.

R: Yes, *what* you is doing it to itself? *What* you could possibly do something that God does not Will?

Q: I guess that's the part I do not understand.

R: That's what I'm trying to help you see.

Q: What I do understand is that I'm tired of listening to that voice and now I listen to another Voice.

R: That's all you need to know! That's why I was saying that the analyzing is not really what it's about. When you remain in the activity of forgiveness, Love will be present and that's all that you are really ever going to learn. You are What Love is.

Q: Yes, I like that.

R: God is Love, God can only create Love. That's What You are! So, that's what you want to practise. All this other stuff about how did it happen, the whole intellectual side of it, you know, it's nice to hear it once, but then just set it down and get on with the Beingness, your willingness to be What God has created. That's what you really want.

Q: No, I guess my question is simple, is this Awakening?

R: Just keep forgiving and don't try to figure it out! What would want to figure it out? Aren't You already What you want to become?

Q: Yes.

R: Yes, but you don't know it, because you're trying to figure it out. You're trying to do the right thing, so that you'll get to that goal and I'm saying, the right thing is to step back from doing all of that and let The Light guide you. OK? So, if The Light is guiding you, you go, "Oh, look, The Light is guiding me. OK, that's all I need to know. What is it guiding me to do? Forgive! Oh, cool, so The Light is guiding me. I feel myself forgiving, I feel myself challenged or tempted to not

- 334 -

forgive and then I practise forgiving and then what happens? I practise forgiving and what happens?"

Q: Happy.

R: Happy Love. Well, what did God create? Well, then I'm realizing Who and What I am as God created Me. Isn't that what I wanted? Well, what do you think your Awakening is? Wow, I should be really cosmic with bombs going off. It would be really nice if, you know, starbirds would be there, and rainbows and dogs – white ones would be really, really nice – and a couple of those sprinkles and a couple of those angels, you know, playing the harp; I always kind of like that, you know, and let them fly around a little bit when they're playing. And I want to hear that Voice, "This is My Son in Whom I'm well pleased." God has that megaphone, "My Son in Whom I'm well pleased." Got to have that!

Q: I would like to ask a very serious question.

R: Is it a question? God loves You. That's a question?

Q: I really want to know.

R: Aren't you the one that was at the hospital and God showed up?

Q: Yes, that's why. I want to connect that to your beginning declaration. What may be the difference between someone who makes the declaration, God loves me, to himself and someone who doesn't? I mean, when I continually make the declaration to myself that God loves me, what rights can I claim from there? What does it imply?

R: It implies that you're agreeing with What God thinks. And eventually you're going to know The Truth of It.

Q: Hallelujah.

R: Oh, finally.

Q: But, if God loves...

R: Hallelujah, Hallelujah... I always wanted to do that with a choir.

Q: Do you get from there the freedom to do what you want?

R: No, You only get the freedom to do What God wants.

Q: So, you can say, I can do this because God loves Me.

R: No, you can't do that. You can't go around killing people because God loves You.

Q: I can jump in the river and say God loves me?

R: Yes, you can do that if you want. I hope you can swim. Or if you can't swim, hopefully you land in a boat and go, "Thank you God, thank you, thank you, that's a miracle."

Q: I want to progress along the path of forgiveness and say to myself that I'm entitled to that because God loves me. Is that right?

R: Yes, you're entitled to progress along the path of forgiveness, because God loves You, that's true. But how long does your progress take, according to God?

Q: A moment.

R: Not longer.

Q: In the beginning.

R: No, stay with the moment, stay with that moment, so it can be right now.

Q: Hallelujah.

R: OK, that's better. Don't worry about what you have written there, stay in the moment.

Q: Yes, but...

R: No but, stay in the moment! Listen, the information is not nearly as important as the Beingness that is true for you. Go for the Beingness, not for the information. It's just data. You're not a computer. You're Love Itself!

Q: Right, OK. Hallelujah. But...

R: OK. No buts. The only butts we have here in Holland are the ones you sit on.

Q. You started this night and you said that Love gives, so that forgiveness...

R: Is the key...

Q: Is the key to Love and that, you said, gives a molecular change.

R: It would, wouldn't it?

Q: You mean, the molecules of your body?

R: Yes. Not only the molecules of your body, the molecules of your whole world. Where is your body, by the way?

Q: Well, you said in the mind.

R: Yes, that's what I said, so where is it?

Q: Hallelujah.

R: Hallelujah! Have I said hallelujah lately? Can I get an amen?

Q: Amen! So, the molecular change is also in the moment?

R: Of course, that's what the moment is.

Q: So, the body changes completely in the moment?

R: It disappears, that's the change. It disappears in a moment, in a twinkling of an eye. How fast is a twinkling of an eye?

Q: Shorter than it takes to say hallelujah.

R: OK, that's cool. So, that's how fast it changes, in the twinkling of an eye.

Q: So, awakening involves a molecular change in the body which is immediate?

R: Transformation is physical, that's absolutely right and when the physical disappears, then what You are left with is What You've always been. Did you ever hear about Resurrection?

Q: Yes.

R: OK. Jesus' body did not disintegrate! Disintegration means, the molecular structure returns to a more simple structure. That's not what happens. That's not transformation. It disappears, it's quantum! Isn't that good news? You are going to have a quantum moment.

Q: Yes, hallelujah.

R: You're going to be known as Quantum Boy!

Q: You said that God loves Me, the second secret? Does God love Everything, because...

R: You are Everything! He only loves You, nothing else.

Q: Because Everything is created by God?

R: That's right.

Q: And God only creates Perfection!

R: And that's You! God only creates Oneness. He only extends Himself. Nothing ever gets away from God. It's all there right in Gods Mind. Isn't that great? It must be a huge Mind. You're in an infinitely small maze. You can't even begin to comprehend what God's Mind is like.

You think It must be something like yours, thank God It's not. Man! I mean, somewhere you're just going to go, "I must have made a mistake. I can't figure that out, think I'll just quit. I'm a quitter, I'm going to quit the human race. No more human race for me, I just want God." All you're going to get is God. OK?

You're upside down. And you can find that in your mind, you know, instead of doing those shitty things that you do. I mean, I'm not here for any other reason than to help you find, in your mind now, the things I'm saying and this is Jesus telling you that, because you believe you're separate, what is required for your mind is a joining. Now, a joining is not writing down what I'm saying. It's finding in your mind what I'm saying. That what I'm saying, you can find in your mind. Like, if I say, God loves You, you should be able to find God loving You, because He's eternally loving You.

But, you'd rather sit here, hearing this and go, "Oh, that's kind of nice. I like him when he says things like that. I don't really know, sometimes I know." You comment. You're like those guys when I watch football, you know. Yak yak yak, yap this and yap that, win this and win that, you know. These guys, they all have the same name, and they get on there, pretending to know something and they get paid for it. Boy, what a rip off that is, you know. Your mind is like that, you have these commentators in there, "Look, isn't that a nice blue? I don't like blue. Yes, that's right, we used to like red, didn't we? Yes, I remember back when I was really young..." There is just that commentator in there.

You know what I'm saying? It's about joining; it's about finding the experience. If I say to you that forgiveness is the key to happiness, those are words – forgiveness...is...the... key...to...happiness – there must be an experience in your mind that is associated with those words. When I say those words, it would be really nice if you found the experience that goes with them. That's what I'm here for! If it was just to say the words, you've got books to say the words and you love books. But, you've got a living being here, who can help you find that experience in your own mind by the frequency that I am.

And you miss it by not looking for the experience, the knowing in your own mind. You'd rather collect pieces of data. Don't you understand that? Look! God man, pooh.

Q: Hallelujah.

R: Yes, that's nice. But Oneness is what Reality is. No one argues with that, do you? OK. Then, does it make sense to you to tear things apart and analyze the parts, if Oneness is Reality? Whose program do you think it is to tear things apart into pieces as small as you can and analyze them and then put them together? Whose program do you think that is? Yes, ego's.

Don't do that! When I sit here and go through this thing, don't tear it apart and look at all the pieces and think you're going to find Oneness. Your job is to join and find all of that in your Mind, in the Oneness of your Mind. And when that occurs you'll know that You're in the Presence of your Creator, because The Creator is going to reveal Himself to You. And of course, you know, through different systems we can talk about whether It's the Holy Spirit and He'll lead You to The Christ. And, when You finally find The Christ, You have the doorway open to God. Yes, that's all true, but it happens so fast, it's not quite like that, because time is an illusion, it's not sequential, it was one moment, one instant, one idea.

Can you hear what it is that I'm trying to convey here tonight? You keep trying to break down everything I'm saying so you can analyze it. That's the ego. That is never going to wake up. It's going to analyze until it dies and it's hoping it can convince you to continue to do that, because that's how you stay in control of your Awakening, which means, you don't awaken! And, then you can go around and you can tell everybody all the ideas that you've heard. Not only that, you can gather them from many different teachers and say, "This one says this and this one says this. And this one says this," and you know, "I kind of like this and this one is probably a little bit off." And all you do is analyze it all. That's the ego. That has nothing to do with The Truth of You, Truth Itself or God, Which is The Truth of You and Truth Itself. It's Singular. Stop trying to break It apart so that you can grasp It.

Reality is beyond your grasp. It's going to get you. It's going to reveal Itself to You. You're not going to grasp It. You're not going to steal God's fire by sneaking up on Him and grasping something that's of value. It's not going to happen. Somewhere you're going to have to wise up and come into a bit more maturity on your spiritual path and let go of these things that you've been doing over and over and over again for many lifetimes. That didn't work then, it is not working now, but you just won't give up. You're just like bulldogs. You get a hold, "Grrr, don't come near my illusion, grrr!" "Nice doggy." "Grrr!"

So, I guess that's enough. I was a little strong there in the end; that's because I'm such a gentle guy. Yes.

Q: What was said is that this life is falling into multiplicity and the only destiny we have is to return to Oneness.

R: Yes, that's the illusion! The illusion is that you fell into anything outside of God and that's *impossible*! Let me say this to you. Please, try to hear this, will you, without analyzing. Please try to hear this. OK, are you ready? Here it comes. [Pause.] Did you get it?

Q: Yes.

R: OK. That's secret number six. Ask yourself a really simple itty-bitty little question. See what happens. It goes like this:

What could possibly experience more than God?

Q: You want the answer?

R: Do you want the answer? I said, ask yourself.

Q: I've got the answer.

R: Do you? I hope it was nothing.

Q: I think so.

R. Yes, that's what you are. You think you're bigger than God. You think you're separate from God. But you just answered, nothing can do that, which means, you're nothing. But, when I say that, you get upset. However, when you say it, that seems reasonable, until you say, "I'm nothing," and then you go... "that can't be true." Nothing succeeded in being separate from Oneness, because if it did, there would be no such Thing as Oneness. When are you going to give up? When are you going to admit you did not succeed? When are you going to say, "I am mistaken"?

R: I'm sorry, you know, I don't know how else to get past your ego, other than to just say, look, you're full of shit! You're the demonstration of the belief that something can be separate from God. That's impossible! *You* are impossible and you don't like that message, because you're so busy taking care of yourself! But you're taking care of nothing! You're giving all your care, all your love, all your money, all your concern, taking care of nothing and you know it and that's why you're not happy. You're wasting time. I'm sorry. Yes, I just should have started there and then left. And then you'd been really mad at me.

But, that's the hard lesson. Ask yourself, what could possibly experience a world of pain and suffering and death? Jesus tells you really, really clear in *A Course In Miracles*. He says, "Stop looking at the effects. Stop trying to figure out the world and ask yourself a simple question, 'what could possibly experience that?'" Because you're saying, you experience it and Jesus wants you to ask that question, what could possibly experience what God does not experience? But no, you don't want to look at that. You want to look at all the world and all its problems and so on and so forth. You want to get as far away from where the real healing is taking place or can take place.

You don't want to look at the self that you've made up and admit that it's not real, it's made up. It's what you call your personality. Everything you've been doing since you were a kid was to try to make a self that could relate to everyone else, and when it wasn't quite right you tried to change it. In some things you just refused to change, because you're in charge and if people don't like it, you'll find somebody else that will like it. You just do all that strange, crazy stuff. What does that have to do with God? Do you think Perfection can create something that needs to grow, that needs to evolve? Does Perfection create something that needs to evolve? It's already Perfect, what is It going to evolve to? You guys love evolution. "We're learning, we're growing!" What crap! That's just part of the illusion. OK? I won't steal it from you, I won't take it away from you, but come on. You know, you can't wear it like a badge, a ribbon. So proud that you're evolving.

God doesn't create things that evolve! He's Perfection, that's The Truth of You. Get over it. What could analyze Perfection? What needs to find the reasonability of God? "I'm an authority here. If God is not reasonable, I'll reject

Him. You'd better act reasonable as far as I'm concerned. God, you're out of here. My world! Hit the road Jack. I'll have it my way, please, Mister McDonald's." Got it?

Q: Yes.

R: Are you with me? I hope you are. I want you to be. I want you to be sitting right there in The Light, recognizing everything that's being revealed. You have spent hundreds of lifetimes wanting tonight and here it is. What do you want to do with this? That's what I would ask myself if I were you. And since I'm You, I ask you to ask your Self, "What am I going to do with this?"

Is it just another Friday night? Or, has a doorway opened for you? Not of information, but a doorway that you can rise through. See, this is not falling in love, you're rising in Love! That's what's been offered to you all night tonight. Freedom from your self-identity, so that you can see the Identity that God gave You; That's What's offered to You. You can stop playing the part of, I don't know, which is the idea that there is a problem and you can start playing the part of, yes Father, I am the solution. So, you can stop focusing on the problem and focus on the solution.

Hello? The secrets that were revealed to you tonight, are the solution. I do this but to myself. God loves me, that's the solution. Forgiveness brings forth Love, that's the solution, that's not the problem. Stop, stop, you know, with your magnifying glasses, magnifying the nature of the problem so you come down to the minutest detail; so you can tell everybody about the infinitely small maze that you're caught in. Instead look at the solution, look at The Truth and offer that to your brothers. Offer them the Love of God, offer them your Love, offer them your willingness to sit with them while they join in finding that Love within them, the place where God will visit You, the Holy Temple that exists within You.

Offer to be with your brother, while he comes into that realization and that recognition. Try that for a change, rather than sharing the latest book that you read, the latest movie that you saw. Try staying focused, instead of letting your mind wander all over the place, so that you'll be present when God is ready to pluck You.

You think, in your spiritual wisdom of your own making, that you can't miss opportunities of the spiritual nature and I guarantee you, you can. There are windows that open and close, possibilities, and you can miss them by wandering around in your mind and getting involved in things that don't allow you to take advantage of that open window where revealing can happen and recognition of the True Nature Itself is available. You have lots of spiritual ideas that are not supporting The Truth of God, The Truth of You and The Truth of your brother. A lot of them.

It's not your job to try to sort them out. Your job is but to step back and let The Light lead you where The Light comes from. As You enter into where that Light comes from, You recognize that You are The Light and the Source of that Light, because The Light that You are is self-effulgent. It has no source, It is What It is. The Light that emanates, that created You, is You. You are The Light. It just extended Itself, that's all that it is revealing to you. What's revealing to You is You. Hello? Yes. You're not going to become Something You're not already, it's impossible. It's just going to dawn on your mind What has always been.

And, what you've made up just disappears! It doesn't disintegrate and become some other form. It disappears because it never was, like a dream, like an illusion, it just disappears. Isn't that good news? The world was made of your beliefs, only.

Q: Yes.

R: So, you're getting the good news? Really, you're getting the good news? You're finding what I'm talking about in your mind? There weren't so many agreements there, hahaha! That's OK, just stay with it, you know. It's all going to play out, it's all going to unfold, it's all very, very beautiful. Your whole Awakening is really, really beautiful. Oh yes, there is another secret, number six,

There is only one Awakening

There is not lots of awakenings, and guess what? It has already happened!

So, you're just a little late in accepting that it has already happened for you, you're reluctant. And I'm here to collect your reluctance. So, just let go of it and I'll collect it. I know what to do with reluctance. It's worthless, it's easy, I know what to do with it. So, if you don't want your reluctance anymore, give it to me, I'll take it. Do you know how to let go?

Have you been practising letting go? Do you know how to let go? Do you know how to let The Light remove energies and thoughts from you? OK, then let it go. I am The Light, I am The Way, I can take it from you if you're willing to let it go. I know what it is. I know what it's not. You think it's a big deal. For me it's like having a drink of water. You don't think about it, you don't do that. If you want to drink water, you just take a drink of water. It's like me. If you want to give me your pain and your suffering, if you want to give me your confusion, I'll just take it.

It's not real to me. I don't have any problem taking it. I do not not take it, because it's not real. So, you can sit there and go, well, he didn't take it because it's not real and I still have it. No, that's just playing around in your mind shit games, you know. But no, I will take it. If you let it go, I will take it. I, The Light, will take it. And as I take it, you will see that You are The Light. That's what The Savior does. And then when you see, You're The Light, it's like tag you're it. Now you are The Savior. And what do You do as The Savior? The same thing. You take the pain and the suffering that you forced your brother to experience, so you could be you.

But, now you see and you want to relieve him of the job you gave him to prove the separation took place. You relieve him of that. You take the pain and suffering. You are your brother's keeper. You take it because he believes in it and you relieve him of that need to believe in it and that's what you call miracles; they are natural. Miracles are natural. When they are not occurring, something has gone wrong. Hello? OK. So, thank you for coming. I know there are lots of things you could have been doing tonight, but you choose to be here instead, and that says something about you.

Some of you brought your bodies here, but you weren't really here very much. You're going to have to learn about that, otherwise you'll continue to suffer. Once this Light is provided to you from where this Light is coming from, the burden that you carry, which is Light, is a lot different than what you've been used to. I guarantee you that that is true. In that sense, The Christ is counting on You to carry this message, to be this message, to share it, so that your world can be relieved from pain and suffering. And if it's not important enough for you to be with this message and to be this message, then somewhere you'd better start admitting that you're OK with all the suffering that you're forcing your brothers to experience. And you know what I say about that? Shame on you!

Shame on you to know better and force your brother to have more pain and suffering. You know better. Right, it's time to grow up, kids. It's time to be more mature in The Light and let The Light use this form, this mind, to reach out and heal all the suffering that's going on. That's what you're here for. Not just for what you think is your own suffering that you would like to see end. But, you're here for the whole world, because it is your own projection.

You're The Savior! You are The Savior. God gave You that job. He's not a dummy. He picked You very specifically and very wisely to carry this message. Honor that responsibility of that Light, by being It and when you find you need help, help is here. You're not alone. *You'll never walk alone.* Why do you think I put that book out? Because, you think you walk alone and it's not true. Let it help you. Look at it from time to time. There is a lot of help in that book. It will help remind you of The Truth of You. Alright?

It's been a fine evening. Hope you all got more than you were looking for. Sure enough. Oh. Look at this one here and this is our real fake one. OK, so, this has been a wonderful evening. I like coming here and visiting you guys, but it would be really nice if You just go Home so I didn't have to come here anymore.

Wouldn't that be nice? Maybe some night we'll all come here together and I'll say something like, "Secret number two is, God loves You,' and that will mean so much to you that your Heart will leap into the Presence of God and You won't know of this world anymore. You see, in my mind, that's possible! I think you think it's a fantasy yet. I don't think you actually see that it is possible that that can happen. And, if we can move you from Reality not being fantasy and your fantasy not being Reality, we could get back on track. You see, you think what I'm talking about is a fantasy, because you think you know of this here and you call it Reality.

So, thanks guys.

A QUESTION

An age-old question that many have asked as well as attempted to answer but which still persists in the minds of many spiritual people, can be found in John 14:12[23].

John quotes Jesus of Nazareth prophesying the activities of those who emulate his Love of God and their willingness to serve:

> *Truly, truly, I say to you, He who believes in me,*
>
> *the works which I do he shall do also;*
>
> *even greater than these things he shall do,*
>
> *because I am going to my Father.*
>
>> Jesus of Nazareth

The question each spiritual person must first ask himself is, "Am I fulfilling the first part of the quote?"

> *"He who believes in me, the works I do he shall do also."*

Are we demonstrating the acts that Jesus has performed? This being the prelude to the next part of the quote:

> *"...even greater than these things he shall do".*

Then they must ask, what are the "greater things" that Jesus suggests we are to demonstrate?

---

[23] *All Bible quotes in 'A Question' are from 'The Modern New Testament from the Aramaic'.*

People have offered many interpretations, but what we do know from Jesus can be found in John 14:26:

> *"But the Comforter, the Holy Spirit,*
>
> *whom my Father will send in my name,*
>
> *he will teach you everything,*
>
> *and remind you of everything which I tell you."*

So, we have a teacher right now who knows everything that we need to learn. The answer to our question can be found by each individual who is following the path set by Jesus through the guidance of the Holy Spirit.

Let's take a quick look at the works of Jesus. He also expects these of his followers:

1. Miracles: water to wine, blind to see, deaf to hear, sick to heal, lame to walk, and of course raising the dead.
2. Establishing the Truth that God is a Fact!
3. Changing the relationship between church authorities and the parishioners.
4. Love the Lord your God with all your heart, and with all your soul, and with all your mind, and with all your power. (Mark 12:30.)
5. And, your neighbor as yourself.[24] (Mark 12:31.)
6. Proof that there is no such thing as death through the act of Resurrection.
7. Further proof of man's true relationship with his Creator through the act of Ascension.

---

[24] *In Aramaic, the word neighbor means everyone you see/meet.*

Looking at this list and knowing so few who are willing to surrender their fears and truly follow the example set by Jesus I can only come to the conclusion that a dramatic event must occur in each follower's mind before the Holy Spirit can lead us to our destiny of "greater things". However, our destiny must be fulfilled because it is the function of the Holy Spirit, whose function was, and is, established by God. It is certain because it is of God!

God bless you in all your endeavors to fulfill your destiny to communicate directly with our Creator!

rananda

REFERENCES

'A Course In Miracles', original edition, 2010[2]
ISBN 978-09764200-5-7

'The Modern New Testament, from the Aramaic', 1998
ISBN 0-87516-716-0

ADVISED FOR READING

'A Course In Miracles',
Text, Workbook for Students, Manual for Teachers
2nd edition, 1996 - ISBN 0-9606388-8-1 Softcover
2nd edition, 1996 - ISBN 0-9606388-9-X Hardcover
3rd edition, 2007 - ISBN 978-1-883360-25-2 Hardcover
3rd edition, 2007 - ISBN 978-1-883360-24-5 Softcover
3rd edition, 2007 - ISBN 978-1-883360-26-9 Paperback

PRAYER OF SAINT FRANCIS

Lord, make me an instrument of Thy Peace;
Where there is hatred... let me sow love;
Where there is injury... healing;
Where there is doubt... faith;
Where there is despair... hope;
Where there is darkness... light;
Where there is sadness... joy;
Oh Divine Master; Grant that I may not so much
seek to be consoled as to console;
To be understood as to understand;
To be loved as to love;
For it is in giving that we receive;
It is in forgiving that we are forgiven;
And it is by dying to self that one
awakens to Eternal Life.

Amen.

ABOUT RANANDA

Rananda was only five years old when he began receiving instructions from Enlightened Masters from out of time and space. Rabbis, pastors and ministers couldn't answer his questions about God, the nature of man and the meaning of life. His travels in search for Truth led him through many experiences and eventually to Guru Maharaji and Master Teacher.

In 1998 Rananda experienced what some call Enlightenment. Since 2000 he has been meeting with groups of people and individuals all over the world to share with them his Knowing, his Love. When in the Netherlands, Rananda conducts, together with his partner Suzanne, meetings designed to help people remember Who They really are.

MAGNUM OPUS MINISTRIES NEDERLAND

MOM–NL was established in 2004 to further the work of Rananda and Suzanne Moran. You can support MOM-NL; we welcome all help. It can take the form of prayer, money, ideas and all kinds of practical assistance. You are cordially invited to join in any of our activities.

For more information visit us at www.mom-nederland.nl.

Rananda's teachings available on CD

CD *Rananda at Bonnefantenmuseum, Maastricht, The Netherlands*

This recording of a Remembering Event with Rananda offers a vivid and intense introduction to his teaching.

CD *Teaching on Relationships*

None of your experiences in an illusion remotely resembles the Love of God. Nevertheless you keep on trying to find Love and Happiness outside yourself in the world. There is another way. – *Rananda*

CD *Teaching on Ramana Maharshi*

Ramana Maharshi is considered to be one of the most important Indian gurus and mystics from the 20th century and one of the clearest exponents of Advaita Vedanta or teaching of non-duality. This fascinating teaching shows the strong correspondence between Advaita, *A Course In Miracles* and Singularity as Rananda teaches it.

CD *What would Love do?*

In every moment of confusion, what is needed is Love. Where is it that we are willing to be less then loving? When it shows up, what will you do? We need to be trained to choose Love. – *Rananda*

Rananda's teachings available on DVD

DVD *The Only Answer*

Do you want to know what is faster than the speed of light? You will never find out by studying what is at the speed of light. You do not find Heaven by studying hell. You do not find what is faster than manifestation by studying manifestation. You've got to go there, that is how you find out. – *Rananda*

DVD *To Live from your Heart*

You, who are teachers of the heart, the task at hand for you is joyful, because it is of the heart and the heart is of joy. Be of good cheer as you make your movements through time to no time. For that indeed is your destiny: no time, no past and no future. How fast, that is up to you. You have been given a vision, you decide what to do with it. – *Rananda*

DVD *Saviorship*

According to Jesus you must play the role of Savior to learn who you are. That is not a concept, you personally have to accept it! God gave you the role of Savior of your world. You are The Light of the world. Not someone else! – *Rananda*

Discover what is asked of you to be a Savior and to be saved. Are you willing to respond to the call?

DVD *Rananda teaches from A Course In Miracles Ch. 28:*

IV. The Greater Joining

DVD *Rananda teaches from A Course In Miracles Ch. 29:*

    VI. Forgiveness and the End of Time
    VII. Seek Not Outside Yourself

DVD *Rananda teaches from A Course In Miracles,*

Review lessons 1-15 – Part 1

    There is Another Way of Looking at the World

Books by Rananda

Gloriana – *The Story of an Atlantean Angel*

With a foreword from the Great White Brotherhood of Light:

"This book is only for the others who know the truth and are not afraid to face fantasy. This book is for all who are willing to weep for humanity, to weep in joy for self and to sing to heaven of the true angels that be."

ISBN 978-90-78582-04-5. Also available in Dutch translation: Gloriana – Het verhaal van een Engel uit Atlantis. – ISBN 978-90-78582-01-4

You'll Never Walk Alone – *Your Resurrection Is Your Reawakening*

In this book Rananda compiled quotes *from A Course In Miracles, Jesus' Course in Miracles* and *The Modern New Testament from the Aramaic* to shed light on the life and meaning of Jesus of Nazareth also called Jesus Christ. – ISBN 978-90-78582-03-8.

To order please visit our website:

www.mom-nederland.nl

or send an email to:

bestellingen@mom-nederland.nl